THE GOVERNMENT OF RISK

The Government of Risk

Understanding Risk Regulation Regimes

CHRISTOPHER HOOD, HENRY ROTHSTEIN, AND ROBERT BALDWIN

OXFORD

UNIVERSITY PRESS

OXFORD

UNIVERSITY PRESS

Great Clarendon Street, Oxford OX2 6DP

Oxford University Press is a department of the University of Oxford.
It furthers the University's objective of excellence in research, scholarship,
and education by publishing worldwide in

Oxford New York

Athens Auckland Bangkok Bogotá Buenos Aires
Cape Town Chennai Dar es Salaam Delhi Florence Hong Kong Istanbul
Karachi Kolkata Kuala Lumpur Madrid Melbourne Mexico City Mumbai
Nairobi Paris São Paulo Shanghai Singapore Taipei Tokyo Toronto Warsaw
and associated companies in Berlin Ibadan

Oxford is a registered trade mark of Oxford University Press
in the UK and in certain other countries

Published in the United States
by Oxford University Press Inc., New York

British Library Cataloguing in Publication Data

Data available

Library of Congress Cataloging in Publication Data

Hood, Christopher.
The government of risk: understanding risk regulation regimes/Christopher Hood,
Henry Rothstein and Robert Baldwin.
p. cm.
Includes bibliographical references.
1. Risk management. I. Rothstein, Henry. II. Baldwin, Robert. III. Title.
HD61. H56 2001   658.15′5—dc21   2001021837
ISBN 0–19–924363–8

1 3 5 7 9 10 8 6 4 2

Typeset in Stone Sans and Stone Serif by
Cambrian Typesetters, Frimley, Surrey
Printed in Great Britain
on acid-free paper by
T.J. International Ltd
Padstow, Cornwall

PREFACE

This book is the product of a journey of exploration into risk regulation—the result of several years spent examining and comparing how risk was regulated across different policy domains. Some of the travel was literal: to talk to government officials and other players in different worlds of risk regulation, and some of it took us far afield. But much of the journeying was metaphorical or virtual, in a search to understand the various tribes, customs, and problems that make up the different worlds of risk regulation.

The three of us embarked on this odyssey from different points and with rather different intellectual baggage—with backgrounds variously in public administration, social studies of science, and public law—but our destination was the same and so was our reason for undertaking the journey. We wanted to see risk regulation at work in a number of different domains, and to come back not just with a set of travellers' tales but also with a systematic way of comparing the regimes we had seen.

In the course of our journey, we published parts of the analysis that this book embodies. An early attempt to sketch out the 'regime' approach to regulatory analysis was published in *Risk Management* (Hood *et al.* 1999a), and in the same year our first analysis of what we then called the 'minimal feasible response' approach to risk regulation was published in *Health, Risk and Society* (Hood *et al.* 1999b). The germ of the idea that became Chapter 9 of this book was published in the proceedings of the 1998 Society of Risk Analysis Paris Conference, and a more developed version was later accepted by *Administration and Society*. We began to collect our thoughts about the appraisal of regulatory regimes in an article on the UK's notorious Dangerous Dogs Act of 1991 published in *Public Law* in 2000. As our journey went on, our approach developed and changed, and this book aims to bring the whole approach together.

Travellers bound on this sort of journey need a lot of help. For financial assistance we are indebted to the Economic and Social Research Council, which helped to fund our inquiries for more than two years as part of its Risk and Human Behaviour Phase II Programme; to the LSE's research fund; and to its Centre for Analysis of Risk and Regulation. We are grateful for research assistance provided by Francesca Davoli, Matthew Grist, Clare Hall, Nigel Taylor, Ligia Teixeira, and Joachim Wehner.

For assistance with information and help in pointing us in the right direction on our journey we are grateful to several hundred players in the regulatory world, who gave generously of their time and expertise in helping us to go beyond the often sketchy accounts of regulatory regimes in official and other published information. We held over 100 face-to-face interviews and several times that number of telephone interviews with regulatory players both in the 'front line' and in policy positions across a range of organizations. Those organizations included various parts of the EU bureaucracy, a range of UK central government departments, agencies and inspectorates, quangos, local authorities and related bodies, business firms, NGOs and professional organizations; and we also talked to academics, independent experts, and consultants. By convention we do not name serving civil servants, but we are deeply indebted to a number of busy people who went far beyond the call of duty in giving us a graphic and detailed picture of how regulation worked in their worlds.

Also important is intellectual help in exposing error, and in challenging muddled interpretations and lack of clarity. We are grateful to those who commented on our ideas and analysis when we presented them at conferences and seminars in places as various as Seoul, Hong Kong, Paris, Canberra, London, and Edinburgh. We had the opportunity to present our ideas to groups of practitioners in the UK Cabinet Office, Health and Safety Executive, Department of Health, Environmental Agency, and the Hong Kong government's civil service training college; to two conferences of the Society for Risk Analysis; and to four ESRC Risk and Human Behaviour conferences. We would particularly like to acknowledge the help and moral support offered throughout the project by Jim McQuaid, formerly of the HSE, Joyce Tait of Edinburgh University, Graham Loomes of Newcastle University, Hazel Kemshall of De Montfort University, and Andrew Evans of UCL. We are deeply grateful also to Andrew Dunsire, David Jones, and Tony Prosser, who read the entire manuscript in draft and made valuable comments.

Above all, we were immensely lucky to have the help of Michael Spackman as guide, philosopher, and friend throughout our journey. The errors and shortcomings that remain in our account are, needless to say, our own responsibility, but there would have been a great many more without Michael's generous assistance. He read all of our drafts with a meticulous care drawn from his background as a transport economist and former mandarin, and tirelessly came up with ways of improving the drafting, tightening the analysis, and patiently correcting our misconceptions. We dedicate this book to him.

Christopher Hood
Henry Rothstein
Robert Baldwin
London, October 2000

CONTENTS

I. Introducing Risk Regulation Regime

II. Explaining Variation in Risk Regulation Regimes

III. Exploring the Dynamics of Risk Regulation Regimes

LIST OF FIGURES

LIST OF TABLES

I

Introducing Risk Regulation Regimes

1

What Are Risk Regulation Regimes?
Why Do They Matter?

> In warfare there are no constant conditions.
>
> Sun Tzu (1983 [originally c.500 BC]: 29)

1. From Risk Society to Variety in Risk Regulation Regimes

This book examines the regulation of risk, defined as governmental interference with market or social processes to control potential adverse consequences to health.[1] It seeks to describe, compare, and explain variation in the way risks are handled by the state. It sets out to show how overarching theories of risk and its management need to be modified or supplemented to account for detailed variations in risk regulation regimes.

Many such overarching approaches to risk and its management have been developed over the past two decades. Perhaps the best known is the work of Ulrich Beck. According to Beck (1992) and others, we live today in a 'risk society'. By that Beck means that risk has a different significance for everyday life from that applying in previous historical eras. Human activity and technology in 'advanced modernity', he claims, produces as a side-effect risks that need specialized expertise to assess and recognize, are collective, global, and irreversible in their impact, and thus potentially catastrophic on a scale never seen before. Some have even claimed there is a 'collective mania with risk' (Sapolsky 1990: 83). The much-discussed bovine spongiform encephalopathy (BSE) issue that has developed since the 1980s and 1990s—that is, the link between the human brain disease new variant Creutzfeldt-Jakob disease (nvCJD) and eating meat from cattle infected with 'mad cow disease'—epitomizes for Ulrich Beck and others the features of the 'risk society'. That is

---

[1] Risk in that sense is conventionally defined as a probability, not necessarily calculable in practice, of adverse consequences. We exclude financial risk from this analysis and business risk more generally is not part of our primary focus, though as we shall see later it intersects with the regulation of health risks. Regulation is taken here to mean attempts to control risk, mainly by setting and enforcing product or behavioural standards.

because it involves a hazard—eating meat—the risks of which are knowable and assessable only through scientific investigation rather than by direct lay observation. Moreover, it involves the application of a recondite language of risk—by scientists and government at least—to ordinary activities like eating and drinking, instead of qualitative and dichotomous judgements, like safe/unsafe, wholesome/unhealthy.

Beck and associated thinkers would add other cases that they see as typical of 'advanced modernity', like the risks associated with genetically modified organisms, reproductive technology, or computer failures that also potentially impact on a wide range of everyday human life. Other contemporary cases in point include the risks of 'adventure tourism' by holidaymakers from the affluent world[2], and the possible risks from mobile phones suggested by—conflicting—reports on their alleged addictiveness, effect on memory, role in brain tumours and dementia, and contribution to road accident deaths.[3] Whether or not the controversial idea of a 'risk society' is theoretically coherent or accurate as a historical generalization is much debated, but there has undoubtedly been an avalanche of discussion and literature on risk, hazard, and blame in recent times, and that phenomenon needs some explanation.

As well as a 'risk society', we are also said to live in a 'regulatory state' (Majone 1994). The idea of the 'regulatory state' is that a new institutional and policy style has emerged, in which government's role as regulator advances while its role as a direct employer or property-owner may decline through privatization and bureaucratic downsizing. The two ideas of 'risk society' and 'regulatory state' could, indeed, be linked in so far as risk and safety is often held to be one of the major drivers of contemporary regulatory growth, for example in the development of EU regulation (see Royal Society 1992: Ch. 6; Scharpf 1996; Beck 1992: 24). In turn, development of risk regulation is interpreted by many to reflect broader political and cultural change. Perhaps the best-known and most controversial is the anthropologist Mary Douglas, whose thinking has been developed by many other students of risk. Building on a 'grid-group' analysis of culture that highlights a dynamic of conflict among four fundamentally different sets of beliefs and attitudes (see Thompson, Ellis, and Wildavsky 1990), Douglas sees risk as a political weapon used by a society poised between the cultures of individualism and egalitarianism, to blame those who wield power in the state and big corporations for what happens to the rest of us. From this perspective the increased salience of risk and regulation reflects a cultural shift away from 'hierarchist' world-views over matters of trust and blame (Douglas and Wildavsky 1982; Douglas 1990: 7).

---

[2] The issue of what advice governments should give to tourists travelling abroad, especially on adventure holidays, was an issue highlighted by a 1999 tragedy in Uganda when eight eco-tourists from the developed world were killed by Rwandan rebels (Leathley 1999).

[3] See Moran (1999); Independent Expert Group on Mobile Phones (2000).

Another interpretation of the link between regulatory development and the social handling of risk is offered by Michael Power (1997: 141). Power sees the development of an 'audit society' in the UK and other states, which responds to risk and regulatory failure by 'greater investment in formal, generalizable systems of control rather than by developing non-standard capabilities for acting on informal sources of intelligence'. The argument is that patterns observable in the financial world, where more elaborate and formal audit systems are adopted after every collapse to offer greater 'assurance' about system robustness, are developing in many other domains of social life.

Such macroscopic and world-historical[4] perspectives on risk and its management may have their uses. But most of them do not explain, or even describe, variety *within* the putative 'regulatory state', 'risk society' or 'audit society'. Yet casual observation, academic inquiry,[5] and official surveys[6] alike indicate substantial variety in the way risks and hazards are handled by the state. We can observe variation both between one state and another and—perhaps even more strikingly—between one domain of risk and another within a single state.

Even across the affluent democracies, with which those writing about 'risk society' and 'regulatory state' are mainly concerned, substantial variation can be observed in the particular risks and hazards that are chosen for regulation and the way regulation works. For instance, after a 1996 campsite tragedy in Spain when 86 tourists died in a flash flood, a study revealed the extent of differences in campsite regulation across the EU countries (AIT/FIA 1998: 11). According to the study, campers in France would find their campsites tightly controlled, with extensive warning systems, and evacuation and contingency plans to deal with gas bottle explosions, avalanches, and floods. In contrast, campers in Greece or Ireland would experience minimal and relaxed regimes. Even neighbouring states may take very different approaches to regulating risk. For instance, for a long time Germany had the most draconian system in Europe for checking the roadworthiness of cars, while France had none; even now neighbouring France and the Netherlands adopt sharply contrasting policies towards hemp products (see van de Wijngaart 1991). Writing a decade or so ago, Kirstin Shrader-Frechette (1991: 100) noted an exact mirror-image in the regulatory systems governing saccharin and cyclamates in neighbouring Canada and the USA, with cyclamates permitted and saccharin banned in Canada, and cyclamates banned and saccharin permitted in the USA. And even where standards are common, enforcement practices can vary sharply among states (see Baldwin and Daintith 1992).

---

[4] Or maybe 'historicist', in the terminology of the late Sir Karl Popper (1957).
[5] Such as Cheit (1990); Shrader-Frechette (1991); Breyer (1993).
[6] Such as Health and Safety Executive (1996; 1998); HM Treasury (1996).

Indeed, mini-trade wars often stem from differences in risk regulation regimes between states. Well-known examples include the conflict between the EU's 'precautionary' approach to regulating bovine somatotropin (BST)—growth hormones used in the production of milk and beef—and the United States' more resilient regulatory approach to this particular type of risk, and the ban on exports of UK beef by the EU during the BSE crisis while the product was permitted for sale within the UK. When we began to gather material for this book a similar international conflict of risk regulation systems was brewing over white asbestos. Canada—the world's largest exporter of white asbestos—was complaining to the World Trade Organization about 'precautionary' bans of this material by France and other EU member states (*Europe Environment* 1999).

Even more striking than these differences between states in handling a given hazard are variations in the ways risks and hazards are handled across policy domains within the same country. Indeed, it often happens that there is a strong international exchange of knowledge, views, and cultures within particular risk domains, such as chemicals, and air and sea transport, but very little cross-domain exchange within states (see Breyer 1993). The result is a policy and intellectual 'archipelago' of risk domains isolated from one another, with very different policy stances across the various domains. For some hazards, governments adopt heavy-duty, anticipative, and intrusive regulatory arrangements reminiscent of the draconian measures taken by early modern states to control plague, as described by Michel Foucault (1977: 195–200) in his well-known *Discipline and Punish*. More recent cases of anticipative and intrusive risk regulation include the ill-fated attempt to immunize every man, woman, and child in the USA in 1976 against a swine flu epidemic that failed to eventuate (see Moore 1995: 110–48), the compulsory slaughter of over a million chickens in Hong Kong in 1997 as a response to a 'bird flu' that was considered to pose a risk of a serious regional or international epidemic, and the UK's ban on beef on the bone in 1997. For other hazards, such as smoking, much lighter and more reactive approaches are adopted.

Risk tolerances may vary as well as anticipation and intrusiveness in regulation. For example, in the UK, which is the main focus of this book, the state in some cases sanctions what seem to be remarkably high levels of risk tolerance, as in the case of cancer risks from radon gas in the home, to be discussed further in this book. In other domains, however, as in the case of pesticide residue risks in drinking water, regulation encompasses extreme risk-aversion (see Morris 2000). In a few cases, producers such as beef farmers have been partly or fully compensated for compliance with costly safety rules. But for most organizations or individuals subject to safety regulation, like restaurant operators, compliance has simply been required, without any compensation, such that producers must either absorb the costs of compliance or pass them on to consumers in part or whole. In some domains of risk regulation—for instance, drinking water quality, distance vision requirements, or maximum permitted blood-alcohol levels for drivers—relatively formal and heavily quantified standards have been applied, while in others, like most other aspects of driver fitness, standards are much vaguer and more general.

Some of the variations we can observe across risk regulation domains involve different approaches to standard-setting. Some domains, notably road safety, are dominated by a 'cost-benefit-analysis culture' in which the costs of additional safety measures are weighed against probable benefits using explicit value-of-life calculations (Evans 1994). For instance, such an approach underpinned the rejection of proposals for the introduction of an automatic train protection system across the entire UK rail network in the wake of a train crash in London in 1988 which killed over 30 people.[7] But this approach is far from universal, and indeed critics of risk regulation policy often point to disparities between state regulatory effort in relation to different kinds of risks. For instance, smoking tends to be less heavily regulated than vehicle emissions although it is normally assumed to be a much bigger killer, and domestic accident risks are much more lightly regulated than occupational risks, even though the former claim ten times more lives a year than the latter in the UK. Some risk domains are dominated by various forms of 'quantified risk assessment' culture, notably in nuclear power plant safety, in which risks are expressed in elaborate numbers but the costs and benefits of various forms of regulation or management are not. By contrast, other risks are handled by a culture of inter-agency bargaining—for example over who pays, how much and when over the EU Drinking Water Directive—or of wholly qualitative 'seat of the pants' approaches to standard-setting, in cases such as the regulation of guns or activity holiday centres.

The design of institutional machinery and boundaries for risk regulation also varies sharply from one domain to another. Some risks and hazards are handled by 'risk bureaucracies', in the sense of state agencies staffed by specialists in risk management, such as fault-tree engineers, toxicologists, and risk-benefit analysts dealing in an alphabet soup of risk management jargon like ALARP and NOAEL, with expert monitoring arrangements and dedicated specialist enforcers. Others are regulated by more generalist agencies, self-regulatory arrangements, or the law courts (see Cheit 1990), and may rely on lay reporting about hazards rather than specialized monitoring. In some cases, one agency or bureaucracy monopolizes an entire risk domain, while in others the domain is divided up among a multiplicity of players for different stages or aspects of the regulatory task, amounting to a control system made up of multiple regimes, or at least sub-regimes.

Such examples indicate that risk regulation regimes can vary widely even,

---

[7] The issue was later reopened after two further major train accidents in London, including a collision near Paddington station in 1999 which killed 31 people.

perhaps especially, within the same 'regulatory state'. To come to grips with such variation, we need to go beyond generalizing perspectives like 'risk society' to a more disaggregated analysis. This book accordingly develops the idea of risk regulation 'regimes' to bring out some of the ways in which risk regulation varies from one domain to another and how it can change over time.

'Regime' connotes the overall way risk is regulated in a particular policy domain—though, as we shall see later, some domains are closely linked to others. We concentrate here on the public management of risks and hazards, but that does not mean an exclusive focus on state officials in a narrow sense, since many regulatory regimes involve some mixture of public and private and semi-public organizations. In principle, we can distinguish varying private risk regulation regimes too—for the USA, Ross Cheit (1990) has brought out some of the variety in standard-setting by industry bodies—and such variations come into our story in so far as these private regimes intersect with state regulation.

In exploring the notion of risk regulation regimes, we draw on several approaches to risk. We are not cognitive psychologists concerned with experiments in risk perception, on which a vast literature has accumulated. Nor are we engineers or professional risk-assessors seeking to estimate risk from particular hazards and develop optimal-decision approaches to managing those risks—the source of another large body of writing. We are not professional moral philosophers or big-picture sociologists either, and there is another growing literature on risk from both of those perspectives. Our aim is different. We want to find a way of describing, comparing, and explaining variety in risk-regulation regimes—a variety that is often observed by commentators, but rarely explored beyond the stage of anecdote or first principles. Accordingly, we seek to describe how these regimes work—and fail—and to examine and understand the forces shaping them.

Our approach is 'institutional' in a broad sense, in that our point of departure is a comparative focus on rules, conventions, and organizations. However, to describe and compare risk regulation regimes properly we need to go beyond the characterization of institutional geography and formal rules, and to draw on several of the perspectives mentioned above. For instance, we need to explore a range of risk-assessment techniques and policy-making approaches to distinguish the different scientific and bureaucratic practices, techniques, and cultures embodied in different fields of risk regulation. Such information as is available on the public salience of different risks and hazards can tell us about variations in the awareness of such hazards on the part of the media and the public. It may also help us to gauge how closely aligned 'lay' and 'expert' views are in different risk domains. We need to explore established attitudes and beliefs, for instance over the adequacy of evidence or what counts as justice, to put flesh on the formal regulatory rules applying to each hazard. So a 'regime' approach is not completely divorced from some of the approaches mentioned above. It is better seen as an angle of vision that cuts across and pulls together many of the conventional ways of looking at risk and its management.

2. The Idea of Risk Regulation Regimes

We use the term 'regime' to denote the complex of institutional geography, rules, practice, and animating ideas that are associated with the regulation of a particular risk or hazard. Institutional geography can vary in features such as scale, from international through national to local jurisdiction; integration, from a single agency handling all features of regulation to highly fragmented administration and complex overlapping systems controlling related aspects of a risk; and specialization, from risk-specific and hazard-specific expertise to general-purpose administration. Rules can vary in formality, from unwritten club rules to statutory codes; targets, from affecting inputs to processes and products; and penalty or incentive structures, from moral exhortation to criminalizing certain types of activity (see Hood 1986; Baldwin 1995; Black 1997). Practice and animating ideas can vary in professional or cultural bias, for instance in reliance on professional or lay reporting of hazards; rigour; and preferred policy instruments, for example a bias towards public education and dialogue, a bias towards market-type incentives like grants or taxes, or a bias towards command-and-control modes of operation. We shall describe a simple way of analysing risk regulation regimes in the next chapter, but three basic features of the regime approach deserve to be noted briefly here.

First, we see risk regulation regimes as *systems*. We view them as sets of interacting or at least related parts rather than as 'single-cell' phenomena. So we are interested just as much in what 'street bureaucrats' and front-line people do on the ground as in the activity of standard-setters and policy-makers at the centre of government, and in the relationship, if any, between the two.

Second, we see risk regulation regimes as entities that have some degree of continuity over time. Of course, regulatory systems are seldom if ever completely static. Risk regulation regimes have their sudden climacterics as well as their incremental adjustments and steady trends. There is admittedly a fine line between what is to be counted as a minor adjustment of an existing regime—for instance, when an air or road accident causes an extra item to be added to the list of routine tests in mandatory checking of aircraft or vehicles—and what counts as a step-change in regime. We prefer to count the latter as involving a quite different set of policy instruments—such as replacement of quarantine requirements for imported animals by vaccination requirements validated by animal passports—or a different conceptual approach. Exactly where such a boundary line is to be drawn is a question that takes us into deep philosophical waters, and the distinction cannot be hard and fast. But the concept of a 'regime' for our purpose implies a set of characteristics that are often retained beyond the tenure in office of any one leader, government minister, or political party.

Third, as with any system-based approach to organization, regimes are conceived as relatively bounded systems that can be specified at different levels of breadth. For example, if we take the risks to patients associated with health care we could conceive the 'regime' for controlling those risks as composed of all the regulatory activities that affect health care directly or indirectly. Those activities include attempts to control the risk from dangerous doctors or other health-care workers, for example by attempts to exclude unqualified, bogus, or incompetent doctors from practice; to control the risk from dangerous drugs or medical equipment, for example by drugs approval procedures testing for side-effects and efficacy; and to control the risk from dangerous medical procedures, for example by controls over use of anaesthetics, blood transfusions, or cloning. To that could be added other sources of risk, such as risk of attack for patients in hospital from other patients or intruders, or risks associated with power failures or hospital acquired infections. While it can be useful to think about regulation regimes from an overall systems perspective, we can also conceive of regimes in a narrower sense as the system of control that centres on a defined sub-set of a broader risk. In the health-care example, we could focus on the 'regime' that is concerned with risks from dangerous doctors as opposed to the regime constituted by the sum of all controls over health care.

We have to specify carefully, therefore, what level of 'regime' is being analysed, and the kind of risk the regime addresses. The health-care example discussed above shows that patients face sources of risk other than those presented by dangerous doctors, and the risk that the dangerous-doctors regime seeks to control is the risk left as a residue after the other controls—on drugs, equipment, procedures, hospital security, and the like—have taken effect. We shall see later that this point is important when trying to analyse the features that shape the content of regulatory regimes that are nested, as in the health-care example, in a larger system of controls.

We are by no means the first to have developed the concept of a regulatory regime in a general sense. The idea has numerous conceptual and terminological cousins in other contexts. The term 'regime' and 'regime theory' has been developed for similar purposes—that is, to describe variety in systems of governance—in several fields. For instance, theorists of international relations have used the term since the 1970s as a convenient way of characterizing different forms of international order as bundles of norms, rules, and decision-making procedures (see Krasner 1983). Students of public policy also use the concept of 'regimes', for example to link the content of regulatory policy with its political context in cross-national comparisons (see Elkin 1986: 49–72), and in urban political science to describe relatively enduring policy styles in city government. The features denoted by 'regimes' in the latter form of analysis include the nature of the governing coalition, the structure of relations between actors, and the resources held by the various players in the system (see Dowding 1996: 82–4). Economists also use the term 'regime' to denote alternative approaches to the conduct of economic policy, especially in the choice of alternative policy instruments and the way those instruments are varied over time (see Bryant, Hooper, and Mann 1993: vii, 5). Policy practitioners and commentators on law and regulation commonly use the term to denote particular configurations of formal rules and practice applying to issues such as business taxation, environmental protection, or human rights. Though diverse in disciplinary origin, all of these different usages of 'regime' incorporate the first of the two features mentioned earlier, that is, a more or less elaborate and explicit 'system' perspective. Most of them embody the second and third features as well, in that they imply a view of regimes as relatively enduring phenomena and of systems that can be nested in larger systems.

The concept of regimes in risk regulation is also related to several other analytic themes, notably in system theory and related fields of organizational and regulatory analysis, even though the word 'regime' may not be used in such analysis. For example, cybernetics, the science of control and communication in natural and artificial systems, offers an analytic framework for understanding control systems and a set of theorems relating to the operation of such systems, of which the 'law of requisite variety' is the best known (Beer 1966).[8] Some leading legal and regulatory theorists have developed a theme in system theory that was originally associated with a branch of biology: the 'autopoietic' notion of systems as inclined to maintain themselves by processes of dynamic conservatism in the face of environmental disturbances. In principle such a perspective offers a basis for modelling adaptive processes in law, politics, and regulation (see Teubner 1987; Brans and Rossbach 1997).

Institutional analysts of a number of stripes have looked for ways of identifying variety in decision-making and implementation styles that are closely related to the notion of 'regimes'. For example, various attempts have been made since John Stringer's (1967) work in the 1960s to map patterns of organization within policy domains as 'policy networks' or 'issue networks' (see Rhodes and Marsh 1992; Heclo 1978; Dowding 1995). Contemporary ideas of 'governance'—for instance, as developed by Rhodes (1997)—focus on different interactions among multiple state and non-state actors, and portray the 'policy network' approach as a departure from what is claimed to be an older pattern focusing mainly on state activity and single organizations.

---

[8] In earlier work, one of us (Hood 1996) drew on cybernetics to contrast two different institutional designs for the management of risk.

Other institutional analyses that can be related to the notion of regimes include catalogues of different types of policy instruments (Hood 1983; Ogus 1994); institutional types and rule types, such as Elinor Ostrom's (1986) account of the 'DNA' of decision-making structures;[9] and of interest-group constellations. For the latter, one of the best-known is the 'Chicago-school' approach[10] that relates regulatory characteristics to the existence of interest-group coalitions with low transaction costs in collective organization. James Q. Wilson (1980) offered a well-known modification of the Chicago-school approach in the form of a typology of regulatory costs and benefits, which we will draw on later in this book in characterizing regulatory regime context.

Finally, cultural and organizational theorists have taken a particular interest in the regulation of risk and hazard, identifying alternative polar 'world-views' that come into play when such issues are in debate (see Adams 1995; Schwarz and Thompson 1990), and the way such worldviews can clash with one another. Table 1.1 indicates some of the variety that a cultural-theory perspective leads us to see in risk regulation, contrasting four polar approaches that could be expected to manifest themselves in different regimes. Cultural theorists would expect such differences to be at the heart of variety in risk regulation regimes.

This discussion of usages of 'regime' and some related approaches is by no means comprehensive. Nevertheless, it shows that many of the ideas underlying our conception of 'risk regulation regimes' are not short of 'giant shoulders' to stand on. What we aim to do is a mixture of reading across and drawing together. By 'reading across' we mean bringing some of the ideas developed in other policy contexts into the domain of risk regulation, and by 'drawing together' we mean linking and developing some of the existing institutional perspectives on risk management. The aim is to produce a meso-level perspective on risk regulation that parallels developments in the analysis of many other policy fields. A meso-level analysis comes between the macroscopic level of whole-society characterizations, à la 'risk society', and the micro-level of single-case studies or debates over the policy settings appropriate for particular risks.

There is, however, no single correct way of conceiving risk regulation regimes. No one has ever seen a risk regulation regime. The concept has many possible dimensions, and the balance of emphasis across those dimensions is bound to vary according to the analytic interest of each observer. A traditional lawyer might give primacy to the formal rule structure, an institutional economist to the underlying incentive structure, an anthropologist to the prevailing pattern of attitudes and beliefs, a political scientist to the distribution of power among actors, an historian to the way the past shapes the

---

[9] Or in other typologies of rules such as those offered by Diver (1983), Baldwin (1995) or Black (1997).

[10] See, for instance, Peltzman (1975); Noll (1987).

TABLE 1.1. *Risk regulation regimes in a cultural theory frame*

	Fatalist	Hierarchist
Stress on	Unpredictability and unmanageability of hazards, unintended policy effects	Expert forecasting and management
Role for government	Minimal in anticipation, respond after the event	Develop anticipative whole-society solutions
Preferred policy instruments	Ad hoc and post hoc responses	Expert quangos and committees
Justice model	'Chancist'—unavoidable elements of luck and lottery	Aggregated social welfare—utilitarianism
Exponent	Wildavsky (1988) on 'resilience'	Royal Society (1992) on enlightened management
Examples	Adventure tourism, common responses to 'natural' disasters	Chemical safety, UK controls on beef-on-the-bone, 1997–9

	Individualist	Egalitarian
Stress on	Market and individual choice processes	Community participation in decision-making
Role for government	Support/develop markets and underpin informed choice	Support/develop popular participation
Preferred policy instruments	Markets and courts, perhaps supplemented by community information-asymmetry-reduction measures	Local participatory institutions, forums, citizen juries
Justice model	'Choicist'—minimize legal intrusion/rent transfer	'Rawlsian'—protect the worst-off, give them priority
Exponent	Tollison and Wagner (1988) on smoking	Shrader-Frechette (1991) on citizen participation
Example	Some developing-country states' approach to vehicle-safety standards	'Agenda 21' on local consultation over global environmental change

present, a geographer to the relation between physical scale and regulation. But these perspectives heavily overlap. It is possible to develop a concept of risk regulation regimes that cuts across a number of them without encompassing all possible dimensions. Moreover, as we will show in the next chapter, a cybernetic framework offers a set of overall organizing categories that can be linked with other features of regulation. Accordingly, we start from a generic trio of components that can be found in any control system in nature or artifice, roughly corresponding with policy-making, monitoring, and enforcement or behaviour modification. We link those three components to a distinction between regime context and regime content, to produce a dimensional snapshot of variety in risk regulation systems.

3. Potential Payoffs of a Risk Regulation Regime Perspective

As noted earlier, a risk regulation regime-centred approach to looking at the social handling of risk and hazard is intended to be a 'middle way' approach to institutional analysis. It is designed to capture the variety that is left out of macroscopic 'risk society' or 'audit society' approaches, which inevitably can deal only in broad-gauge interpretation. At the same time, it is designed to achieve a broader and more general perspective than is yielded by microscopic approaches, which tend to focus on the setting of safety standards alone, or on the details of a particular hazard, or both. In adopting a comparative-regime perspective, we do not deny the value of those other approaches. To argue that one type of lens can be useful is not to downplay the complementary value of others, as any wearer of bifocal glasses can testify. Rather, our aim is to provide a middle-range lens on risk regulation to pick up variety that cannot be readily seen either through the telescope of the 'risk society' sociologists or through the microscope of single-case or single-feature analysis. Apart from bringing out variety that is otherwise hard to see, our angle of vision has at least three other related uses. It brings out systemic interaction; it helps us to identify puzzles and questions that are invisible from other perspectives; and it can serve as a policy tool to explore the justification for regulatory variety.

The first and most prosaic value of a regime perspective is simply as a method of comparing cases to identify commonalities and differences in institutional risk profiles. Ernest Rutherford once said, 'Science is divided into two categories, physics and stamp-collecting' (Cohen and Cohen 1993: 329); and if that is true the risk regulation regime approach is closer to the latter than the former. By treating regimes as dimensional rather than unified phenomena, our approach offers a way of unpacking their constituent parts systematically—'analysis' in its literal and original sense.

The second potential value of a regime perspective is as a means of bringing out the relationships among the different parts of a regulatory system. In that sense, a dimensional account of risk regulation illuminates parts of regulatory systems that portraits based only on standard-setting cannot reach. In the world of policy analysis an intellectual movement stressing implementation analysis developed nearly 30 years ago in reaction to an earlier tendency to focus on standard-setting or legislative politics (see Pressman and Wildavsky 1973; Hood 1976; Bardach 1977). The argument was that a policy-study approach which focused largely or exclusively on legislative or standard-setting processes missed much of the 'action' and indeed much of the politics of public policy. That point can be made with particular force for risk and hazard regulation. Much debate about, and analysis of, risk regulation still focuses largely on the policy-setting component. But over-concentration on the executive or legislative process of setting standards, in Brussels or Washington or elsewhere, can obscure what, if anything, those standards do to modify behaviour on the ground (see Baldwin and Daintith 1992). In some institutional conditions, particularly where different levels of government and different professional and organizational cultures operate in standard setting and implementation, the nominal 'implementers' may in practice be setting standards, applying their own ethical benchmarks, and conducting their own private cost-benefit analyses (see Hawkins 1984).

A classic example, described by Brian Wynne (1989), was the review of 2,4,5-T by the UK Pesticides Advisory Committee in 1979. The use of 2,4,5-T was endorsed by the standard-setting experts on the wildly unrealistic assumption that farmers on the ground would be willing and able to read and follow all the detailed operating instructions, use the correct equipment, and wear the recommended clothing. More recently, a UK Parliamentary inquiry demonstrated how far the actual practice of slaughterhouses deviated from the official rules for preventing BSE-contaminated offal from getting into the food supply between 1989 and 1995 (see, for example, Calman 1998: ¶145). We will give more examples of such disjunction in risk regulation later in this book.

A system perspective can also bring out what, in another context, Baldwin and Hawkins (1984: 582) have described as the toothpaste-tube-like characteristics of regulatory systems, that is, their tendency, if squeezed in one place, to bulge out in another. So if the standard-setting component of a regulatory system experiences a 'squeeze', for example in pressures for greater rigour or transparency, we need to look carefully for corresponding 'bulges' in other components, for example in increasing discretion or opacity of the implementation process, as the system adapts to the disturbance. For example, a 1990 report by WHO (1990: 82) suggests that the response to the development of safety protocols for the spraying of pesticides in some developing countries was deliberately not to train operators in the protocols. Increased legal liability, for instance in relation to advice to the public about the handling of risks, may cause advice to be abandoned rather than improved, in the same way that the French government for a long time avoided giving any advice about the dangers of radon gas in the home out of concern for

legal liability (Massuelle, Pirard, and Hubert 1998). Indeed, powerful imperatives for 'blame-shifting' in both public and private organizations may make
it politically convenient for standard-setting and implementation to be
located on different institutional planets—an issue we shall be discussing later
in the book. What a 'regime' perspective does is to reconnect those elements
and bring them together into a single analysis.

Third, a regime approach is a means of identifying puzzles and questions
that are not easily visible from other approaches. As we will show in Chapters
2 and 3, a risk regulation regime approach is not just a tool for analysis—a
lens that comes between the microscope and the telescope—but also a challenge for explanation of observed variety. To the extent that it is capable of
bringing out clearly the variety of ways in which different forms of risk and
hazard are regulated, the question of what accounts for that variety is
inevitably raised. That question cannot be satisfactorily answered either by
historicist whole-society generalization—because that approach explains 'too
much'—or by deep-trench case studies—because that approach explains 'too
little'.

Indeed, several related questions are prompted by the risk regulation
regime approach. How much of the variety in regimes can be explained 'parsi-
moniously' by any one explanation, and how far do we need to invoke multi-
causal explanations? How far are features applying to one element of a
regulatory regime, such as standard-setting elements, shared with other
components? How far can we explain observed variety in risk regulation by
the nature of the risks and hazards themselves? How much depends on
'market failure' characteristics associated with risk, such as information
deficits or monopoly? Or are more orthodox 'political' explanations a better
predictor of observed variety in risk regulation regimes? We shall be grappling
closely with these questions in Part II of the book. As we will show in the
following chapters, looking closely at variation in regimes exposes the limits
of conventional explanations of why the state regulates risk in the way it
does, whether those explanations come from received folk-wisdom in policy
communities or expert cultures or from orthodox academic perspectives.
Hence, the value of the regime approach does not lie only in its ability to
produce more comprehensive comparative descriptions of the profile of state
actions across different risk and hazard. It helps us to arrive at a more dimensional and disaggregated analysis of what happens when the risk society
meets the regulatory state.

The fourth value of a regime approach is that it has potential policy significance in at least two ways. It highlights the consistency or otherwise with
which risks and hazards are regulated in different policy domains, and the
justification or rationalizations that are given for differences from one
domain to another (see for example Breyer 1993). Such policy issues—increasingly preoccupying the courts, central agencies of government, and 'risk

bureaucracies' themselves, as well as interest groups and the media—are at the heart of concerns about 'better regulation' in the UK and other OECD countries. Central issues include why risks to life are reduced at much higher cost in some policy sectors than others, why the value of a life is officially set at very different levels in road transport and nuclear safety, or why cost-benefit considerations figure heavily in standard-setting for some fields of risk regulation but not in others. Such interests are reflected in cross-government official inquiries such as the UK's Interdepartmental Liaison Group on Risk Assessment (ILGRA) (Health and Safety Executive 1996; 1998) and its counterparts in the USA and EU.[11] The regime approach offers a way of developing those frameworks conceptually and empirically.

The other potential policy payoff of a regime approach is in the way it can be used to track the activity of regulation in each domain of risk and hazard across the various institutional boundaries and organizations active in the field. Those organizations may include different levels of government, public, and private actors, and various types of intermediaries such as the advisers and consultants who are part of many regulatory regimes. Such regime maps, as we will see in Chapter 3, vary in complexity from one risk domain to another. But their policy value is to direct attention to overlaps—or underlaps, at least as common in the regimes we investigated—among the activities of the various organizations engaged in risk and hazard regulation. Here too crucial questions arise as to how, if at all, the observed variety can be justified and rationalized.

4. The Plan of the Book

This book's exploration of risk regulation regimes is divided into three parts. The first part is devoted to conceptualizing, analysing, and comparing risk regulation regimes. This chapter has aimed to indicate how the concept of 'regimes' can help refine our understanding of risk regulation or indeed 'risk society'. The next chapter moves on to develop a relatively simple framework for describing and comparing risk regulation regimes, combining a distinction between regime context and regime content with an analysis of the fundamental components of regulatory control.

The following chapter uses that analytic framework to draw systematic comparisons among nine different domains of risk regulation. While this book draws on observations of risk regulation in different contexts from secondary literature, its main empirical foundations are built on an in-depth

---

[11] See, for example, Presidential/Congressional Commission on Risk Assessment and Risk Management (1997) and Health Council of the Netherlands: Committee on Risk Measures and Risk Assessment (1996).

analysis of regulation in nine domains—or sub-domains—carried out over several years in the late 1990s. Those nine domains were chosen to give a spread of cases—for example, high-tech and low-tech risks, occupational and consumer risks—and they include the regulation of risks from dangerous dogs, radon gas, benzene, released paedophiles—repeat sex offenders against children—road traffic, and pesticide residues in food and water. We shall be introducing these cases in Chapter 3, specifying the risks and domains involved, and using them throughout the analysis in the rest of the book as samples of variety among risk regulation regimes.

Having developed a mapping instrument for risk regulation regimes and brought out the degree to which regime contours vary from one risk domain to another, we devote the second part of the book to considering how that variation might be explained. Accordingly, Chapter 4 separates the elements of regulatory regime context and regime content and in particular considers how far three elements of regime context could be expected to explain regime content. Those elements are the functional logic of market failure presented by different sources of risk, public preferences and attitudes, and the impact of interest groups. We devote a chapter to each of these elements of regime context in Part II, and examine how far they can plausibly explain or shape variations in regulatory regime content. Chapter 5 analyses the 'market failure' characteristics of different risks and hazards, showing that the observed pattern of risk regulation regimes is only partially explained by the degree of market failure. Chapter 6 looks at the pull of public preferences and attitudes about risk, to which 'responsive government' in a liberal democracy is expected to pay attention in shaping risk regulation regimes. Chapter 7 follows a well-trodden path in political science and examines the role of organized interest groups and professional communities in shaping risk regulation through lobbying power or institutionalized expertise or both. Chapter 8 concludes our examination of how to account for variety in regulatory regime content by assessing how much of the observed variety in regime content can be explained by variations in regime context, and to what extent it seems to come from the 'inner lives' of regulatory regimes, in the sense of the attitudes, beliefs, and conventions of the various technocratic and bureaucratic 'tribes' in the regulatory machine.

These first two parts of the book are concerned with the comparative statics of risk regulation regimes, and the focus is on description and explanation rather than normative evaluation. In the third and final part, we change the emphasis and focus instead on regime dynamics and on evaluative questions about regimes. Accordingly, Chapter 9 considers those received official and academic interpretations of contemporary risk regulation that see it as developing cumulatively in rationality and transparency. We consider how far observed developments fit a quasi-evolutionary view of risk regulation dynamics as a staged retreat away from an inertia position, and contrast this view with an alternative 'lateral mutation' or shifting-sands perspective on regulatory change. The latter perspective is more challenging for conventional nostrums for evaluating regulation, such as 'proportionality' and cost-benefit, but it cannot be dismissed.

Chapter 10 concludes the book by returning to our starting-point and reviewing how a 'risk regulation regime' perspective can refine our understanding of risk regulation and how such an approach can be developed. What is offered by a regime perspective is not claimed to be a panacea. Like any other approach, it has its limits. Nevertheless, the regime lens has a value in several ways. As outlined earlier in this chapter, it offers a middle-range approach to the understanding of risk and how it is handled by the state, thus helping to develop earlier cross-domain comparisons of regulatory systems. It can help to generate fruitful questions that are not readily visible from other viewpoints, and in particular it prompts closer scrutiny of the scope and limits of different overarching 'theories' of regulation in accounting for the various elements and components of regulation. It can also help us to evaluate contemporary ideas about 'better regulation'.

2

The Comparative Anatomy of Risk Regulation Regimes

Entia non sunt multiplicanda praeter per necessitatem.

(attributed to William of Occam)

1. A Basis of Comparison

The last chapter gave some examples of the variety of regulatory regimes to be found across different risk policy domains and argued for systematic analysis of that variety to move beyond the broad-gauge generalities of the 'risk society' literature. Accordingly, this chapter looks at ways of analysing and comparing risk regulation regimes.

We have already noted that regulatory 'regimes' are analytic constructs, not directly observable entities.[1] They can be conceived at different levels of breadth or generality and are also potentially *n*-dimensional, capable in principle of being described at up to infinite levels of complexity. This chapter, however, begins with some fairly simple and broad-gauge ways in which risk regulation regimes can vary. As we argued in the last chapter, taking a dimensional view of regulatory regimes means characterizing them as more than a single all-encompassing essence, but that does not mean we need to identify every conceivable feature on which risk regulation regimes might vary.

A dimensional comparison of risk regulation regimes should ideally have at least three related features. First, it should begin at a fairly simple and self-explanatory level, making distinctions that are broad enough to cover a wide range of the regulatory landscape. Second, its basic categories should be capable of being progressively disaggregated into more fine-grained differentiations. That is the way biologists have traditionally sought to classify plants and animals *per genus et differentiam*, a method often applied to other schemes of comparison as in Bentham's (1983) 'chrestomathic table' of types of knowledge. Third, it should connect to live debates about how regulation works or should work.

---

[1] Risk regulation regimes might be considered as Platonic essences—entities accessible to philosophy though not directly visible. But our starting point is more modest and selective.

With these desiderata in mind, our anatomy of regulatory regimes begins with two fairly simple dimensions, both of which figure large in description and analysis of regulation. One dimension is the three components that form the basis of any control system—that is, ways of gathering information, ways of setting standards, goals, or targets, and ways of changing behaviour to meet the standards or targets.[2] As we have already noted, much debate on risk regulation understandably tends to focus on the *standard-setting* issues, because standard-setting raises dramatic questions about the valuation of human life or the way one risk is weighed against another. From a control-system perspective, however, *information-gathering* and *behaviour-modification* are just as important to the government of risk. Indeed, as we shall see later, they are the components by which risk regulation regimes can often best be judged.

A second basic dimension on which regulatory regimes can be compared comprises their instrumental and institutional elements, starting with a simple distinction between regulatory regime 'context' and regime 'content'. *Regime context* means the backdrop or setting in which regulation takes place, such as the different types and levels of risk being tackled, the nature of public preferences and attitudes over risk, and the way the various actors who produce or are affected by the hazard are organized. *Regime content* means the policy settings, the configuration of state and other organizations directly engaged in regulating the risk, and the attitudes, beliefs, and operating conventions of the regulators.[3]

Linking those two dimensions forms a starting point for comparing the anatomy of regulatory regimes. That framework is summarized in Table 2.1, which includes examples to illustrate sources of variety in each of its six cells. Such a schema cannot embrace every possible way of conceiving regulatory regimes. Nor are the distinctions among the three basic components of control and between context and content always clear-cut. For instance, it is well known that the mere gathering of information can sometimes alter behaviour—as with the placing of cameras to detect street crime or speeding on highways—such that the *information-gathering* and *behaviour-modification* elements of control are distinguishable only in an analytic, not physical or institutional, sense. Nevertheless, as a starting point for conceiving the anatomy of regulatory regimes, the two-dimensional schema summarized in Table 2.1 has several advantages.

One is that it provides a way of describing and comparing regulation across

---

[2] Henceforth we use the shorthand terms 'information-gathering' (IG), 'standard-setting' (SS) and 'behaviour-modification' (BM) to denote these three control components.

[3] The distinction between regime context and content can be thought of as contrasting 'characteristics of the risk' and 'characteristics of the regulation', or 'states of the world' and 'policy choices', a distinction commonly used in policy analysis in the 1960s and 1970s (see Dorfman 1962).

TABLE 2.1. *Control components and regulatory regime content and context*

	Control components		
	Information gathering	Standard setting	Behaviour modification
Context: e.g., type and level of risk being tackled, nature of public or media attitudes, configuration of lobbies and organized interests	*Example*: risks individuals can assess at low cost vs risks assessable only by professionals or at high cost	*Example*: risks involving high stakes for organized groups vs risks with no lobby groups	*Example*: risks where mass public opinion resists state control vs regulation 'with the grain'
Content: e.g., regulatory stance, organizational structure, operating conventions and regulator attitudes	*Example*: active vs passive information-seeking by regulators	*Example*: cost-benefit vs technical feasibility approaches to goal setting	*Example*: price signals vs command approaches to control

risk domains on the basis of a few simple distinctions—which, it will be recalled, was our first desideratum. A second advantage is that the basic categories of Table 2.1 can be progressively unpacked, as we shall show later, to make more fine-grained distinctions among regimes—our second desideratum. A third is that it picks up regime features that are central to a range of debates about how regulation is or should be conducted—our third desideratum. For example, the link, or lack of it, between *standard-setting* and other aspects of regulation is the major focus of the literature on policy implementation and institutional coordination that we referred to in the last chapter. Similarly, the distinction between *regime context* and *regime content* is central to a debate between those who seek to explain how regulation works or develops by reference to its technical or social environment and those who stress the way the 'inner lives' of public organizations shape their decisions, in a way that is not readily predictable from environmental conditions (see March and Olsen 1989; Powell and DiMaggio 1991).

The rest of this chapter develops the basic anatomy of regulatory regimes depicted in Table 2.1, while the next chapter puts the approach to work, using it to bring out variations and commonalities among nine different risk regulation regimes.

2. A General Control Theory Perspective: Regimes as Combinations of Control Components

One of the standard ways of understanding regulation, widely and increasingly used in the sociology of law and policy studies, is to view it from a cybernetic angle (see for example Hood *et al.* 1999*a*). From such a perspective, any control system in art or nature must by definition contain a minimum of the three components depicted in the column axis of Table 2.1. There must be some capacity for *standard-setting* to allow a distinction to be made between more and less preferred states of the system. There must also be some capacity for *information-gathering* or monitoring to produce knowledge about current or changing states of the system. On top of that must be some capacity for *behaviour-modification* to change the state of the system.

If any of those components is absent, a system is not under control in a cybernetic sense.[4] Following the 'law of requisite variety' mentioned in the last chapter, each of the components must also have sufficient variety—different possible states—to match the variety of its environment if control in a cybernetic sense is to be achieved. It also follows that for a system to be under

---

[4] In this sense, control means the ability to keep the state of a system within some preferred subset of all its possible states (Hood 1986: 112).

control, there must be some way of linking those three components together—which is often the Achilles heel of control systems in human organizations, with their frequent underlaps, conflicts, and communication failures (Perrow 1984). A control-theory perspective thus raises fundamental issues about the effectiveness of risk regulation.

Information-Gathering

The gathering of information is central to all regulation, and particularly to risk regulation when issues of probability and consequence are in question. Indeed, when the politics runs hot in risk regulation it is often the *information-gathering* element that is in contention. That applies, for example, to the wide variation in levels of official monitoring of environmental pollution amongst EU Member States. More generally, there has been a long-running debate in risk policy over the quality of information that is used to detect and assess risk. For instance, sometimes information about tests or near-misses can be faked, fabricated, or suppressed by state or private organizations, as with the fabrication of toxicological test results in the US by Industrial Bio-Test in 1976 (see Millstone 1986: 99). Controversy can also be found over the extent to which historical records or animal experiments can be used to make reliable inferences about risks to humans,[5] or the extent to which risk distributions can be drawn from the way data is recorded for incidents such as road or industrial accidents (see Adams 1995). Moreover, there is a long-running debate about how scientific information is interpreted and used by different actors of different professional, institutional, and cultural backgrounds.[6]

Information about risks can be gathered in many ways. For instance, it can be obtained by regulators conducting their own analyses and experiments, by imposing legal requirements to report, test, or register on others, or by paying others to provide information. It can be provided voluntarily by complainants or whistleblowers or individuals willing to contribute to common learning, as in the case of anonymous reporting systems for errors or near-misses. Or it can be obtained willy-nilly through physical surveillance devices like black-box flight recorders or spy satellites. Often the information-gathering component of a regulatory regime consists of a mixture of such methods.

Risk regulators also vary in the extent to which they gather information by active, reactive, or interactive methods. An active approach, sometimes

---

[5] For instance a controversial 1980s study found only 37 per cent of chemicals known to be carcinogenic to humans produced cancer in laboratory animals in long-term feeding tests, making inferences to human health from such tests less accurate than a tossed coin. A recalculation of the analysis produced a 75 per cent correlation, still leaving a one in four chance of erroneous inference (see Salsburg 1983 and discussion in Millstone 1986: 97).

[6] See Robbins and Johnstone (1976); Nelkin (1979); Wynne (1982); Collingridge and Reeve (1986); Jasanoff (1990).

known as 'police patrol' in the oversight-systems literature (McCubbins and Schwartz 1984), means regulators scan the environment, seeking out and assembling information about the policy issue in question. A reactive approach, sometimes known as 'fire alarms' in the oversight literature, means regulators rely on others to come forward with information. Interactive approaches, less commonly discussed than the 'police patrol' and 'fire alarm' approaches, come somewhere in between the two, typically through regulators imposing periodic reporting requirements on others and then responding to the content of the reports, as often happens in occupational safety regimes. Power (1997) claims the advent of an 'audit society' has triggered a boom in interactive forms of information-gathering in many fields of risk regulation.

Standard-Setting

Central to regulation is the setting of standards, goals, targets, guidelines. As already noted, much writing about risk and its regulation focuses on *standard-setting*, since it raises distinctive issues about the value of life and acceptable levels and distributions of risk (see Heimann 1997). Philosophers, amateur and professional, have had much to say about issues such as implied consent and distributive justice in risk-policy settings. As noted in the last chapter, many critics have pointed to inconsistencies and discrepancies among safety standards in different countries and policy domains.

There are many different ways of setting standards in risk regulation. Standards sometimes emerge from a technocratic process applying received technical approaches, drawing on systematic tests or inquiries or reading across from other domains or countries, as in the case of nuclear safety (see Cheit 1990). In other cases, standards sometimes emerge from bargaining among participants with different interests, producing solutions that represent a compromise between rival positions or the interests of different parties, such as in the case of greenhouse gas or occupational safety standards. By contrast, in other cases standards may come from stab-in-the-dark activity, when regulators pluck numerical or qualitative criteria out of the air in some way.[7] Risk regulation often involves a mixture of such standard-setting approaches.

Andrew Dunsire (1990), drawing on cybernetic analysis, distinguishes between simple steering, homeostatic control, and control through opposed maximizers—he terms the latter 'collibration'. Simple steering comprises standards or targets that are set by direct judgement and often not separated

[7] For instance, when the US Federal Drugs Administration introduced regulations for food contact plastics in 1958, many chemicals were approved for use under 'prior sanction', meaning that substances used before 1958 could still be used irrespective of whether or not there was any supporting scientific evidence of risk or safety (Rothstein 1994).

institutionally from *information-gathering* and *behaviour-modification*.[8] Cases of simple steering can be identified in risk regulation, but perhaps the central debate over standard-setting in contemporary risk regulation concerns the rival merits of homeostatic and collibration approaches, for example over the adoption of 'no observable adverse effect level' approaches to the regulation of chemical risks (see Royal Society 1992; Hood 1996). A 'homeostatic' standard involves specifying an acceptable level of risk in quantitative or qualitative terms, with the intention of keeping the state of the system at or below that level. Familiar examples include limits on food additives or minimum vehicle braking-efficiency standards. Such acceptable-risk standards do not consist of a balancing act that needs to be conducted among rival principles in every case, but of a threshold or maximum to be observed.

By contrast, a 'collibration' standard consists of some process in which rival and contradictory desiderata—for instance, of risk against cost, risk against risk, or risk against time and convenience—are maintained in some sort of tension, with a balance-tipping or optimization mechanism. Regime standards that impose deliberative processes weighing different criteria against one another rather than determinate targets are commonplace in risk regulation. One much-cited example, reflected in the reforms to occupational health and safety regulation proposed by the Robens Committee in the UK in 1972, is the idea of handling workplace safety through an obligation to deliberate in worksite-specific safety committees as opposed to uniformly-applied maximum or minimum standards for every process or activity. Another is the use of systems that oblige new or existing regulatory standards for improving safety to be evaluated in terms of cost-effectiveness or cost-benefit.[9] As noted in the last chapter, such an approach has come to be used in many countries for determining local road safety priorities. The relative emphasis placed on 'homeostatic' as against 'collibratory' methods of *standard setting* is thus a pervasive design issue in risk regulation.

Behaviour-Modification

How to change individual and organizational behaviour is another issue that figures large in the politics and public debate surrounding risk regulation. Business and other critics of regulation often fulminate against mechanical implementation or enforcement systems that are claimed to ignore the particularities of each context or lose sight of the original purpose of the standards involved in a process of bureaucratic 'goal displacement' (Merton *et al.* 1952;

---

[8] It seems to correspond with what Mintzberg (1983) terms 'simple structures' in his analysis of organizational types.

[9] Cost-effectiveness conventionally means analysis to find the least-cost way to produce a given outcome or the most effective way to spend a given budget, while cost-benefit analysis means ways of helping to determine whether a given expenditure would produce a net social benefit.

Grabosky 1995) or 'tunnel vision' (Breyer 1993). For instance, a study of EU rail safety regulation noted a case of a minor Swedish railway line that was closed because new standards required an expensive automatic train protection system, even though the closure of the line could be expected to increase road traffic and associated risks of more road deaths and injuries. The railway safety regulator would not be held in any effective way responsible for such a reduction in transport safety (NERA 2000: 85 n. 57).

As such examples show, *behaviour modification* can often be a highly problematic component of risk regulation. Not only can the preferences and incentive structures of bureaucrats produce distortions (Clay and Schaffer 1984: 10; Dunleavy 1991), but the attitudes and beliefs of those regulated can unexpectedly shape the outcome produced by implementation instruments. For instance, within a compliance culture, official bans or warnings about dangerous products or practices can be expected to discourage the consumption or activity in question. Within an opportunistic culture, such policy tools will work only if accompanied by a substantial investment in detection and the application of sanctions. Within a defiance culture, they may produce the reverse of the intended effect, by increasing the attractiveness of the product or practice to those who wish to defy authority, such as youth smokers or bare-headed bikers. The plasticity and unpredictability of cultural shifts often makes such effects hard to gauge in advance.

One of the most prominent debates over behaviour modification in the law and regulation literature concerns the relative merits of 'compliance' and 'deterrence' as ways of applying legal or regulatory standards (see Hawkins and Thomas 1984). Moreover, variations in the predisposition to compliance or deterrence have often been observed as a feature of national regulatory cultures. For instance, it is often claimed that European and UK regulatory regimes in domains such as occupational safety tend to be more compliance-oriented than the more deterrence-focused US system. 'Compliance' doctrines rely heavily on diplomacy, persuasion, or education rather than routine application of sanctions to produce a compliance culture on the part of those affected by regulation. By contrast 'deterrence' doctrines, going back to Bentham and Beccaria, rely on the credibility of penalties or punishment, expressed in the 'expected cost' of non-compliance to violators, to prevent those regulated from breaking the rules. Some regulatory designers such as Ayres and Braithwaite (1992) argue for a hybrid approach, advocating 'compliance' responses towards those regulatees identified as poorly-informed or morally concerned about the regulatory requirements and 'deterrence' approaches to those regulatees who demonstrate themselves to be opportunistic or amoral. The overall bias of a regulatory regime towards emphasis on compliance or deterrence can be expected to be a key feature of its behaviour-modification style.

3. The Context and Content of Regimes

Cutting across the control-component dimensions of regulatory regimes are variations in the context and content of regulatory regimes: a distinction often drawn in various ways in policy literature. As noted earlier, *regime context* denotes the backdrop of regulation, comprising, for example, the intrinsic characteristics of the problem it addresses, public and media attitudes about it, and the way power or influence is concentrated in organized groups. *Regime content* denotes regulatory objectives, the way regulatory responsibilities are organized, and operating styles of regulators.

Context and content can be considered as one fundamental dimension of regulatory regimes because, as was noted earlier, much of the debate about how regulation works centres on the relationship between the two. 'Contextualists' of various kinds see regime content as a product of the policy backdrop. They look for environmental factors—technical, political, or social—to explain what the content of regulatory policy is and why it changes. In contrast to the contextual approaches is a school of thought that sees regulation as shaped by the inner lives of regulatory institutions—lives that are partly independent of the policy backdrop and are expressed in deeply-rooted microcultures, traditions, conventions, and patterns of discourse.[10] Whatever may be the more convincing way of explaining and predicting policy settings and regulator behaviour, a robust basis for comparative description of risk regulation regimes cannot wholly discount either approach and needs to be able to pick up variety in both context and content. We therefore need to be able to give an account of both elements.

Table 2.1 depicted a simple distinction between *regime context* and *regime content*, and Table 2.2 breaks down each of these elements into a further level of disaggregation. We will briefly discuss the six row components of Table 2.2 here, to set the scene for a more detailed examination in the next six chapters.

Elements of Regime Context

The *context* of risk regulation regimes could in principle be characterized in any number of ways. But in the risk regulation literature, three contextual elements tend to be most heavily stressed. As shown in Table 2.2, those basic elements are:

- type of risk: the inherent nature of the hazard and associated risks (see Royal Society 1992: Chs 1–5);

---

[10] See Meidinger (1987); March and Olsen (1989); Brans and Rossbach (1997); Hall, Scott, and Hood (1999).

TABLE 2.2. *Elements of regime context and content*

		Control components		
		Information gathering	Standard setting	Behaviour modification
Regime context	Type of risk Public preferences and attitudes Organized interests			
Regime content	Size Structure Style			

- public preferences and attitudes; and
- organized interests.

The first contextual element, *type of risk*, involves the inherent features of the risk or hazard itself. Those features, much discussed in the literature on risk perception, include its source or cause, how familiar and well-established it is, how easily it can be quantified, its timing or impact, the severity of its consequences, and the probability of occurrence. But if the essence of regulation is interference in markets or other social processes, perhaps the most basic type-of-risk features are the level or severity of risk in the absence of regulation—the combination of consequence and probability—and the extent to which the risk is capable of being handled through market processes or by the ordinary civil law of tort or delict. Market processes include insurance and other private ways of detecting and dealing with risk, and civil-law processes work through contracts and suits for damages by those adversely affected by creators of hazard. Opinions will vary from one observer to another about the extent to which any particular risk is inherently capable of being handled by market, civil law, or immanent social processes. Cultural theorists (for example, Thompson, Ellis, and Wildavsky 1990), whose approach we mentioned in the last chapter, expect egalitarians to see market and tort-law 'failures' almost everywhere and individualists to find such failures almost nowhere. But even allowing for such differences, there are wide observable variations in how much it would cost individuals to assess a risk for themselves and how much it would cost them to avoid or mitigate the hazard, as we shall see in Chapter 5.

Public preferences and attitudes overlap to some extent with type of risk, since one way of describing risks would be in terms of how they are viewed by the public. From the perspective of many influential risk experts, however, the two elements are separable to some degree (see Douglas 1986; Breyer

1993). Certainly, risk domains vary widely in terms of the level of overall public concern, varying from high anxiety to deep apathy, and of how 'hot' or 'cold' they are in media coverage. Regulation in a context of media silence and public apathy is likely to be very different from regulation conducted in the heated atmosphere of high media and public salience. Similarly, public opinion that is consensual provides a very different policy context for regulation from that presented by conflicting opinion, as we shall see later in the book.

The nature of organized interests surrounding a risk domain also overlaps with public and media attitudes. But risk domains can vary widely in who creates and who is exposed to the hazard, and in the ways that victims and risk creators are organized. For instance, how is risk distributed between producers and consumers, between employers and workers, or between other sets of actors, such as landowners and trespassers, or drivers and pedestrians? Such distributional questions are often central to risk regulation politics, since they raise issues of relative power and mobilization among the groups affected. Again, risk regulation in a context of no significant interest group activity is likely to be different from regulation conducted in a domain where all the affected stakeholders are highly mobilized, or where some affected groups are more highly organized than others with different interests. So the extent and distribution of group mobilization can also be considered a key element of policy context.

These three elements—type of risk, public preferences and attitudes, and organized interests—encompass much of what is commonly identified as the main features of regime context in risk regulation. Other contextual elements could nevertheless be added to this basic trio, and the trio can itself be progressively subdivided. We shall be breaking down each of these elements further in Chapters 5–7 as we look more closely at the relationship between context and content.

Elements of Regime Content

Like context, the *content* of risk regulation regimes can be characterized in many different ways, and the literature on the content of public policy tends to be more diffuse than that focusing on contextual elements. Nevertheless, some broad recurring themes can be discerned. At the most general level, much discussion of *regime content* relates to three overlapping elements that also appear in Table 2.2. These three basic elements are:

- size;
- structure; and
- style.

Regime size means broadly how much regulation is brought to bear on any risk through the given regime. Size can be conceived in at least two separate ways. One is what we shall later term 'aggression', denoting the extent of risk toleration in standards and behaviour-modification, and how far regulators go in collecting information about the risk. Another is the overall scale of investment that goes into the regime from all sources, in the form of direct tax-financed state spending, state employment, or compliance costs imposed on business firms or non-state actors. Regulatory size is what is broadly at issue for those who are concerned about the balance between the state and the market, the threshold of risk toleration in regulation, the degree of 'anticipationism' in risk regulation, or the extent of regulatory bureaucracy. Many what-to-do debates on risk policy turn on questions of under-regulation versus over-regulation and, as we shall show in the next chapter, risk regulation regimes vary markedly on several dimensions of size.

The second element of regime content is *structure*. Structure overlaps with size to some extent. It refers to the way regulation is organized, what institutional arrangements are adopted, and the way resources invested in regulation are distributed. Like size, structure can be conceived in at least two ways. One is the extent to which regulation involves a mix of public and private sector actors—for instance, with non-state organizations operating as intermediaries, auxiliaries, or self-controllers—particularly in the distribution of compliance costs between regulators and regulatees. Another is how densely populated the regulatory space or policy community is by separate institutions, and how far the risk involves multiple overlapping systems of regulation, as in the health-care example we gave in the last chapter, where each specific regime may reinforce or affect one or more of the others.

Regulatory structure is much debated by policy and public administration specialists, going beyond issues of state versus market or how aggressively regulation should be pursued. Structure is what is broadly at issue for those who are concerned about the balance between direct and indirect enforcement of regulation, the distribution of compliance costs, and 'joining up' regulatory activity across different organizations, systems, or levels of government. Redundancy—the existence of multiple overlapping systems of control—is also much debated, for instance as between the difficulties it can present for clear-cut lines of accountability and the advantages it can present for reinforcement and robustness (see Sagan 1993). As we shall see later, risk regulation varies markedly from one domain to another in structure. At the more complex end of the spectrum we may find not only multiple interlinked regulatory systems, but also marked institutional diversity across control components, with different sets of organizations involved in standard setting, information gathering and behaviour modification. In the latter kind of regime each control component may involve a different pattern of administrative geography, a separate pattern of regulatory 'capture' or lobbying, and different administrative or technical cultures.

The third broad element of regime content, which overlaps with the other two, is *style*. This element denotes the operating conventions and attitudes of those involved in regulation, and the formal and informal processes through which regulation works. Like size and structure, style can be conceived in at least two ways. One, familiar in socio-legal discussions, is the question of how far the operation of regulation is rule-bound or discretionary, and how far it is based on direct 'command and control' approaches rather than other policy instruments. Another is the attitudes and beliefs of the various regulatory actors and in particular the degree of zeal they show in pursuit of policy objectives.

Though this element may seem less tangible than some aspects of size and structure, it is the central issue for those who see culture and attitudes as all-important in the way regulation works, and here too we can observe substantial variety across different risk domains. Some risks, for instance, are regulated by 'zealots' (Downs 1967) with a lifetime commitment to, and passion for, a particular approach to policy, while for others regulators only go through the motions and are sunk in apathy or fatalism. Some risks are handled by bureaucratic generalists, operating as fixers whose main concern is to cut deals that satisfy different stakeholders, while others are owned by a distinctive professional community. For instance, NERA (1998: 30 n.37) described the food and chemical toxicology community within UK government as 'a club bridging several departments, enjoying typically more cohesion within itself than with other regulatory fields in those departments', and the same could probably be said of the US federal government. Again, some risks are regulated by strict 'rule and rote', as in the case of air safety, space travel, and weapons safety; for others there is a gap between the formal rules and what happens in practice, as in the case of police enforcement of speeding rules; and for yet others rules are much vaguer and less dense. Some risks are regulated within a professional community that crosses the boundaries between regulators and regulatees, while others involve more distance, or even outright conflict, between the regulators and the regulated.

4. Disaggregating Regime Context and Content

The six elements of regime context and content discussed here are broad-brush in character. They cover a wide range of ways in which regulatory regimes can vary, and link to numerous debates about how regulation does or should work, but at a fairly high level of aggregation. To pick up variation among regulatory regimes in more detail, for example to bring out differences among broadly similar regimes, we may need to disaggregate those elements further. Table 2.3 shows how they can be further disaggregated, at two successive levels. Space precludes a detailed line-by-line discussion of the two right hand columns of Table 2.3. We can simply note that the second and third disaggregations of regime context and regime content shown in Table 2.3 touch issues at stake in a wide range of debates about regulatory design and variety. Nor need the process of disaggregation end there. In principle, if the page was wide enough we could continue the disaggregation process to an nth or infinite level of decomposition by successive binary division of each element.

We do not need to make finer distinctions to bring out substantial regime variety in the nine risk domains we took as our empirical cases, which are to be discussed in the next chapter. We can stay at a fairly broad-brush level of analysis and still readily identify variety in risk regulation that cannot be picked up at the general level of the 'risk society' approach. Indeed, for the purposes of describing a wide range of contemporary debates about regulatory design and operation we do not need to go below the first or second level of disaggregation of *regime context* and *content*. We follow the 'Occam's razor' principle contained in the epigraph to this chapter, the idea that analytic schemes should accord with the principle of parsimony and be confined to the smallest number of moving parts or separate elements that can compass a subject.[11] However, as noted earlier, we would need to move to a further level of disaggregation for other analytic purposes or with different case material.

5. Summary and Conclusion

Building heavily on existing and earlier work and starting with a simple two-dimensional conception of regulatory regimes, this chapter has sketched out a basic method for describing and comparing variety. That method is designed to bring out some of the variety in the ways that risks are handled and controlled by the state within the so-called 'risk society'.

We have described the comparative anatomy of regulatory regimes at a relatively low level of complexity here, in order to map out its basic features. But, as we have argued, the basic approach lends itself to successive category disaggregation to draw ever finer distinctions, and the degree of discrimination that is appropriate depends on the material to be compared and the

---

[11] Occam's razor is a respected maxim in science. But it does not tell us what to do in circumstances such as those in which explanation *A* accounts for, say, 80 per cent of observed variety, while explanation *B* accounts for, say, 85 per cent but is many times more complicated than *A*. Which explanation to prefer comes down to a question of aesthetics. Some might prefer *A* because its explanatory power is high relative to its simplicity and the marginal gain in explanatory power offered by *B* is slight compared with its much greater complexity. Others might prefer the version with the greatest absolute explanatory power irrespective of its power-weight ratio, so to speak. Our own preference veers towards the first position.

TABLE 2.3. *Disaggregating regime context and content*

	Basic elements	Second disaggregation	Third disaggregation
Regime context	Type of risk	Degree of residual risk: risk not handled by other regulatory systems or without regulation	Overall level of risk: probability and consequence Certainty or disputed/uncertain nature of risk
		Degree of market—and tort law—failure	Degree of information failure Degree of opt-out failure
	Public preferences and attitudes	Media/public salience	Media salience Mass public opinion salience
		Degree of uniformity or coherence of opinion	Degree of consensus Degree of coherence
	Organized interests	Presence of dominant organized groups	Degree of business capture Degree of professional etc. capture
		Degree of mobilization of affected stakeholders	Level of mobilization Level of militancy
Regime content	Size	Policy aggression: how active regulation is, how much risk is tolerated and how much change is aimed at	Extent of policy 'proactivity' Degree of policy ambition
		Overall regulatory investment: the overall scale of resources going into regulation from all sources	Level of money costs Level of time, skill, and attention
	Structure	Non-state share of regulatory resources: how regulatory costs are distributed between the state and regulatees	Level of compliance costs Level of third-party contributions
		Organizational fragmentation and system complexity: interfaces with other regimes	Number and density of regulator organizations Degree of jurisdictional overlap and system complexity
	Style	Rule-orientation: the overall extent to which regulation is governed by rules	Density of formal regulatory rules Degree of operational rule-following
		Regulatory zeal: the extent to which regulators are 'zealots' for policy positions rather than neutral and detached in their approach	Extent of regulator commitment to policy Extent of regulatory lifetime 'vocation'

purpose of comparison. As with any tool, how we use the idea of regime anatomy as a method of comparing types of regulation depends on what we are applying it to and what we are using it for. The more similar the systems being compared, the further down the scale of disaggregation the comparison will need to go if their distinctive fingerprints are to be identified. In principle, moreover, those regime fingerprints could be digitized to express each regulatory regime in numerical terms as a vector of the various cell components of which it is composed—roughly equivalent to the ecologist's grid-squares for recording biomass and species variety.[12]

How far we need to disaggregate regimes to greater levels of complexity also depends on how many 'degrees of freedom' there are in regulatory regimes—that is, how far variation in one element of a regime is linked to variation in another, or how far we can predict what one dimension of a regulatory regime will be like from knowledge about another dimension. If there are infinite degrees of freedom in regulatory regimes, we need very complex ways of describing and comparing them; if there are only a few degrees of freedom, a parsimonious characterization will suffice.

Making this point prompts empirical questions about the ranges of variation among risk regulatory regimes and the factors that account for those variations. We turn to those questions in the next chapter, comparing nine different risk regulation regimes that we observed in some detail. In Part II we explore factors that may account for the range of variety in regimes, to investigate how far and in what ways *regime context* shapes *regime content*.

---

[12] In our empirical analysis, as will be shown in the next chapter, we used qualitative scales, but those scales could also be expressed in numerical form.

3

Nine Risk Regulation Regimes Compared

The study of form may be descriptive merely, or it may become
analytical. We begin by describing the shape of an object in the
simple words of common speech . . .

Thompson (1961 [orig. 1917]: 269)

1 Introduction

This chapter applies the regime approach to compare nine UK and EU risk
regulation regimes that we observed in the late 1990s. First, following the
method described by D'Arcy Wentworth Thompson in the epigraph to this
chapter, we give a brief overall description of those risk domains and identify
the regimes under scrutiny.[1] Then, turning to a more 'analytical' method,
albeit far cruder than Thompson's, we show how their regulatory profiles can
be compared on the lines sketched out in Chapter 2. Third, we reflect on the
observable variety and the various clusters or family groups of regimes that
can be identified. We conclude by setting the scene for Part II of the book.

2. Nine Risk Domains and their Associated Regimes:
A Brief Portrait

The nine risk domains explored here were chosen to give a spread of cases
which varied in the level and type of risk they posed to individuals. They
included 'voluntary' and 'compulsory' risks, 'natural', 'social' and 'man-
made' risks, risks imposed by the state and risks imposed by other bodies, risks
created by large corporate bodies and risks created by individuals, and 'high-
technology' and 'low-tech' risks. The associated regulatory regimes were also
chosen to give a spread of types, from broadly-conceived regimes comprising

---

[1] Further information for each regime, including information about bibliography and legislation, is found in Appendix I at the end of the book.

most or all of the state's activity pertaining to a particular risk, to more narrowly-conceived regimes acting concurrently with other state activity designed to affect the risk in different ways. The cases are as follows:

(1) Attacks by dangerous dogs outside the home.
(2) Lung cancer caused by emissions of radon gas from the ground or building materials in the home and (3) in the workplace.
(4) Cancer from emissions of benzene from vehicle exhausts or other sources, and also (5) from workplace exposures.
(6) Attacks on children from convicted paedophiles released from prison into the community.
(7) Injuries and deaths from motor vehicles on local roads, in so far as these can be abstracted from road safety regulation more generally.
(8) Adverse health effects from exposure to pesticide residues in food and (9) in drinking water.

(i) Attacks by Dangerous Dogs Outside the Home

Attack by dangerous dogs is not the first type of risk that comes to mind in discussions of 'risk society'. It is not a product of technological development. Nor does it require special technical apparatus to detect the snarling dog attached to your ankle. It is a 'traditional' type of risk, harking back to the monsters and dragons feared by our ancestors. In modern times, the level and distribution of risk of attack from dogs may change as a result of urbanization, motorization, changing social behaviour—for instance, drug dealing—and the introduction of new canine breeds. The control of large fighting dogs has come on to the regulatory agenda in many countries over recent years, often associated with child deaths or serious injuries, as in the UK and Germany. But dog dangers are not a risk that has been much affected by 'globalization', apart from the development of internet sites and the like, and such dangers do not preoccupy EU or international regulators. The risk creators, apart from the dogs themselves, are for the most part individual dog owners rather than high-tech corporations, though some organizations—police, security firms, and the like—use large dogs as tools of trade.

Nevertheless, attack from dogs is not a trivial or imaginary risk. A big dog can kill a child in seconds or inflict horrific injuries. Good statistics of the incidence of dog attacks are hard to come by but what figures exist suggest that deaths from dog attack in the UK are in single figures each year (Podberscek 1994). Hospitals in the UK treat about 230,000 cases of dog bites each year, with about 2,000 of those in England and Wales involving serious injury (Thomas and Banks 1990; Baxter 1984; Hervey 1977). Children and the elderly seem to be most at risk from death or serious injury from dog attack.

There is no strong consensus on what the key risk factors are for dog attack. There is some evidence suggesting that attacks are disproportionately associated with certain larger breeds such as German Shepherds, Rottweilers, Dobermans, and pit bull terriers (Podberscek and Blackshaw 1993: 182; Klaasen *et al.* 1996). But size is not everything and may become a risk factor only when combined with a disposition to attack. Some breeds are thought to be more aggressive than others, such as fighting dogs or those bred for catching runaway slaves, like the Dogo Argentino. But against the 'nature' argument is a 'nurture' claim that training and treatment by owners are critical factors in determining whether individual dogs will be aggressive or pacific.

The biggest risk of dog attack appears to be in the home from the family pet (Sherwell and Nancarrow 1991), but public policy debates tend to focus on the risk of attack from dogs at large. Public concern about dog attack risks is reflected in UK poll responses indicating substantial majorities in favour of banning 'dangerous dogs'.[2] As we shall see later, dog attack risks are a classic instance of occasional media 'feeding frenzies' highlighting tragic accidents, alternating with times of lower interest. And dogs are politically significant in most countries if only because a substantial proportion of the electorate owns them.[3]

The 'regime' examined here comprised the general criminal and statutory framework relating to dangerous dogs in the UK, as it developed from Victorian 'administrative' law—the Dogs Act 1871—into a criminal-law framework in the 1980s and 1990s, through Dangerous Dogs Acts in 1989 and 1991. This framework imposed duties on owners to keep their dogs under control and involved special provisions for pit bull terriers and three other specified dog types. It involved nearly all the regulatory constraints affecting the risk of being harmed by a dangerous dog in public, and in that sense was a 'broad' regime.[4]

(ii) and (iii) Radon at Home and Work

Radon gas from the ground can produce a significant risk of lung cancer over a long period of exposure when it is concentrated in buildings, mines, or caves.[5] Excessive lung disease has been known to afflict miners since the sixteenth century, but radon was not identified as the cause until the mid-twentieth

---

[2] *Observer* (1991); *UK Press Gazette* (1991); MORI/Better Regulation Task Force (1999); Today (1991).

[3] According to the Pet Food Manufacturers' Association (1999), the UK has about seven million dogs in around five and a half million households, and the USA has been estimated to have about 40 million dogs.

[4] Even so, there were other statutes affecting risks of dog attacks in public, notably those requiring local authorities to round up strays and the Guard Dogs Act 1975, introduced after a child was killed by a guard dog in Scotland, requiring control and licensing of guard dogs.

[5] Radon derives from uranium that occurs in small quantities in all rocks and soils but the level of radon emissions from the ground is highly dependent on local geology. In the UK, particularly high levels are recorded in the South-West and Midlands of England and parts of Scotland.

century. In modern times, increasing use of building insulation techniques can exacerbate radon concentrations and hence risks. Hence what is new about such risks, making radon a partial example of the sort of hazard associated with the 'risk society' debate, is the development of scientific awareness of the linkage between radon and cancer, building technology that may exacerbate the risk, and technical capacity to detect and measure the incidence of a gas that is odourless and colourless.

Radon risks are also contested to some extent. John Adams (1999) claims radon risks are 'virtual' in the sense that scientists disagree about them, though his term 'virtual' is unsatisfactory and it would be more accurate to describe the risk as 'contested'. In contrast to dog attack risks, they might also be considered 'virtual' because dead bodies and 'bleeding stumps' of radon victims cannot be unambiguously identified, and, as noted earlier, the hazard is chronic rather than acute—that is, significant risk comes from exposure over a long period. In the early twentieth century radon was thought to be beneficial to health, with 'radon spas' popular as a cure for tuberculosis and other ailments (Edelstein and Makofske 1998: 35). Few scientists would subscribe to this view today but some claim radon risks are overstated and that epidemiological data fails to reveal an association between high radon levels and above-normal incidences of lung cancer.[6] A part government-funded epidemiological study in England (Darby *et al.* 1998), however, lends support to the orthodox view of the international nuclear science community which rates radon as a serious risk. That orthodox view is represented by the UK's National Radiological Protection Board, which estimates that about 2,500 lung cancers are caused or aggravated by radon each year: about 5 per cent of all lung cancers (NRPB 1990: 25). Most of these deaths are said to arise from exposure in the home, but as many as 250 a year may arise from exposure at work. If that orthodox assessment is accepted, radon is a significant killer, broadly comparable in magnitude to the number of local road deaths—though not injuries—in the UK each year. But the risk is easy and, at about £30 per test, cheap to detect and can be substantially reduced by feasible and relatively low-cost measures like the installation of membranes and ventilation fans in buildings.

Nevertheless, in the UK at least, radon exposure is not a risk that gives rise to much political concern. Unlike emissions from artificial sources of radiation like nuclear plants or submarines, it does not appear to excite popular fears; and, as we shall see later, media coverage is consistently low—no 'risk amplification' seems to take place here, but rather 'risk attenuation'.

---

[6] See Cohen (1982; 1985); Martell (1987); and see the review and meta-analysis by Lubin and Boice (1997).

The radon regimes for emissions at home and work that are examined here were both 'broad' in the sense that they encompassed all state activity bearing on this risk. That state activity comprised building regulations applying to new homes, voluntary action levels originally dating from the 1980s specifying levels of radioactivity above which home-owners were recommended to undertake remedial action, and legally enforceable action levels for workplaces—introduced in the 1980s to replace a previous voluntary limit—that came within the occupational health and safety system.

(iv) and (v) Benzene in the Air and in the Workplace

Benzene is a leukaemia-inducing chemical that enters the atmosphere mainly as a combustion product in vehicle exhausts and through evaporation from gasoline of which it is a minor constituent. Unlike some air pollutants, such as particulates, benzene emissions are readily dispersed, and therefore present a local pollution problem primarily associated with areas of high traffic density, and petro-chemical facilities such as filling stations and some chemical works. Other sources of benzene include smoking—which may be very significant for heavy smokers—as well as gas cookers and contaminated food and drink (EPAQS/DOE 1994). As with radon, scientific awareness of benzene as a carcinogen has only recently developed, and its presence can be detected only by technical apparatus. Also like radon, exposure to benzene is a chronic rather than an acute risk. However, unlike radon, exposure to ambient benzene is wholly a product of modern industrial technology and, in particular, of a society based on widespread use of petrol-fuelled motor vehicles. Those who produce this risk thus comprise not only a majority of voters at one level, but, at another level, large and politically well-connected corporations like oil companies and motor manufacturers.

While there is relative scientific consensus that benzene causes leukaemia at high levels of exposure,[7] there is less agreement about the effects of long-term exposure at the low levels found in ambient air and most workplaces. For ambient air, WHO risk estimates imply a range of around 0.1–10 leukaemia deaths in the UK per year on worst-case exposure assumptions.[8] European Union estimates put the additional number of leukaemia cases due to exposure to airborne benzene in the workplace in the UK at low single figures per year on worst-case assumptions.[9] The uncertainties are so great, however, that UK government departments refuse to quantify the risk at all

---

[7] For instance, in the 1970s the potential of exposure to benzene at work to cause leukaemia was discovered in a study of leather workers exposed to the chemical in glue.

[8] Namely, that the UK population is constantly exposed to five microgrammes per cubic metre, and, according to the risk estimates used by the EC Working Group on Benzene, of between 5×10^{-6} and 5×10^{-8} /$\mu g/m^3$ (Commission of the European Communities DGX1 1999:17).

[9] Namely, that between 12,000 and 17,000 workers (Health and Safety Commission 1995: 11) were exposed to over 1ppm for 40 years (Commission of the European Communities 1993: 99).

for either ambient air (DOE/SO 1997: 86) or workplaces (Health and Safety Commission 1995: 50), and some studies and scientists suggest the risks may be lower by orders of magnitude.[10] But although ambient benzene has—even more than radon—distinct features of a 'risk society' hazard, it does not exhibit high political salience as an issue on its own. As we shall see later, UK public opinion polls showed evidence of widespread public concern with air pollution in general, but not with benzene in particular.

In contrast to the dog and radon cases, the 'regimes' for benzene considered here were narrowly construed, consisting of overall limits for airborne benzene exposure in the workplace and the ambient air set by a mixture of UK and EU regulators. Benzene risks were affected not only by these measures, but also by other 'upstream' or concurrent controls. For ambient benzene, those other controls included limits on vehicle exhaust emissions, limits on benzene in gasoline, and restrictions on emissions from industrial or commercial processes. For workplaces, there were also specific controls that affected levels of exposure to benzene, such as controls on vapour recovery equipment in the handling of petrochemicals, affecting the exposure of workers such as tanker drivers and filling station attendants. So in this case we examine general limits that operated in the context of other overlapping and more specific controls.

(vi) Paedophile Ex-offenders Released from Custody

The risks to children and families from attack by paedophiles released into the community after serving a custodial sentence involve what is in one sense a 'natural' hazard like radon or dogs. Sexual abuse of children is not a new or high-tech phenomenon, so it is not central to 'risk society' themes. What is new about this risk is the degree of recognition and public discussion it has attracted over recent decades. But unlike benzene or radon, which are also newly-discovered risks, risks presented by released paedophile offenders are of high political and media salience across much of the developed world. Within the UK, that salience contrasts markedly with a lower, albeit growing, level of public attention and concern about child sexual abuse within the home by close family members.

The scale of risk is hard to assess. There are no officially published statistics on offences by released child sex offenders in the UK. Official statistics for all sexual offences against children in England and Wales indicate about 4,000 cautions or convictions are issued per year, though some have suggested the true number of offences could be nearly 20 times greater, at up to 72,600 each year (Grubin 1998: 3, 12). Surveys suggest that, as with dog attack, the risk is greater at home than on the streets: about 80 per cent of

---

[10] For example, CONCAWE (1996: 4); Munby and Weetman (1997).

offences are estimated to occur in the home. Between 25 and 40 per cent of offenders are estimated to exhibit repeat patterns of paedophile-type behaviour (Grubin 1998: v). If those estimates are correct, the implication is that at least 1,000 child sex offences a year might be expected from released offenders. The scale of the problem facing governments that want to track convicted offenders on release can be indicated by the fact that in England and Wales in 1993 over 100,000 men—not much fewer than one in 200—had a conviction for a sexual offence against a child.[11]

Paedophile risks share some features with those from dangerous dogs, but they also contrast with dog risks in several ways. People tend to travel more than dogs, so issues of national and international cooperation are more salient for the control and monitoring of this risk. Moreover, though at one level the creators of the risk are individuals, at another level the state is the creator of the risk, since it is responsible for releasing convicted sex offenders into the community on parole or after custodial sentences. Third, risk/risk tradeoffs figure larger in the management of paedophile risks than they do for dog risks. That is, measures to reduce the risks to children from attack—such as obliging those who have been convicted for paedophile offences to wear distinctive uniforms so that children could readily identify them, to take an imaginary example—are liable to increase the risk to released offenders from attacks by the general public, and some such measures, unlike our imaginary uniform example, might also endanger innocent people mistakenly identified as offenders. Fourth, the assembly of information about the risks and tactical decisions over management cuts across a range of agencies in the domains of welfare and criminal justice, presenting a particular challenge to the normally fragmented character of public bureaucracies.

As with benzene, our analysis here is concerned with a narrowly construed regime for the control of paedophiles. We do not examine the general provisions of the criminal law and numerous child protection and welfare measures. Instead we are concerned only with measures directly controlling the conditions under which ex-offenders are released from custodial sentences, such as the assessment of risk posed by each offender on release and the monitoring of ex-offenders.

(vii) Local Road Safety

Death and injury from vehicle accidents on local and suburban roads is a familiar and palpable risk, not a 'virtual' one. The risk grew in the twentieth-century—though road accidents also occurred in the era of horse-drawn vehicles and trams—and it is a product of technological development. It does not, however, figure large in 'risk society' discussions. One possible reason is that

---

[11] Of that number, only 15,000 had convictions involving life sentences (Marshall 1997:1).

this risk does not seem to arouse feelings of dread and bewilderment in individuals. Another is that, like aviation accidents, serious accident rates have fallen across most of the developed world in both absolute and relative terms: that is, relative to vehicle miles travelled.[12]

State-collected aggregate statistics in principle make risk quantification in this field easier than in cases like radon or benzene where risks are emergent or part of a cocktail of factors producing cancer. However, the framework of categories used by the state to collect the numbers heavily shapes the sort of risk quantification that is possible. For example, available UK accident statistics do not allow definitive conclusions to be drawn about the changing balance of risk between in-vehicle and out-of-vehicle road users—vulnerable road users such as pedestrians and cyclists—even though Adams (1985) and others see that balance as central to the contemporary politics of road risk. However, official transport statistics record that accidents on local roads—all roads maintained by local authorities—claim around 2,500 lives a year in Great Britain. That means local roads are approximately equal with radon in their annual kill-rate and at least ten times more dangerous than dogs in serious injuries at over 30,000, though approximately equal with dogs in numbers of slight injuries.[13]

This risk domain is heavily marked by distributional risk/risk politics, for instance between 'invulnerable' and 'vulnerable' road users such as truck drivers relative to cyclists, between local residents and commuter drivers from elsewhere, and between those who impose and those who pay the costs of safety, as in the case of children confined indoors instead of playing in the street. Hence it involves many interest groups of varying scale and political sophistication. It is also marked by official tradeoffs of risk against cost, in at least two ways. One is official acceptance in most countries of some death and injury on the roads as a price to be paid for the benefits of motor vehicles—though what is acceptable and how benefits should be measured are contentious. The other is the fact that many measures for reducing risks involve expenditure by the state. Hence, like paedophile release, risk reduction involves major costs to the state and, like benzene, its management touches on matters of high importance to a mass of middle-income voters, making it a key element in both local and national politics.

As with benzene too, the regulation of road risks involves multiple overlapping systems of control, over vehicles, drivers, and roads. For example, regulatory requirements on vehicle construction are designed to reduce road risks by making cars, buses, and other vehicles safer for their occupants and

---

[12] In contrast, the developing world accounts for 70 per cent of total global road crash deaths with only 30 per cent of the world's vehicle fleet, and is set to take an increasing share (International Federation of Red Cross and Red Crescent Societies 1998; Ross 2000).

[13] See DETR (1999: 7, 14). Even then, some claim that official figures underestimate the risks (see Simpson 1996; Davis 1992: 163).

those outside in the event of a collision.[14] But in looking at the 'regime' for regulating risks on local roads we focused on controls over drivers and roads, covering a wide range of activity by central government, local authorities, and the police, but not every part of state activity affecting road risks. In particular, we focused on measures to reduce road risk by highway engineering—typically involving substantial state expenditure—attempts to modify the behaviour of drivers and other road users, and police enforcement of multiple road traffic laws designed to reduce accident risk.

(viii) and (ix) Exposure to Pesticide Residues in Food and Water

Our final two cases concern health risks from pesticides, in the form of residues in food and water. Along with benzene, these cases are perhaps closest to the risks emphasized by the 'risk society' literature within our set. Health risk from pesticides is a product of technological developments in agribusiness and is central to the twentieth-century shift to intensive farming methods. Pesticides in their nature are 'designer toxins', with about 20,000 deaths a year worldwide from pesticide poisoning, around a million cases of non-fatal poisoning, and 37,000 cases of cancer caused by exposure to pesticides in developing countries alone, according to WHO estimates (WHO 1990: 85–8).

Pesticides, like radon and benzene, involve dangers that are not detectable except through scientific testing equipment and overall risks that are assessable only by experts. But 'expertise' is perhaps more controversial in this case than for benzene or radon. Scientists do not have a settled or common view of the dangers pesticides present, as is shown by the ever-changing debates over matters like the causes of 'Gulf War Syndrome', or risks associated with use of organophosphate sheep dips. From the standpoint of public attitudes, there is evidence that pesticides come into the mysterious category of 'dread risks', in the language of a well-known study of risk perception conducted by researchers in Oregon some two decades ago (see Slovic, Fischoff, and Lichtenstein 1981). And pesticides have been a central theme in the development of the environmental movement since the 1960s.

In this case, creators of the risk are corporations or organizations, notably agribusiness, food, and water companies, rather than individuals, though the farming sector and the small-business end of the food retail sector crosses that divide. Some of those risk-creators are powerful multinational agribusiness corporations, others are local monopolies like water companies, and there are numerous commercial intermediary organizations too. As noted earlier, this

---

[14] However, the scale of vehicle manufacture, concentrated in a few powerful corporations, means that such measures are undertaken in an international context and may be a major shaper of vehicle markets.

risk domain is heavily populated by experts and professionals and, like local road safety, there are multiple interest groups ranging from 'dark greens' to multinational corporations, and substantial media attention on the risk and its regulation.

As with benzene and road risks, there are multiple overlapping systems of control affecting pesticide residue risks. For example, pesticide products must be approved for use after safety testing, as with drugs. Controls are placed on conditions of use for such products, such as 'buffer zones' preventing their use within a specified distance of water. Those controls interlock with occupational safety regulation, both to limit risks to those working with pesticides and to limit the risk of high pesticide concentrations entering groundwater or the food chain.[15] But our focus here is mainly on 'downstream' controls involving overall limits for pesticide residues in food and drinking water imposed by EU and UK regulators. As we shall see later, overall limit regimes for food and water involved different conceptual approaches and different systems of enforcement.

Overall

These brief portraits are intended to bring out some of the salient features that divide or unite the nine risk domains, though necessarily at an impressionistic level. As we have seen, some of the risks in question were regulated by a complex of regimes, while others involved simpler stand-alone arrangements, and the risks themselves varied on features such as detectability, public salience, speed of onset, collective-consumption characteristics, and causal agents. In the next section, we move from describing the risk domains *seriatim* to comparing a selection of the regulation regimes that were observed in these risk domains in the UK and EU. We will use the dimensions we discussed in Chapter 2 as the basis of our comparison.

3. From Domains to Regimes: Comparing Nine Risk Regulation Regimes

It will be recalled that Chapter 2 set out two basic dimensions on which risk regulation regimes could vary. One dimension comprised the *context* and *content* of regimes and the other comprised the *information-gathering, standard-setting* and *behaviour-modification* components of control. Table 3.1 uses that framework to compare the regulatory regimes applying to the nine risk

---

[15] In the water case in England and Wales, the controls also interlock with the economic regulatory regime for the water and sewerage industry.

TABLE 3.1. *A dimensional comparison of nine European Union and United Kingdom risk regulation regimes*

Regime context		Ratings for all regulatory control dimensions				
		High	Medium-high	Medium	Medium-low	Low
Type of risk	Degree of risk, without relevant regime	Local road risks Domestic radon risks	Occupational radon risks		Paedophile release Dangerous dog risks	Occupational benzene risks Ambient benzene risks Pesticides in food risks Pesticides in drinking water risks
	Degree of market and tort law failure re above risk	Paedophile release risks Ambient benzene risks Dangerous dog risks Local road risks Pesticides in drinking water risks Pesticides in food risks		Occupational radon risks Occupational benzene risks		Domestic radon risks
Nature of public and media opinion	Media/public salience	Paedophile release risks	Pesticides in food risks Pesticides in drinking water risks	Local road risks Dangerous dog risks	Ambient benzene risks	Domestic radon risks Occupational radon risks Occupational benzene risks
	Degree of uniformity of coherence of opinion	Paedophile release risks Domestic radon risks Occupational radon risks Occupational benzene risks	Pesticides in food risks Pesticides in drinking water risks	Dangerous dog risks		Local road risks Ambient benzene risks
Extent and distribution of organized groups	Presence of dominant organized groups	Pesticides in drinking risks Pesticide in food risks Ambient benzene risks	Occupational benzene risks	Dangerous dog risks Paedophile release risks	Local road risks Occupational radon risks	Domestic radon risks
	Degree of mobilization of affected stakeholders	Pesticides in food risks Pesticides in drinking water risks Occupational benzene risks Local road risks Ambient benzene risks		Dangerous dog risks Paedophile release risks	Occupational radon risks	Domestic radon risks

Regime content — Ratings for individual regulatory control dimensions

Regime content		Standard setting					Information gathering					Behaviour modification				
		High	Medium-high	Medium	Medium-low	Low	High	Medium-high	Medium	Medium-low	Low	High	Medium-high	Medium	Medium-low	Low
Size	Policy aggression	Food, Water		Amb. ben., Occ. ben., Paedoph's, Dogs	Roads	Dom. rad., Occ. rad.	Water, Roads	Occ. ben.	Food, Dom. rad., Amb. ben., Paedoph's	Occ. rad	Dogs	Water, Food		Occ. ben., Roads	Amb. ben.	Dom. rad., Occ. rad., Dogs, Paedoph's
	Overall investment in regulation	Food, Roads	Occ. ben., Paedoph's	Water, Amb. ben.	Paedoph's	Dom. rad., Dogs, Occ. rad., Occ. ben.	Water, Food, Paedoph's, Roads		Occ. ben., Dom. rad.	Amb. ben., Occ. rad.	Dogs	Roads	Water	Food	Occ. ben., Dogs, Paedoph's	Dom. rad., Occ. rad., Amb. ben.
Structure	Proportion of investment in regulation from private or third sector sources	Food		Amb. ben.		Dom. rad., Dogs, Occ. rad., Paedoph's, Water, Roads	Occ. ben., Food, Water, Dogs		Occ. rad.		Dom. rad., Amb. ben., Paedoph's, Roads	Dom. rad., Occ. rad., Occ. ben., Food, Water, Roads		Dogs	Amb. ben., Paedoph's	
	Degree of organizational complexity or fragmentation	Food, Water, Amb. ben.	Occ. ben., Paedoph's	Roads	Occ. rad., Dogs	Dom. rad.	Water	Paedoph's, Food	Amb. ben.	Occ. ben., Roads, Occ. rad., Dogs	Dom. rad.	Amb. ben., Paedoph's, Water	Paedoph's, Roads	Food	Occ. ben., Dogs, Occ. rad.	Dom. rad
Style	Rule orientaton	Water, Food, Occ. ben.	Occ. rad., Occ. ben.	Paedoph's, Roads, Amb. ben.	Dogs	Dom. rad.	Water, Occ. ben., Occ. rad., Food		Paedoph's, Roads, Amb. ben.	Dogs	Dom. rad.	Occ. ben., Occ. rad., Water, Food, Dogs, Paedoph's	Amb. ben., Roads	Roads	Dom. rad.	
	Zeal of regulators	Food, Water, Occ. ben., Amb. ben.	Occ. rad., Occ. ben.	Paedoph's, Roads, Dom. rad.	Paedoph's	Dogs	Water, Roads, Amb. ben., Dom. rad.	Food, Paedoph's, Dom. rad.	Occ. ben.		Dogs, Occ. rad.	Water	Occ. ben., Paedoph's	Food, Roads, Amb. ben.		Dom. rad., Dogs, Occ. rad.

See Appendix C for notes on methodology.

Amb. ben. = ambient benzene risks Dogs = dangerous dog risks Dom. rad. = domestic radon risks Food = pesticide residues in food risks Occ. ben. = occupational benzene risks

Occ. rad. = occupational radon risks Paedoph's = paedophile release risks Roads = local road safety risks Water = pesticide residues in drinking water risks domains described earlier. It compares regime context and regime content at the second level of disaggregation discussed in Chapter 2 (Table 2.3), though for reasons of data limitation it breaks down only regime content and not regime context among the three control components.[16] It is intended to show how the framework can be put to work to bring out some basic commonalities and differences among systems of risk regulation.

We will comment briefly on the absolute differences among these regimes in the next section. What needs to be stressed here is that Table 3.1 indicates *relative* differences, with the nine cases rated against one another, rather than on an absolute or objective scale. It is like lining up a group of children according to their different features like age, height, or weight, with the oldest/tallest/heaviest at one end and the youngest/shortest/lightest at the other. That is, we scaled the regime features across a five-point scale, and the 'highs' and 'lows' represent the extreme points we observed in our set. Even a relative comparison of this type has to involve some tricky judgements, particularly where the available data is patchy, and we do not claim that all the placings in Table 3.1 are uncontestable, though we based our judgements on careful debate and the best information we could assemble. Our aim here is not to claim infallibility for all the placings in Table 3.1, but to demonstrate the application of the comparative method that was sketched out in Chapter 2.

Examples of Regime Differences

Limits of space, and no doubt readers' patience, preclude us from going through Table 3.1 line by line, but it is worth picking out a few of the distinctions it draws among our cases. Take regulatory 'aggression', for instance. As explained in Chapter 2, *aggression* is a second-level disaggregation of regime content that measures the extent to which the state seeks to intervene in modifying a risk and how actively it does so. Some regimes ranked relatively high on aggression across all control components, such as the overall limits on pesticide residues in drinking water—'Maximum Admissible Concentration', in the jargon—for which the official goal was near zero tolerance of risk, there was extensive checking for residues, and the residue limits appeared to be met (DWI 2000). Domestic radon came close to the opposite profile, with official action levels entailing very high toleration of risk, as we shall see in Chapter 5, and little behaviour-modification activity, although it rated rather higher on information gathering as a result of extensive state-funded testing.

---

[16] In most cases policy context features were not readily disaggregatable among the control components. That did not apply to some key type-of-risk features that we discuss in Chapter 5. In general, the regulators concerned had low levels of information about both their own costs and the compliance costs they imposed on regulatees.

Other regimes, however, had a greater spread of relative placings. For instance, the dogs regime ranked medium on standard setting, in so far as it was intended to reduce the risk from dog attack by some unspecified amount, but ranked low on information gathering[17] and low on behaviour modification, since police gave low priority to dog risks and there was no evidence that the 1991 Dangerous Dogs Act had reduced overall risks of dog attack in public (see Klaassen *et al.* 1996). The local road safety regime, by contrast, ranked very high on information gathering, in that there were elaborate arrangements for collecting data not only about accidents but also public attitudes and preferences, but lower on standard setting and behaviour modification, in that the standards—and results achieved—involved a roughly one-third reduction of road deaths and other injuries over ten years (DoT 1987; DETR 2000). This brief discussion of regulatory aggression shows the advantages of using a dimensional approach to compare regimes. Regimes that are similar on one component may be different in others, and aggression over standards was not always matched by equivalent aggression in the other components of control.

The same point can be made about the 'organizational complexity' element of *regime content*. Some regimes, like those governing ambient benzene and pesticide residues in food, had high levels of organizational complexity in the standard-setting component of control, because they spanned EU and national levels of government, involved an elaborate structure of expert committees and multiple government departments, and built on a complex array of other sub-regimes in the same policy domain, as noted earlier. Other regimes, such as that governing dog risks, manifested few of those complexities on the standard-setting component of control, other than normal public-sector conventions of consultation across government and interest groups. However, when attention is turned to the information-gathering component, the dog risk regime was only marginally less organizationally complex than the ambient benzene regime. Information gathering for benzene involved a mixture of central and local government surveillance on top of other control systems for checking vehicle exhausts and industrial emissions. For dog risks, such information gathering as occurred involved a mixture of police, customs officers at ports and airports, the private operators of a mandatory register for a number of proscribed fighting dog types, plus other sub-regimes applying to stray dogs and guard dogs. This example shows that whether a risk regulation regime is to be counted as organizationally 'complex' or 'simple' may depend on the control component at issue.

Similar dimensional variety can be identified in the regime context elements of Table 3.1. Some policy domains, like domestic radon, scored

---

[17] No information was collected on dogs in the UK except for four fighting breeds that were required to be registered and for 'aggravated offences' in Northern Ireland. Background research was low and dog bites were not notifiable incidents, unlike the situation in some other countries.

consistently low on most elements of regime context, but others were more dimensionally variable. For instance, the local road risk domain scored high on both type-of-risk elements—seriousness and 'spillovers'. But it rated medium-low on public preferences and attitudes—medium on opinion and media salience, relatively high on conflict—and registered a mixed score on the interest-group elements—high on group mobilization, medium on domination by any one organized group outside government. The paedophile risk domain, on the other hand, had a very different regime context profile. It scored only medium on the type-of-risk elements, relatively low on seriousness since the probability of attack is low compared, say, with local road risks, although high on opt-out difficulties. It rated very high, however, on both 'public preferences and attitudes' elements and medium on the degree of interest-group organization and dominance by a single group.

Hence, even at the medium level of aggregation at which the analysis in Table 3.1 is pitched, a dimensional approach to looking at risk regulation regimes brings out variety that is invisible from a world-historical or macro-social perspective, let alone explicable by such perspectives. It shows that risk domains vary not only in type and level of risk, but also in policy settings and regulatory stances. It shows, moreover, that features of the standard-setting component of control, such as high levels of aggression, do not necessarily carry over to the information-gathering or behaviour-modification component. As we shall see later, knowing a regime's relative score for one regulatory control component on any one of the six policy content elements shown in Table 3.1 gave us a better than even chance of predicting its relative score on another control dimension—but not much better.

Disaggregating the Picture

The analysis of regime differences in Table 3.1 is set at a medium level of aggregation, going beyond the basic categories we began with in Table 2.2 in Chapter 2, but only at the second level of disaggregation indicated in Table 2.3. As we have already noted, however, the level of aggregation can be increased or decreased, dependent on whether we want to focus on fine-grained differences or look broadly at several features simultaneously. In the next section, we will do the latter, using a wider-angle lens that helps us to see across a range of features, but at a lower level of detail.

For some purposes, as noted in Chapter 2, we need to do the opposite, using a zoom lens to bring out detailed differences more sharply. Table 3.2 gives an example of two types of disaggregation that enable us to see finer differences among regimes. The first example given in the table rows (1) and (2) of Table 3.2 takes three regimes—dangerous dogs, paedophile release, and ambient benzene—that achieved similar scores in Table 3.1 for 'aggression' in standard-setting, as shown in row (1). Row (2) indicates how those regimes

TABLE 3.2. *Disaggregating regime features and risk policy domains*

	Relative regulatory aggression				
	High	Medium-high	Medium	Medium-low	Low
(1) Standard-setting 'aggression' overall, reproduced from Table 3.1			Ambient benzene Paedophile release Dangerous dogs		
(2) Policy proactivity separated from overall 'aggression', as in third breakdown of Table 2.3	Ambient benzene		Paedophile release		Dangerous dogs
(3) Behaviour modification 'aggression' for the whole risk policy domain	Pesticide residues in drinking water				Dangerous dogs
(4) Behaviour modification 'aggression' for different parts of the risk policy domain	'Public' water supplies	Fighting dogs		General dogs	'Private' water supplies

compare when we move to a further level of disaggregation in 'aggression', as shown in Table 2.3, to examine the degree of 'proactivity' in standard-setting on its own. When we look at proactivity on its own, separated from policy ambition, the three regimes no longer appear similar. On proactivity, the dangerous dogs regime represented a minimal state policy presence that mostly fired into action only in response to high-profile dog tragedies. The paedophile regime represented some degree of response to tragedy or media events too, but with a larger state policy presence and more continuous policy conversation among various established policy professionals. The regime for ambient benzene, however, was a case where there was a substantial policy presence with continuous policy conversation taking place largely independent of tragedy or media events. That example shows how we can separate regimes that appear similar at the level of analysis represented by Table 3.1 by greater analytic disaggregation of the elements of regime context or regime content.

The other form of disaggregation illustrated by the bottom two rows of Table 3.2 breaks down risk policy domains rather than the elements of policy context and content. The aim here is to show that the rating of a regime on institutional and instrument elements can depend on how broad a risk domain we look at. The two examples, shown in rows (3) and (4) of Table 3.2, are the domains of pesticide residues in water and dangerous dogs. Taking those two domains as a whole, the two cases appear quite different on the 'aggression' element of regime content for behaviour modification as shown in row (3). However, a more complex picture emerges when we divide them up into sub-domains, splitting the dangerous dogs domain into fighting dogs and dogs in general and splitting the pesticide residues in drinking water domain into 'public'—that is, networked—and 'private' water supplies. Divided up in that way, fighting dogs came to approach the level of regulatory aggression shown for 'public' water supplies, while the level of aggression applying to 'private' water supplies was well below that applying to dogs in general.[18] In principle we can disaggregate in both of these ways at once, breaking up both the elements of regime content and the parts of different risk domains to produce ever finer distinctions among forms of risk regulation.

Identifying Variety and Linkages Across Control Components

Another way of refining the picture of regime variety depicted in Table 3.1 is to look at the way the three basic components of regulatory control relate to one another for each regime, particularly for the elements of regime content. After all, the extent to which arrangements for information gathering, standard setting, and behaviour modification relate to one another—or fail to do so—is a key question for policy design. Mismatches or underlaps among those control components are often identified in the aftermath of regulatory failures or disasters and the idea of coherent linkages between them figures large in recipes for better or more 'joined-up' regulation.

When we calculated 'relational variety'—the degree of similarity or difference in the placing of a regime across the three components of control—for the six regime content elements depicted in Table 3.1, we found none of the regimes approximated 'perfect congruence' in the relative placing of their

---

[18] Whereas fighting dogs like pit bull terriers were subject to draconian rules such as neutering, insurance, and muzzling in public places, only general behaviour controls applied to other dogs. Equally, whereas controls over public drinking water supplies were rigorously enforced by a specialized enforcement agency, namely, the Drinking Water Inspectorate, in England and Wales, local authorities were responsible for enforcing control over private water supplies and put much less effort into enforcing the rules, according to our interviews.

TABLE 3.3. *Organizational integration and cultural cohesion across the three components of regulatory control*

	Relative integration and cohesion				
	High	Medium-high	Medium	Medium-low	Low
Organizational integration: extent to which organizational boundaries overlap across control components	Occupational radon Occupational benzene Pesticide residues in drinking water	Local road risks	Pesticide residues in food Ambient benzene	Paedophile release Domestic radon	Dangerous dogs
Cultural cohesion: extent to which those working in different dimensions of control share common outlook and practices	Occupational benzene Pesticide residues in drinking water	Pesticide residues in food Paedophile release Local road risks Ambient benzene	Occupational radon	Domestic radon risks	Dangerous dogs

regime content elements across the three control components. Some regimes, however, such as local road risks and occupational benzene, were much less congruent than others—notably pesticide residues in drinking water. Table 3.3 looks at 'regime coherence' in a different way, by rating the nine regimes we observed for the degree of institutional linkage or overlap on two elements of regime content that were not included in Table 3.1. Those two elements are the extent of shared regulatory culture—attitudes, understandings, and working practices—across the three control dimensions, and the degree of organizational integration: that is, the extent to which formal organizational responsibilities overlapped across those control dimensions.[19]

As can be seen from Table 3.3, some regimes displayed high organizational integration across control components and a shared regulatory culture, such as the regime for pesticide residues in water or the occupational safety regime for benzene. Others scored low on both features, such as the regime for dog risks and domestic radon. Only in a few cases was there much difference

---

[19] The former element is related to Rhodes' well-known distinction between 'policy communities' (exhibiting continuity and cohesion) and looser forms of policy networks (see Rhodes and Marsh, 1992).

between regimes' scores on overall cultural cohesion and on organizational overlap, though we found different views of the same risk could in some cases be held by different parts of the same organization. For example, generalist health and safety inspectors within the UK's Health and Safety Executive tended to view workplace radon risks as less important than did specialist inspectors and policy staff. We can generally conclude, however, that cultural mismatch in regulatory regimes is typically associated with organizational underlaps, though whether the underlaps cause the mismatch or the mismatch causes the underlaps is not a question we will pursue at this point.

4. Absolute Variety and Types of Regimes

Hitherto we have been comparing regimes only on relative scales, looking at the cases we observed against one another. But many of the differences we can observe seem to be substantial even in absolute terms, and are not the product of hair-line distinctions among systems that might appear nearly-identical from other perspectives. For example, as we will show in more detail in Chapter 6, the nine regimes we observed went right across the spectrum of media and public salience, from massive to minimal media coverage and from high public concern to almost total indifference. The nine regimes also ranged from cases where official policy was near-zero tolerance of risk, to cases where official action thresholds were above the risk levels that would be considered tolerable for other hazards by orders of magnitude. Some of the regimes were entirely devoid of interest groups in a conventional sense and amounted to 'policies without publics' (May 1991), while others involved a handful of transnational corporations with high stakes in shaping regulation, and still others involved a host of highly-mobilized and antagonistic stake-holder groups. Those variations are substantial by any standards.

There were, however, some features of regime content where the absolute variety we observed seemed more limited. For example, there were no cases of complete or near-complete organizational integration or inclusiveness across regulatory control dimensions in our set, as depicted in Table 3.3. That observation may reflect the set of civilian risks we selected, and it is possible that other cases, such as the control of nuclear weapons risks as studied by Sagan (1993), might produce higher organizational integration or inclusiveness scores than the civilian risks we examined. Similarly, in their regulatory style elements, particularly regulatory zeal, many of the UK and EU regimes we observed seemed to be variations on 'accommodativeness'—a policy style often said to be characteristic of regulation in the UK and perhaps Europe in comparative perspective (see Hutter 1997; Vogel 1986.) If that is true, observation of regimes from other cultures or countries might stretch the scale of variation that we observed.

Comparing risk regulation regimes also prompts taxonomic questions about what broad differences in 'family groups' can be observed among regimes. At one level, every regulatory regime can be considered unique in the same sense that all of us are unique as human beings, and the more we disaggregate policy features or policy domains or both, the more differences we can expect to see. But equally, if we increase the degree of aggregation, making only broad-brush distinctions, the more likely it is that the cases will divide into a limited number of types, just as we can divide up human beings for some purposes into broad categories like short and fat, tall and thin, and so on. Family patterns among the regimes compared on Table 3.1 could be detected by digitizing the relative scores into some regulatory approximation of DNA profiles and subjecting the data to a cluster analysis or similar techniques. We adopted a modified form of that approach to show up some of the family patterns in our limited set of cases.

For this purpose, we move up rather than down the scale of aggregation from the level used for comparison in Table 3.1. That is, we put all the regulatory control components together and use more aggregated institutional and instrumental elements than those shown in Table 3.1. Thus Table 3.4 characterizes our nine regimes according to only six broad elements of regime context and content rather than the twelve shown in Table 3.1. For regime context, it depicts just three composite elements: overall regulatory risk, that is, the seriousness and market-tractability of the risk in the absence of the specific regime at issue; the opinion salience of risk, taking an amalgam of public preferences and attitudes; and interest group configuration, an amalgamation of the extent to which stakeholders are mobilized, and the extent to which a particular organized group can ordinarily expect to be preponderant on the basis of its high stakes and comparative advantage in organizing. For regime content Table 3.4 likewise takes just three broad features related to size, structure, and style. Size is an amalgamation of aggression and investment, to give an idea of the scale of regulatory intervention and resourcing. Structure is an amalgamation of the degree of organizational complexity—number of organizations and associated sub-regimes in the same risk domain—and the extent to which regulatee organizations share the costs of regulation across the three regulatory control components as discussed in the previous section. Style is represented by intensity or formality, a broad amalgamation of the rule orientation of the regime and the extent of zeal displayed by regulators in pursuing their goals.

Aggregation at this level inevitably means accepting some loss of definition as regimes that are different on the features shown in Table 3.1 start to blur into one another. But when we look at our cases in a further aggregated form, into single elements of regime-context and regime content, they divide into a number of different broad groups, which are depicted in Fig. 3.1. The regulation of pesticide residues in drinking water and food scored high or

TABLE 3.4. *An aggregated comparison of nine United Kingdom and European Union risk regulation regimes on six institutional and instrumental elements across all regulatory control dimensions*

Institutional and instrumental elements	Relative rating of regulation regime		
	High	Medium or mixed	Low
Regime context			
Overall risk: pre-regulatory vulnerability	Local road risks, Pesticides in drinking water, Pesticides in food, Domestic radon, Ambient benzene	Occupational radon risks, Paedophile release, Dangerous dogs	Occupational benzene
Overall opinion salience: heat of public concern	Paedophile release, Pesticides in food, Pesticides in drinking water	Dangerous dogs, Local road, Ambient benzene	Domestic radon, Occupational radon, Occupational benzene
Overall interest group pressure: concentrated lobbying pressure	Occupational benzene, Ambient benzene, Pesticides in food, Pesticides in drinking water	Paedophile release, Dangerous dogs, Local road	Occupational radon, Domestic radon
Regime content			
Size (scale)	Local road, Paedophile release, Pesticides in drinking water	Pesticides in food, Occupational benzene	Occupational radon, Dangerous dogs, Domestic radon, Ambient benzene
Structure (complexity)	Pesticides in food, Pesticides in drinking water, Occupational benzene, Local road	Ambient benzene, Paedophile release	Occupational radon, Domestic radon, Dangerous dogs
Style (intensity or formality)	Pesticides in drinking water, Pesticides in food, Occupational benzene risks, Ambient benzene	Occupational radon, Paedophile release, Local road risks	Domestic radon, Dangerous dogs

See Appendix C for notes on methodology

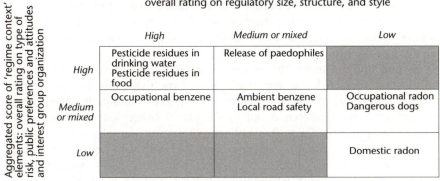

FIGURE 3.1: Nine risk regulation regimes
See Appendix C for notes on methodology

fairly high on both the aggregated regime context and regime content elements. Ambient benzene and local road safety were cases that were medium or mixed on both the aggregated regime context and regime content elements. Paedophile release was high on context but only medium or mixed on content, whereas occupational benzene was high on content but only medium on context. In contrast to occupational benzene, occupational radon was still medium or mixed on context but was low on content, and the same pattern applied to dangerous dogs.

The first two 'family patterns', noted in the top left and bottom right cells of Fig. 3.1, seem to involve relatively pure symmetry between regime context and regime content, while the others suggest a more complex relationship between those two elements in risk regulation. None of the regimes we observed were clear cases of high regime context profiles matched to low regime content profiles or *vice versa*. As can be seen, the top right and bottom left cells of Fig. 3.1 are empty and there was not even a case combining low context profiles with medium content profiles. To the extent that these nine cases are representative, it suggests a broad relationship between regime context and regime content. We explore that relationship more fully in the next part of the book.

5. Conclusion

Three conclusions can be drawn from the analysis in this chapter. First, it offers some empirical underpinning for our claim in Chapter 1 that there are substantial differences to be observed among contemporary regulatory regimes for risk and hazard. Even within a single country there is no uniformity in the way the state goes about regulating risk. Nor are those variations trivial or in some way beneath the notice of those inclined to look at a world-historical 'big picture' rather than the small print of bureaucratic detail. Both regime context and regime content can vary widely in risk regulation, as the analysis of the nine cases shows.

Second and relatedly, this variation suggests that 'risk society' analysis cannot easily reach some important parts of the risk regulation problem. A comparative description of risk regulation regimes along the lines of the anatomical scheme sketched out in Chapter 2 brings out differences that cannot be accounted for in terms of general propositions about how modern societies construe and approach risk compared with societies of the past. To tackle such questions about contemporary variation in risk regulation, we need an approach that is both methodologically more conservative and more ambitious than the style of most 'risk society' analysis; Barzelay (2000) has made such an argument for the analysis of public management policy. The approach needs to be methodologically more conservative, in the sense of drawing on conventional and fairly well-developed meso- and micro-analytic ways that policy scientists have developed to account for policy variation over time or between domains. Those standard forms of explanation include analysis of organized group activity, of the transactional nature of goods, and of public attitudes and opinion.

Third, though a systematic comparative description of risk regulation regimes is a necessary precondition for anything more than impressionistic explanations of observed regime variety, the categorization of risk regulation regimes, or regulatory regimes more generally, is something that is still in its infancy. We are a long way from possessing any generally accepted international, multidisciplinary, or even mono-disciplinary, *lingua franca* or analytic framework for understanding regime variety, as the first chapter showed. In that sense, the analysis of regulatory regimes today is in the sort of position that organizational studies was in the 1950s, before the development of the dimensional style of analysis associated with contingency theory or modern institutional economics. The dimensional analytic framework sketched out in Chapter 2, and the attempt to put some empirical flesh on its bones in this chapter, is intended to be a modest step in the development of better comparative understanding of the variety of regulatory regimes. In the next part of the book we pursue the analysis further by examining the extent to which regime context shapes regime content.

II

Explaining Variation in Risk Regulation Regimes

4

How Far does Context Shape Content in Risk Regulation Regimes?

> The forces to be dealt with are so numerous that it is best to take a few at
> a time . . .
>
> Alfred Marshall, quoted in Price (1968: 12)

There are many possible ways of explaining variation in regime content, but prominent among the 'usual suspect' explanations that can be rounded up are the three main elements of regime context sketched out in Chapters 2 and 3: types of risk, public preferences and attitudes, and the nature of organized interests. Accordingly, in the next four chapters we separate the context and content of regulatory regimes to see how far variations in the latter are explicable by variations in the former.

1. Regime Context: A Triangle of Shaping Elements?

Everyone has their own favourite approach to explaining what shapes policy and institutional design. But the three basic elements of regime context, albeit under different names, link to a familiar trio of accounts of what shapes regulatory policy, both in what regulatory practitioners told us in interviews and in the literature on public policy and jurisprudence. Each can also be related, to some extent at least, to a normative theory of regulation as well as a positive one, as we shall show later. Broadly, we could think of the three regime context elements as incorporating functional or market failure, populist or opinion-responsive, and corporatist or interest-driven answers to the question of what shapes regime content, though each can be nuanced beyond those stereotypes.

The functional or market failure answer says regime content varies mainly because types of risk vary, producing different sorts of correction that regulators need to make to deal with market failure. The 'populist' answer says regime content varies because public preferences and attitudes differ from one

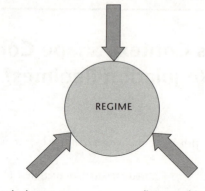

'Market-failure' pressures:
pressure for government in liberal-capitalist societies to
adopt 'proportionate' responses to correct serious
failures in markets and/or tort law processes

REGIME

'Opinion-responsive' pressures: 'Interest-driven' pressures:
pressure for liberal-democratic   pressures for government in institutionally
governments to respond to general   developed societies to respond to
public opinion   pressures from organized groups

FIGURE 4.1: Three shapers of risk regulation regimes

risk to another, as has been documented by at least a generation of systematic sociological and psychological survey research. The corporatist or lobby-driven answer—'it's the politics, stupid'—says regime content varies because of different distributions of power among group interests across risk domains.

It is no accident that the three basic elements of regime context map on to this commonly-recurring trio of answers about what shapes regime content. They featured in the comparative anatomy for just that reason. We can put them together and think of risk regulation as a 'space' within which this trio of influences operate, as depicted in Fig. 4.1.[1]

To set the scene for the next stage of our investigative journey, the rest of this chapter briefly discusses the three shapers *seriatim*, before returning to the triangular 'space' depicted in Fig. 4.1 and considering ways the shapers can interact. Then we briefly consider some possible alternatives to the three primary elements of regime context as explanations of variations in regime content, to which we will return in Chapter 8.

---

[1] The idea of 'regulatory space', which is commonly used in contemporary literature on regulation, is conventionally traced back to the work of Hancher and Moran (1989), though that work has its roots in more general work on 'policy space' dating from the 1960s, and arguably goes back to even earlier ways of thinking about government. Moore's (1995) conception of public management also employs a 'space' metaphor.

2. Regulating Risk the Functional or Market Failure Way

The 'functional' or market failure explanation of regulatory regime content conventionally surveys risk problems from the standpoint of market liberalism. The assumption is that governments in market-liberal societies will ordinarily not intervene where markets or civil law processes can operate without 'failure' (see Breyer 1982; Ogus 1994). Regulation will—and, from a conventional market-liberal view of the world, *should*—reflect what public authorities need to do to correct failures in such processes. In a perfect market, risk will be factored into product prices or handled through insurance and trade in futures. Likewise, in a perfect civil law system litigation or the threat of it will expose those who create risk, or are in the best position to avoid it, to the full costs of their acts of commission or omission (Posner 1986). There are, however, many instances where such processes will fail, including information deficiencies or asymmetries, inequalities of bargaining, monopoly power, or spillover effects. From a market failure perspective, it is at those points where government intervention can be expected to be concentrated. That means the 'type of risk' element of regime context would be the best predictor of regime content, particularly the element of regulatory size or scope.

Numerous criticisms have been made of 'market failure' accounts of regulation,[2] but those approaches can by no means be lightly dismissed. As prophets of globalization like to stress, functional or market failure approaches to regulation are heavily entrenched in much of the basic architecture of international institutions such as the EU and the various world trade and aid organizations. The principle of 'proportionality'—that the extent to which the special legal power of the state is invoked should be matched to the mischief being addressed—is entrenched in EU law and has become a central feature in the appraisal of regulatory appropriateness by the OECD and UK as well.[3] There are also several related approaches to analysing market and tort law failures that have developed over recent decades.[4] States that 'interfere' in risk domains that can be handled by the market, supplemented by the general law of contract or tort, can therefore plausibly be expected to face substantial pressures to withdraw or reduce such intervention.

---

[2] For instance, some argue that what counts as 'market failure', 'public goods', or 'externalities' can be culturally and professionally variable (see Malkin and Wildavsky 1991). Many have argued that 'government failure' in regulation, through various forms of capture, incompetence, bureaucratic game-playing, and the like, needs to be set against the expected reduction in market failure by state intervention.

[3] We will discuss this principle further in Chapter 10.

[4] Those approaches include the economic approach to law (Posner 1986), the public choice analysis of the nature of goods (Sproule-Jones 1982; Ostrom 1974), and socio-legal analysis of alternatives to so-called 'command and control' regulation (Breyer 1982).

3 Regulating Risk the Populist or Opinion-Responsive Way

The 'populist' or opinion-responsive way of explaining regime content builds on the idea that public policy follows public opinion and preferences. This answer may overlap with the functional or market failure approach, since markets are conventionally regarded as discovery systems for establishing individual preferences, within a given distribution of income; those concerned to correct market failures often seek to find surrogates for such discovery, notably by willingness-to-pay studies. And like the functional or market failure approach, this explanation also links to a normative theory of regulation: the idea, as old as democratic theory, that government should follow 'the will of the people'. When we talked to practitioners about differences in regime content, they used the populist approach to explain those differences at least as often as the functional one, telling us that regulation reflected the way the general public felt about the risks involved. For example, if the general public for some reason fears risks associated with carcinogens more than those associated with neurotoxins (Breyer 1993), the opinion-responsive government hypothesis would predict more stringent regulation of the former than the latter. But, as we shall see later, what regulators meant by 'public opinion' or 'public preferences' was variable and ambiguous.

As with the market failure approach, the idea of regulatory regime content as reflecting public opinion is open to familiar objections, both as a positive and as a normative theory.[5] But in a world where public policy is often said to be heavily shaped by public opinion and focus groups, it might seem strange if the nature of public and media opinion bore no relation at least to the size of regulation and perhaps to its style as well. Sometimes the way legislators respond to new risks such as those associated with genetically modified foods is put down to the force of public opinion. The same is sometimes said to apply to responses to near-misses or disasters narrowly averted. Equally, the tendency of regulation to develop as a set of monuments or a cemetery commemorating past disasters and tragedies is often attributed to the desire of politicians to be in line with public or media sentiment (see Bernstein 1955; Schon 1971). Public attitudes may even help to explain why some disasters are given elaborate and permanent regulatory tombstones, while others have much more modest monuments or even unmarked graves.

---

[5] Those objections include: the difficulty of avoiding inconsistent and ill-informed policy choices and the difficulty of registering intensity of preferences, in the absence of deliberative mechanisms; the ability of agenda-setters to bias public opinion by manipulative framing of issues; and the limitation of public attitude surveys that consider attitudes to risk reduction in a 'free lunch' mode without paying attention to the costs individuals are willing to pay to reduce the incidence of risk.

4 Regulating Risk the Corporatist or Interest-Driven Way

The corporatist or interest-driven way of explaining regime content is the *Realpolitik* idea that regulatory activity reflects the interplay and lobbying of organized interests. Contrary to the idea that the state pursues general welfare through correcting market failures[6] or that its activity reflects popular attitudes, the third approach sees regime content as a product of the activities of organized interest groups and their competition to press the hardest on the windpipes of public officeholders.

The corporatist or interest-driven approach, long entrenched in political science, is less clearly associated with a normative approach to regulation than the two approaches considered earlier. To some extent it links to pluralist doctrines of good government and even more to corporatist ideas that the state should embody the most powerful organized interests in society. In risk regulation those doctrines are commonly applied to occupational safety, with the occupational-safety regimes in many countries embodying labour unions and employer groups bargaining over wages and working conditions.[7]

Explanations of regulation in terms of the configuration of organized interests now conventionally begin with the 'Chicago school' approach which developed in the 1960s and 1970s. This approach, which formalized and developed earlier political-science approaches, saw regulation as reflecting the interests of the best-organized group in the policy domain. That group was ordinarily expected to consist of those business firms whose profits were most affected by regulation: for example, railway companies, banks, or truckers whose fortunes could be affected by price control or restrictions on entry to their markets. Such groups were likely to be best-organized, according to this school of thought, because they had higher stakes in influencing regulation settings than other players, and because they tended to have a comparative advantage in organizing compared with more diffuse groups like consumers or pollution victims. The conclusion was that regulation would normally operate in the interests of the business producer groups being regulated. It would normally be used to protect the markets of such firms against new entrants, underwriting prices and profits, and compelling consumers to pay more for products than they might wish or even to buy products they did not want.

Numerous objections have been offered to this way of explaining regulation (see Hood 1994: Ch. 2), and modifying the Chicago-school approach to

---

[6] As in the Hegelian view of the state pursuing the general social welfare of the society under the direction of selfless public servants, or the variant of Marxism that views the state as a 'super-capitalist' somehow programmed to look after the general interests of the capitalist order.
[7] Even in the UK, which is often claimed to have abandoned tripartite corporatism under the Thatcher government, but never did so for occupational safety regulation; see the Health and Safety at Work etc. Act 1974.

take account of them makes its predictions less determinate. For instance, who sees what as being in their interests may be more culturally variable than the original analysis allowed, and so may be the ability of 'latent' groups to survive, as Mary Douglas (1987) has shown. Moreover, not all regulatory policy domains are populated by rent-seeking business interest groups, by groups possessing the information, expertise, resources, or commitment to act in rational, self-serving ways, or indeed by any organized interest groups at all. In a refinement of the original Chicago theory, James Q. Wilson (1980) argued that the conditions for capture of regulation by producer groups were far from universal. Such an outcome could only be expected when the benefits from policy capture could be concentrated on one or a few organized groups and the costs diffused among the public or taxpayers at large. In three other circumstances he explored—where benefits were diffuse and costs were concentrated, where both benefits and costs were diffuse, and where both were concentrated—some other style of politics could be expected.

Distribution of costs of state intervention

	Concentrated	Diffused
Concentrated	**INTEREST GROUP POLITICS** *Organized lobby activity*: high but contradictory *Expected outcome*: deadlock, compromise, policy see-saw *Example*: roadworthiness checks for trucks (concentrated truckers' interests and concentrated vehicle manufacture and repair interests). Some health and safety policy	**CLIENT POLITICS** *Organized lobby activity*: high but one-sided *Expected outcome*: stable capture *Example*: roadworthiness checks for cars (diffused car-owner interests and concentrated repair interests)
Diffused	**ENTREPRENEURIAL POLITICS** *Organized lobby activity*: low unless 'policy entrepreneur' intervenes *Expected outcome*: inertia bias may be offset by entrepreneur activity *Example*: regulation of smoking, mobile phones and food safety (concentrated producer interests, diffuse victim interests)	**MAJORITARIAN POLITICS** *Organized lobby activity*: low *Expected outcome*: inertia bias except after calamity *Example*: global warming flood risks (diffuse victims and and beneficiaries)

Distribution of benefits of state intervention is the row label spanning Concentrated and Diffused.

FIGURE 4.2: Risk regulation and Wilson's matrix of cost/benefit distribution
Source: adapted from J. Wilson (1980: 357–74) .

Wilson's typology, often cited in the public policy literature, is reproduced and illustrated in Fig. 4.2, and readers will recognize that the features of interest group configuration discussed as part of regime context in Chapters 2 and 3—the extent to which groups are mobilized and the extent to which one single group dominates—relate closely to Wilson's analysis. Such a typology has the advantage of clarifying the 'win window' for dominance of a regulatory regime by conventional interest groups.

Under the conditions of the bottom right-hand corner of the matrix, in which no organized interest groups in the conventional sense operate—conditions argued by May (1991) to apply to a number of key risk policy domains—we need to look to other forms of explanation to understand what shapes regime content. Outside the 'majoritarian politics' category, however, many elements of regime content might be expected to reflect organized group pressure, as noted in Chapter 1. And even where no interest groups of a conventional kind—business lobbies, labour unions, or cause groups—are found, there may be micro-interest groups entrenched within the structure of government. Regulation often involves competing professional groups inside government, such as economists, lawyers, scientists, or engineers, competing over who 'owns' the policy domain and who should dominate it. Such issues take us outside the traditional interest-group framework of the original Chicago school, but they do figure in the policy networks literature and, as we shall show in Chapter 7, they cannot be ignored in the government of risk.

5 The Interaction of Regime Context Elements and the Search for Critical Cases

The 'market failure', 'opinion-responsive', and 'interest-driven' approaches to explaining regulation echo the three elements of regime context in our comparative anatomy and are analytically distinguishable up to a point, but that does not mean they are empirically separable in practice. Often they mix and blur into one another. For example, there are often conditions where the dominant organized group in a policy domain is a risk producer that has an interest in keeping regulation to the correction of market failures narrowly conceived and general public opinion is aligned with such a regulatory stance. At the time of writing those features seem to apply to the regulation of mobile phones, as noted in the opening chapter. Such intermixing of the regime context elements means we need to look carefully for 'critical cases' in which those elements are not aligned; and those cases may often be time-limited, since dominant organized interests finding themselves on the opposite side to general public opinion are likely to try to bring public opinion into line with the groups' preferred position. We pay particular attention to such cases in the chapters that follow.

6. Beyond the Regime Context Triangle

We took the trio of regime context elements as our point of departure for explaining regime content in this section of the book because they reflected the answers we most commonly received from our interlocutors in the nine worlds of risk regulation we examined, and are well established in the public policy literature. As we have already noted, though, that trio does not exhaust all the possible ways of explaining regulatory variety. At least two other types of account can be considered.

One is that other elements of regime context might be added to, or substituted for, the elements in our triangle to explain variety in regime content. Adding more contextual factors would mean turning the regime-shaping triangle discussed earlier into something more geometrically challenging. For example, ideas are often argued to be a powerful shaping factor over regulation: an old theme in policy analysis that came back into vogue in the 1980s after 30 years or so out of fashion, and was applied particularly to the regulatory changes of that era (see Derthick and Quirk 1985). Some of the ideas that might be candidates as shapers of risk regulation include developments in value-of-life analysis, the rise of the 'precautionary principle', the 'polluter pays' doctrine, 'risk communication' ideas, and new ideas about the shape of normal distributions in science (Peel 1999).

However, the problem with any strong case for ideas as contextual factors in shaping policy has often been stated: 'The theoretical snarl is that the strong case—that the "power of the idea itself explains its acceptance"—first must demonstrate that interests are interpenetrated by ideas, but then ideas must be shown to exert influence untainted by the interests they have just been shown to interpenetrate . . . . The move is untenable . . . ' (Goldstein 1993: 2, quoted by Jacobsen 1995: 286). The conclusion drawn by many policy analysts is that ideas cannot be clearly separated from interests; indeed, as noted earlier, ideas may shape what individuals see to be in their interests. The same goes for the idea of 'entrepreneurship' as a shaper of policy, in the form of the leadership activity of those who can spot 'windows' for innovative policy developments and bring together ideas, political support, and institutional machinery at a crucial point.[8] Nevertheless, when we examine how interests work in the government of risk in Chapters 7 and 8, we shall look at how they link to interests and how policy entrepreneurs galvanize interests.

Apart from modifying the basic trio of contextual elements, another possibility to be considered is that regime content might not be readily explicable

---

[8] Such a view of the policy process, paralleling the study of entrepreneurship in economics going back to Joseph Schumpeter's work, has been presented by Kingdon (1984) in a well-known analysis and has been particularly developed for the analysis of public policy development in the USA (see Doig and Hargrove 1987; Marmor and Fellman 1986; Greenfield and Stricklon 1986).

by context at all, as noted in Chapter 2. Specifically, 'institutionalists' of various stripes claim context cannot readily explain the decisions and outputs produced by dense institutional processes, because institutions form a barrier or membrane between social context and the details of public policy. For March and Olsen (1989), the density and unpredictability of complex organizations, particularly what they term 'organized anarchies', makes their activity hard to predict from social context. Many institutionalists also stress the idea of path-dependency or punctuated equilibrium; the idea is that policy and administrative routines tend to be heavily influenced by their historical point of origin, with inertia leading to persistence of original form, patterns of development that are path-dependent and often characterized by sudden abrupt changes rather than smooth adaptation to changing context.[9] Those who stress the force of 'autopoiesis' in complex institutional structures likewise see policy as dominated by internal 'discourse' within professional or other networks that will tend only to reproduce itself when faced with external 'disturbances' (see Brans and Rossbach 1997). Other accounts of policy development also lay the stress on processes of institutional or policy self-destruction as much as contextual factors (see Merton 1936; Wildavsky 1980: 62–85; Hirschman 1982).

7. Conclusion

Chapter 8 will return to the idea that intrinsic forces rather than contextual factors can shape regime content in risk regulation. Before that, however, the next three chapters examine the more determinate and falsifiable trio of regime context elements in our exploration of what shapes variety in regime content in the next three chapters. After all, the X-factors are potentially infinite and to analyse we must simplify. We cannot examine everything at once. So following the dictum which forms the epigraph to this chapter, taken from Alfred Marshall's *Principles of Economics*, we start with the simplest or most determinate forms of explanation before considering the more complex or less determinate ways of accounting for what we want to explain.

---

[9] The punctuated equilibrium perspective, which has strong parallels in biology and evolutionary science has come to be associated with 'historical institutionalism' in political science (see Steinmo, Thelen, and Longstreth 1992) and has been used by Baumgartner and Jones (1991) to explain the dynamics of nuclear power policy in the USA. It has produced some powerful analyses of the effects of path dependency and points of origin through the medium of institutions.

5

Exploring the 'Market Failure' Hypothesis

The preferred remedy is to improve the operation of the market by
reducing or eliminating . . . imperfection.

Elkin (1986: 51)

1. Introduction

This chapter explores a variant of the functional or market-responsive explanation of variation in regime content. The 'market failure' (MF) hypothesis is that in a liberal-capitalist society, government will experience pressure to restrict its economic interventions to the minimal response necessary to correct market failures. For this purpose we take a narrow and individualist interpretation of 'market failure', since, as we noted in Chapter 4, such failure can be politically construed in very different ways.

From this viewpoint, regulatory regime content will reflect the inherent nature of each risk, and specifically the extent to which it is technically feasible for markets, including insurance, or the law of tort to operate as regulators of risk. This logic would imply that the regime context elements of severity and market tractability of risk discussed in Chapters 2 and 3 would predict regulatory size and that regime structure would reflect the scale of the relevant hazards. It would imply that risks with the strongest 'public bad' features[1] would be more heavily regulated than others and attempts at voluntary collective activity would be preferred to state compulsion, with the latter adopted only when the former had demonstrably failed. We would also expect measures designed to make markets or tort-law processes work efficiently—for instance, by no-win-no-fee and class action regimes—to be preferred to 'command' regulation.

The market failure approach is widely considered to be a 'rational' basis for regulatory design. It has often been advanced as a normative doctrine of government activity, for instance in the idea of 'positive non-interventionism'

---

[1] By 'public' bad features we mean inescapably collective exposure, difficulties in making risk creators pay for the expected costs of the risks they produce, and risks in which one person's loss does not diminish the likelihood of losses by others.

advanced towards the end of British colonial rule in Hong Kong (see Huang *et al.* 1993). From orthodox economic assumptions, making the minimum state response necessary to correct specific market failures can be expected to maximize Pareto-efficiency in the economy, and that approach is reflected in doctrines of 'proportionality' as a test of good regulation in both law and economics.

Our concern here, however, is positive rather than normative: how far does the market failure approach enable us to predict regulatory content in practice? To explore that issue, we distinguish two dimensions of regulation that the MF hypothesis could be expected to explain. Then we sketch out what the regulatory content of the nine risk domains we studied could be expected to be like from an MF perspective, and compare those expectations with what we observed. As we shall see later, we found the MF hypothesis was more useful as a method of analytic benchmarking than as a reliable predictor of regulatory content.

2. Two Dimensions of Market Failure in Risk Regulation: Information and Opt-out Costs

The value of an MF analysis for our purposes is that it does not suggest the state will adopt a one-size-fits-all response to each risk domain, but rather points to the ways the state can be expected to deal with each risk on the minimal feasible scale and deploy the least intrusive and extensive regulatory response that matches the specific market-failure problem at issue in each case. However, to bring any predictive determinacy to the MF approach, at least three restrictive assumptions need to be made.

One is that egalitarian preoccupations with income redistribution do not ordinarily dominate risk regulation. The assumption is that in wealthy societies most people live at well above subsistence level and hence have at least moderate financial resources to respond to many risks that may affect them by market choices, including purchase of insurance, or legal action. Accordingly, the state is expected to respond to the problems of the minority of the population that is seriously poor by correcting their income deficit through transfer payments rather than responding to every risk with heavy-duty regulation designed to cater for this minority.

A second MF assumption is that state regulation of risk does not invariably need to be directed towards the most incompetent members of society, notably children or adults who are mentally incompetent. As with the issue of income-distribution and poverty, the assumption is that the state deals with the incompetence problem by policies aimed directly at that general issue. That means forms of state intervention designed to ensure the responsible care of the least competent individuals, for example, in measures to remove children from cruel or negligent parents or to care for the insane or vulnerable elderly, that form the background to other more specific risk regulation regimes. If instead regulation of every risk was designed to cater for an incompetent minority, all regulation would tend to be substantial in size and scope and there would be no room for doctrines of 'reasonable care' on the part of workers and the like.

For instance, insanity is not unknown among college professors, though opinions might differ on the extent and frequency of such mental debility. But we do not deal with the professorial insanity problem by university workplace regulations designed to ensure that academics could never hurt themselves or other people, for example by denying all access to sharp objects or sources of combustion. Such an approach would among other things make laboratory science impossible. Instead, regulations are designed on the assumption that the relevant employees are of sound mind and separate provisions are made to cater for the insanity problem, notably by general contractual terms dealing with fitness to work. The market failure principle is not, however, incompatible with risk regulation directed at the 'incompetence level' when the least competent individuals in society are disproportionately exposed and vulnerable to particular risks, such as hazardous toys for children or abusive carers of the frail and elderly.

Third, an MF approach does not need to assume that the danger posed by all hazards can be expressed in terms of well-understood quantifiable risk, or that everyone is perfectly informed about every danger. But it does rest on the assumption that individuals are capable of taking reasonable steps to inform themselves about the hazards that may affect them. It also assumes that the general law, as it evolves through statute or case decisions, will place obligations to collect or produce information about risk in the hands of those who are best-placed to do so, for instance in settling the expected balance of information-gathering responsibilities among employers and workers (see Posner 1986: 167).

Each of these three assumptions is problematic at least at the margin, and some analysts may see all of them as reflecting an unacceptably individualist cultural bias. Without them, though, the MF approach lacks all determinacy and could be consistent with almost any state response to risk. The value of a narrow conception of MF is that it can serve as a sort of benchmark: a basis for identifying the minimal conceivable state response to the 'market failure' presented by each hazard. To the extent that observed regime content differs from what might be expected from an MF perspective, we can turn to other explanations of the kind discussed in Chapter 4.

To pursue the implications of the MF approach for the expected content of risk regulation regimes, we select two major costs that can lead markets or tort-law processes to fail in handling risk, namely, information and opt-out costs.[2]

Information costs are faced by individuals in their efforts to assess the level or type of risk they are exposed to, for example in making decisions about purchasing genetically modified, irradiated, or organic food. Even if we assume that in a fairly wealthy and well-educated society most people have significant resources for informing themselves about risk, individuals wishing to obtain useful information about the different risks they face will find the cost of doing so ranges from trivial sums to costs that would be beyond even a billionaire's pocket. An example of low-cost risk information acquisition would be the cost of placing a detector patch above a household gas boiler to monitor carbon monoxide, while a high-cost example would be the efforts made in seeking to assess the risks of a melt-down in a nearby nuclear power plant. So from an MF perspective, we would expect regulatory size to be larger for high-cost cases than for low-cost ones.

The other selected way that ordinary market or tort-law processes might fail to operate as effective regulators of risk is through the costs of *opting-out* of the relevant risk, or avoiding exposure to it by civil-law processes.[3] The 'opt-out problem' is the inverse of the 'free rider' problem conventionally discussed in public goods analysis. For example, the cost to an able-bodied pedestrian of opting-out of most traffic risks—by crossing busy roads only at safe places—is low compared with the costs of opting-out of the risks of a nuclear winter caused by natural or man-made catastrophes.

The cost of individually opting out of a hazard can be reckoned in absolute terms, but it can also be considered relative to a collective opt-out strategy— for instance, building one's own house on stilts to opt out of flood risk versus participation in collective flood defences. They can be directed at escaping a given risk altogether, as in the case of building a house on stilts, or at escaping some of its consequences, for example by taking out flood damage insurance. They can also be expressed in more than one 'currency'. Even, perhaps particularly, for those of an individualist bias, cases where exposure to risk can be avoided simply by extra expenditure without restrictions in lifestyle are different from opt-out costs which involve substantial restrictions on lifestyle or behaviour. An example of the former, noted in Chapter 3, is the cost of substantially reducing radon concentrations in private homes, which rarely exceeds a few hundred pounds. An example of the latter is the cost of abandoning or moving away from a well-loved home to avoid coastal flooding

---

[2] Information and opt-out costs in practice cover most market imperfections associated with risk regulation. Thus the effects of externalities—impacts that affect others but not those who create them—should be amenable to unregulated market solutions or legal redress if there are no associated problems of information and opt-out costs.

[3] A much-cited example of the latter is Coase's (1960) case of farmers entering into contracts with railway companies to install spark suppressors to steam locomotives to reduce risk of fire damage to crops growing in fields adjacent to railway tracks.

risks. Of course, there are opt-out costs whose level is debatable or culturally variable, like the use of condoms to avoid exposure to HIV/AIDS. Moreover, as that example indicates, lifestyle or behavioural restrictions are inherently difficult to cost when we go beyond the cost of purchasing the relevant equipment or defences.

If the MF approach to risk regulation is followed, regulatory size will be substantial only for risks where opt-out costs and information costs are high, and only for the specific control component that is affected by high costs. Thus, if both information and opt-out costs are low, the MF approach would lead us to expect regulatory size to be small, not going beyond low-level activity like official statements about safe standards or advice about the nature of hazards. No substantial state investment in information-gathering or behaviour-modification activity would be expected.

If information costs were high but opt-out costs were low, MF logic suggests regulatory size would be high for information-gathering but low for behaviour-modification. Conversely, if information costs were low but opt-out costs were substantial, regulatory size would be expected to be low for information-gathering but high for behaviour-modification. However, if *both* costs were high MF logic would lead us to expect regulatory size to be high both for information-gathering and for behaviour-modification. Indeed, even though the MF approach can be considered to proceed from individualist assumptions, those are the conditions in which it would predict high regulatory aggression, far removed from simple *laissez-faire*, leave-it-to-the market approaches. Figure 5.1 summarizes the overall approach, which predicts that regulatory size will increase as risks move south-east on that table.

		Cost of obtaining information on exposure to risk	
		Low	*High*
Costs of opting-out of exposure to risk by market or contractual means	*Low*	Minimal regulation	Regime content high on regulatory size for information gathering, with behaviour modification through information dissemination
	High	Regime content high on regulatory size for behaviour modification	Maximal regulation

FIGURE 5.1: The logic of a market failure approach to regulatory size

3. Expected Regulatory Content for Nine Hazards in 'Market-Failure' Analysis

We now apply the MF logic sketched out in the last section to the nine risk domains described in Chapter 3. The aim is to identify what regime content might be expected for each of these domains from a strict MF perspective, so that we can compare expectations with observed regime content in the next section.

Dangerous Dogs Outside the Home

As noted in Chapter 3, the hazards of dangerous dogs outside the home are more familiar and readily observable than many other sources of risk. Hence the MF hypothesis would lead us to expect little emphasis on state information-gathering. The cost of informing oneself about the dangerousness or otherwise of a dog could be considered low, amounting to no more than lay evaluation,[4] provided, as discussed in the previous section, it is assumed that parents or those responsible take care on behalf of children or other vulnerable people and/or teach them to exercise proper caution towards dangerous dogs. Moreover, compared with many hazards, dog dangers appear stable and predictable, though the introduction of strange new breeds might create difficulties for lay evaluation of the risks they pose.

More problematic for the MF hypothesis are the opt-out costs presented by dangerous dogs. Leaving aside the cost of opting-out of the risks of being bitten by your own dog—by forgoing dog ownership or heavily restricting the choice of animal—the costs of opting-out of risks presented by dogs in the street are potentially high. Contract solutions between risk producers and victims—for example, in the form of contracts with everyone in the neighbourhood not to keep fierce dogs or to keep them chained up—are generally infeasible because of the very high transaction costs involved. Such contracts may also be particularly hard to negotiate between owners and third parties when there are conflicting and strongly held views on the scale and acceptability of the risk posed by a particular animal. These opt-out difficulties suggest that dangerous dogs can be considered as an intense 'public bad' to a local neighbourhood.

Individuals might in principle opt-out of 'neighbourhood dog risks' by obtaining suits of armour and wearing them whenever they left the house. These costs would be substantially higher than those of opting-out of radon risks, to be discussed below. The cost of equipping a family of four with full

---

[4] There is a contrary view that dog dangers cannot be reliably assessed by lay evaluation, but dog experts are divided on the matter. We therefore assume an MF approach would default to the view most amenable to minimal state regulation.

police-standard body armour to protect them against attack by their neigh-bours' savage dogs would be around £2,000, at least six times the typical cost of treating domestic homes affected by radon; titanium-reinforced body armour used by the London Metropolitan Police costs about £500 per suit. But even that sum is unlikely to reflect the true cost of opting-out in terms of the lifestyle restrictions involved in being obliged to go round in full body armour. So even on quite restrictive MF assumptions we might expect regu-latory size—regulatory aggression and investment—for dangerous dogs to be greater for the behaviour-modification component than for the information-gathering component. That pattern could be expected because of the heavy transaction costs and potential deadlocks in handling the enforcement or behaviour-modification problem through the market or through the law of contract or tort.

Radon in the Home

From an MF perspective, neither the information nor the opt-out costs of domestic radon risks could be considered high. As we noted in Chapter 3, the cost of testing for radon in the home is fairly low at around £30 per dwelling and, in general, can be considered a once-only expenditure.[5] Similarly, the annualized costs of remedial work to eliminate domestic radon risks are low relative to property values, averaging less than £100 a year, involving the installation of protective membranes and operation of ventilation fans if needed (National Radiological Protection Board 1994: 23–4). There seem few serious obstacles to the handling of domestic radon risks by an efficiently operating market linked to an effective tort law system. Problems arise only if heavy emphasis is placed on 'infant industry' considerations to justify direct state activity, or on the difficulties faced by victims in damage suits—for instance, of tenants against landlords—in circumstances where, as in the case of smoking, serious effects typically occur decades after the initial exposure. But analogous difficulties have not prevented major class action suits on behalf of smoking victims, and it is not impossible to imagine a more litigious and market-oriented radon culture fostering the commercial supply of expert advice on the market, and radon tests being required by insurers or mortgage lenders.

Given the absence of substantial market failure in this risk domain, the MF hypothesis would suggest regulatory size would be small. It is true, though, that radon is a relatively unfamiliar risk, the significance of which has become apparent only in the last decade or so (Lee 1994). Accordingly, from an MF perspective, the state might perhaps be expected to follow the approach

---

[5] Even for properties found to have high radon levels the test only needs to be repeated once every few years.

adopted for smoking risks, engaging in standard-setting and consciousness-raising activity.

Radon at Work

Though radon has the same technical properties at home and at work, the structure of regulatory regime content for occupational benzene risks might be expected from an MF perspective to be somewhat different from that applying to radon risks at home. In this case the issue arises as to whether the onus of collecting information falls on employees or employers, rather than landlords and tenants. As for the domestic radon case, we would not expect any substantial state information-gathering activity, but we would expect the onus of monitoring radon risks to be laid on employers, as the party best placed to gather information, rather than employees. In this case, opt-out costs are relatively low for employers, as for domestic householders, but they could be considered medium for employees if opting-out means giving up an established or locally available job to escape the risk if employers do not remediate. Accordingly, we would again expect the obligation to remediate to be laid on employers as the party best able to reduce the risk, given the obligations on the part of employees to take care. The content of a risk regulation regime could thus be expected to focus on setting a standard roughly in line with acceptable risks in other domains, imposing monitoring and remediation obligations on employers and limited inspection and enforcement activity over those obligations.

Ambient Benzene

From a strict MF perspective, information costs about benzene risks might be considered low, since benzene in general is associated with vehicle exhausts and those emissions can be readily detected by lay observation, by those who are aware of benzene risks. If we go beyond lay observation, though, the precise assessment of each individual's exposure to benzene would require complex, technically sophisticated, and expensive monitoring, which, like the suit-of-armour approach to dog risks, is intrusive in lifestyle terms as well as cash costs. Individual testing of air samples currently costs in the region of £250 in the UK, meaning that even a daily test would cost over £90,000 a year.[6] This cost, prohibitive to all but the mega-rich, might perhaps be reduced by a mixture of voluntary cost-sharing and a periodic sampling approach to benzene testing in particular locations rather than a daily test, taking into account daily and seasonal variables, traffic flows, and so forth.

---

[6] That cost might decrease with scale in a well-functioning market, as might also apply to testing for pesticide residues in water, to be discussed below.

Even so, the way many people move among different environments over the course of a day means multi-location testing would be needed to inform them about their exposure. Accordingly, from an MF perspective, the state could be expected to place at least medium emphasis on information-gathering.

However, individual opt-out costs from benzene exposure seem to be unambiguously high. At the time of writing there were no filters available at any price that could be used to minimize individual exposure to benzene on the street or in a vehicle. Coase-type contract solutions between risk producers and victims also appear infeasible because of the transaction costs involved, since individuals cannot feasibly enter into contracts with all drivers who might drive past their house, for example. Reducing exposure to benzene tends to involve solutions that are highly expensive both in absolute costs and in terms of restriction on lifestyles, such as giving up a city job and going to live in a remote area or moving house to an area of lower traffic density. Exposure to benzene risks is unavoidable for people living or working in urban connurbations, and affects millionaires in their chauffeured limousines just as much as humble pedestrians or cyclists (Leung and Harrison 1999). Hence benzene is a case where even strict MF assumptions would lead us to expect high regulatory aggression for behaviour-modification, placing it in the bottom half of Fig. 5.1.

Benzene at Work

For occupational exposure to benzene risks, an MF perspective would lead us to expect regulatory regime content along the lines described for radon in the home. The high information costs to individual employees of benzene monitoring could be considered much less prohibitive to employers, and hence there would be even stronger reasons to expect monitoring obligations to be placed on employers rather than employees. Opt-out costs for employees in this case could be considered similar to those applying to occupational radon: the cost of obtaining other employment. So the MF expectation would be for regulatory regime content to comprise standards that reflect the absence of any safe level of exposure, coupled with obligations on employers to monitor for the risk and take steps to protect employees from exposure.

Release of Convicted Paedophiles into the Community

It might seem laboured to apply an MF framework to the paedophile issue, given that in this domain conventional market measures such as willingness to pay may seem of doubtful applicability. Neither markets nor civil law processes can handle without difficulty the central issue of balancing incompatible risks—of harm to children and to those who have been convicted of paedophile offences. However, information and opt-out issues are both central to paedophile regulation. The risks associated with release of convicted paedophiles into the community impose high information costs on potential victims—and their parents—and relatively high opt-out costs too. Moreover, in this case there are no intermediaries, such as employers, on whom the main burdens of information-gathering and behaviour-modification can be imposed. Accordingly from an MF perspective we might expect regulatory regime content in this case to belong in the bottom right-hand 'maximal regulation' corner of Fig. 5.1.

To assess the risk of abuse from released offenders in public places, children or their parents would face very high costs of gathering detailed information on everyone they might meet and establishing their whereabouts. The surveillance costs—for instance, in hiring private detectives or paedophile tracking services—would be substantial. To reduce those information-gathering costs to manageable levels, there would therefore have to be collective action by children or their parents, and a market would have to develop in paedophile tracking services. Given the chances that voluntary collective action might fail due to free-rider problems, an MF perspective would predict substantial state activity to cut the information costs to individuals in some way. As we noted earlier, such information cost-reducing activity might consist of obligations on convicted paedophiles to wear distinctive badges or uniforms after their release—but the enforcement, not to mention civil-libertarian, difficulties associated with such a measure would be substantial. Alternatively or additionally, an MF perspective would lead us to expect the state to compile and maintain a public register of released paedophiles.

Opt-out costs for this risk also appear to be high for children or their parents. Close confinement of children in secure conditions to limit risk of exposure to released paedophiles predisposed to reoffend imposes high costs on both children and parents, and not even the body-armour potential route for opting out of dog risks is available in this case. Moreover, as with dangerous dogs or benzene, Coase-type contract solutions between risk producers and victims are likely to be unworkable, given the number of potential players. Accordingly, an MF approach would predict that regulatory size would be substantial for behaviour-modification.

Local Road Safety

For local road risks, particularly those concerning the relationship between road users in vehicles and those out of vehicles, information costs seem to be variable. Some of the information needed to assess road risks could be considered as a matter of lay evaluation of the sort embodied in road crossing codes. Some of it is more like the information needed to assess paedophile risks, in the sense of information about 'rogue' drivers, incompetent drivers, or other road users likely to act dangerously. How far it is within the capacity of any actor, including the state, to collect such information is doubtful. Moreover, in this case the restrictive MF assumption discussed earlier—that incompetence is capable of being tackled directly rather than risk-by-risk—is problematic, given that a substantial proportion of road users is likely to be drunk, senile, insane, or juvenile. Accordingly, from an MF perspective we might expect state activity combining consciousness-raising activity, of the type discussed earlier for radon, with more specific information-gathering about risk-creators like lunatic drivers, or high-risk locations like accident black spots.

Opt-out costs, particularly for out-of-vehicle road users to escape from the risks to them from vehicles, appear to be high in this domain. It is true that individuals can take steps at fairly low cost to greatly reduce their risk of being mown down by motor vehicles, but not to avoid the risk altogether. As with ambient benzene risks, only an eccentric or wealthy few can afford to opt out of the modern world and live in a wholly car-free environment. Coase-type contract solutions between individual pedestrians, cyclists, and drivers are again infeasible in this case. Given the likelihood that voluntary collective solutions will fail given the large number of actors and the potential for anonymity in big cities, an MF perspective predicts that regulatory size would be substantial for behaviour modification. The expected profile would accordingly be similar to that discussed for dangerous dogs above, though the degree of risk is much greater.[7]

Pesticide Residues in Food and Water

As Chapter 3 noted, pesticide residues in food and water are like radon in that the risk is hard to detect by taste or smell. Risks from pesticides are more contested, however, than risks from radon. Moreover, unlike radon, the costs to individuals of testing water for pesticide residues are substantial. At the time of writing it cost about £250 in the UK to have a single water sample tested for this purpose. Even if a well-functioning market were to reduce such costs, individuals concerned about pesticide residues would need to have their water tested regularly—unlike radon, where a one-off test will ordinarily be all that is required—with weekly testing running at around £13,000 a year at current price levels. It would cost even more to test individual foodstuffs before consumption. Such costs would ordinarily be affordable only by the super-rich. So the MF approach would lead us to expect regulatory regime content to incorporate information-gathering provisions at least in the form of obligations on water and food suppliers to inform their customers about pesticide residue levels in their products. Such disclosure would enable those customers to make intelligent choices about consumption.

---

[7] Not just because there are more than three times as many cars as dogs in the UK, but also because the risk of death and serious injuries is much higher for cars than dogs.

Opt-out costs for pesticide residue risks are harder to determine. A contract or tort-law solution to the problem is likely to be difficult, given that harm may be incurred through cumulative long-term exposure as well as sudden acute exposure. A tort-law solution would require individuals, or their bereaved relatives, to sue food or water companies for exposure over decades, in a similar fashion to recent class-action suits against tobacco companies in the USA. In the present state of scientific knowledge, the cost of such a tort-law solution appears substantial, in overcoming evidential hurdles, establishing causation, and resolving uncertainties in the law in the absence of any regulatory standard.

Opting out of the risk through the market is less problematic in transactional terms, but can involve substantial costs. In principle, of course, those who wish to escape from the risks of pesticide residues in food can buy organic food at a premium. But according to the UK Soil Association's unpublished figures, the 'organic premium' for most foodstuffs in the UK was up to 50 per cent and more in some cases, meaning that the costs of opting-out of pesticide risks in food were far from trivial. To opt-out of pesticide residue risks from piped water, individuals can install filters in their water supply-pipe or buy bottled water—though that can also be contaminated. Given that two litres of drinkable tap water a day cost a mere 35 pence a year at the time of writing, the individual filter opt-out solution is 500 times more expensive[8] and the bottled-water opt-out solution is approximately 1,000 times more expensive.

Such costs do not seem beyond the means of many households in a fairly affluent society, as witness the almost universal use of bottled water for drinking in many continental European countries, and its increasing use in wealthy countries. Indeed, the opt-out costs for risks of pesticide residues in water seem lower than those for pesticide residues in food. But individualized opt-out solutions to pesticide residue risks in water are costly relative to efficient centralized systems of cleaning up water, as noted in the previous paragraph. So even if individualists start with a lifestyle bias against collective solutions however arrived at, the relative costs of individual as against collective opt-out measures for pesticide residue risks in tap water mean that individualist principles do not come cheap in this case. We can also note that, unlike opting-out of dog dangers, substantial lifestyle restrictions do not have to be factored into the costs in this case. Hence from an MF perspective, we might expect regime content for this case to lie somewhere between the top and bottom right-hand cells of Fig. 5.1.

---

[8] The cost of installing filters was approximately £200, plus annual maintenance of between £100 and £200: slightly more than the cost of maintaining and powering fans for radon remediation. Jug filters were even cheaper to buy, but laborious to operate and not necessarily adequate for filtering pesticide residues.

4. MF Expectations Compared with Observed Risk Regulation Regimes

Figure 5.2 (a) summarizes the regime content that would be expected in the nine cases from an MF perspective; as we saw in the last section, some cases are ambiguous, notably the behaviour-modification component of the regime for pesticide residues in water and the information-gathering component for benzene. By comparison, Fig. 5.2 (b) also indicates the observed regimes for each of the cases, showing the degree and direction of difference between MF expectations and observed regime content. We will not go through all the cases summarized in Fig. 5.2, but concentrate on a few selected cases that were surprising from an MF perspective.

Dangerous Dogs

The UK's 1991 Dangerous Dogs Act was often cited as a classic case of 'how not to do it' in regulation (see Better Regulation Task Force 1998: 5). Indeed, it entered British folklore as a supposed example of an excessive knee-jerk government response to media hype (but cf. Hood, Baldwin, and Rothstein 2000). One official in the government department mainly responsible for dangerous dog regulation—the Home Office—observed to us that: 'In the cold light of day, the legislation was probably a bit of "summer madness" ' following high publicity to dog attack tragedies in 1991 (D4).[9] But paradoxically the overall regime for dangerous dogs fitted fairly closely with MF expectations, with observed and expected size and scope of regulation being fairly similar. The one part of the dangerous dog regime, and the part attracting most attention, that did not altogether seem to fit with the MF hypothesis were some breed-specific regulations introduced in the 1991 Dangerous Dogs Act. This Act imposed special and draconian safety requirements for some types of 'luxury' fighting dogs that were new to the country and hence unfamiliar to most UK citizens—notably American pit bull terriers, which had become popular with drug dealers and other criminals, especially in London. It imposed no such requirements, however, on existing or familiar dog breeds associated with savage attacks, such as German Shepherds. It is hard to see a clear MF logic behind this approach, although the breed-specific requirements in the Act were only part of a statutory framework including general behaviour requirements on the owners of all dogs, backed up by criminal sanctions, that broadly fitted MF expectations.

---

[9] Sources of interview quotes in this book have been anonymized and coded in Appendix B according to risk domain, institutional location, and responsibility of each regulatory actor.

(a) *Expected regime content*

Information costs and expected market failure state emphasis on information-gathering

	Low (lay observation sufficient to permit individual responsibility for detection)	*Intermediate or variable* (e.g. lower for employers or intermediaries)	*High* (gross technical and/or financial obstacles requiring heavy state detector activity)
Opt-out costs and resultant expected state emphasis on behaviour-modification activity *Low* (permitting individual opt-out decisions)	Domestic radon		Pesticide residues in drinking water
Medium (requiring duties on non-state actors)		Occupational radon Occupational benzene	Pesticide residues in food
High (requiring heavy state effector activity)	Dangerous dogs outside the home	Balance of road risks	Paedophile release Ambient benzene

(b) *Observed regime content*

Observed size of state information-gathering effort

	Low	*Intermediate or variable*	*High*
Observed state emphasis on enforcement and behaviour-modification *Low*			Domestic radon Ambient benzene
Medium		Occupational radon (but standards out of line with other radiation risks) Occupational benzene (but out of line with ambient benzene exposure risks) Pesticide residues in food (with standards out of line with those for residues in water)	Paedophile release (register not transparent)
High	Dangerous dogs outside the home (but 'deviations' over standards)		Pesticide residues in drinking water Balance of road risks

FIGURE 5.2: Expected and observed regulatory size from a market failure perspective

Occupational and Domestic Radon

Regulatory regime content for domestic and occupational radon exposure fitted MF expectations for regulatory size in several ways. But the observed radon regimes were out of line with MF expectations in at least three ways. First, the officially-recommended UK Action Levels for remediation of radon build-up in the home, first established in 1990, were set at what seemed like an extraordinarily high level in comparison with other state-regulated risks. In fact, the official Action Levels comprised an estimated extra lifetime risk of between 1 and 10 per cent, for non-smokers and smokers respectively (National Radiological Protection Board 1990: 25). Moreover, there were substantial risks below this Action Level, and those risks affected regions of the UK other than those officially designated as 'radon-affected' areas.[10] Puzzling from an MF perspective is the question of why official standards of acceptable risk in this domain should be set at levels considered intolerably high in other risk regulation regimes. A similar 'surprise' applied to the occupational radon regime, where controls on radiation due to radon 'kicked in' at a higher level of risk than applied to other sources of radiation at work.

A second surprise was the low emphasis on radon testing and remediation in the workplace. One informal estimate by a radon official (R1) suggested that at the current rate of progress it would take 22 years for all workplaces in England and Wales to be tested and no figures were available for remediation. A third—and for the MF hypothesis perhaps more important—surprise about the radon regimes was the existence of a large-scale state-funded programme for detecting and gathering information on domestic radon, concentrated in high-risk regions. Given the low cost of radon testing, as noted earlier, this emphasis on information-gathering seemed 'excessive' from an MF perspective. It looked excessive because the state was gathering information that most individuals could readily have purchased for themselves. In addition, the existence of a voluntary and free state-funded testing service necessarily 'crowded out' any private market in radon testing, especially when official action levels were set at such a high risk threshold. The radon regulators justified this government activity in terms of what they saw as apathy on the part of the general public. One local authority Environmental Health Officer wearily referred to his dealings with homeowners as 'head against the brick wall syndrome' (R8) and a central government official said, 'We wanted to establish the nature and extent of the problem. We offered free measurements because the Great British Public might accept a freebie but not pay for it. The problem is that the public thinks if it is natural it can't be wrong . . . ' (R3).

---

[10] Areas were designated 'radon-affected' if a certain proportion of properties exceeded the Action Level.

Ambient and Occupational Benzene Regulation

What was surprising about ambient benzene regulation from an MF perspective, given the high opt-out costs and infeasibility of individually based contract solutions for avoiding the risk, was the relatively small size of regulatory effort over behaviour modification, and the inconsistency of standards between the ambient and occupational regimes. For ambient benzene, the UK government from 1991 published the results of benzene readings across the country. Controls were also imposed on benzene levels in gasoline, hydrocarbon emissions from exhausts, and on other, localized or more minor, sources of benzene air pollution like gasoline filling stations, petrochemical works, and industrial plants. But standards were set surprisingly late and enforcement followed even further behind. Only in 1997, decades after benzene was first identified as a genotoxic carcinogen, were official target standards set for ambient benzene levels and those targets were not to be subject to any enforcement activity until 2004 (Statutory Instrument No. 928 2000).

In this case, against an MF benchmark, regulation seemed 'too small' on behaviour modification, and surprisingly slow for standard setting. Equally striking was the fact that acceptable risk standards set for ambient benzene were a thousand times more stringent, or more restrictive, than those for occupational benzene. It seems difficult to justify such a difference on grounds of lower opt-out costs for employees than the public at large, and indeed the difference in standards represented the opposite bias from that set for domestic and occupational exposure to radon.[11] The difference seems to reflect the way costs and benefits were distributed in the two cases, as well as different patterns of expert and lobby-group activity, as we will see in Chapter 7.

The Release of Convicted Paedophiles into the Community

Regulatory size in this case largely fitted MF expectations. The main 'surprise' concerned behaviour-modification activity, namely, the absence of any provision of information to the general public on a routine basis to enable parents to make more informed choices about risks to their children. As noted in Chapter 1, in contrast to practice in several US States, the UK's statutory register of sex offenders was kept strictly confidential, with vigorous efforts by the public authorities to resist attempts made through the courts to oblige them to disclose the information. Official information conveyed to the general public consisted of media statements and the like, usually about the handling of individual offenders, but not of routine information. Several officials that we talked to defended this approach on the grounds that the general public

---

[11] For the controversy over the way ambient benzene standards were set, see ILGRA (1997).

tended to exaggerate the risk from paedophiles at large, as opposed to sexual abuse at home. They thought publicizing the whereabouts and identity of sex offenders would tend to spread public alarm and undermine the efforts of police and local authorities to keep sex offenders under control. Critics had much less faith in the ability of the regulators to manage the risks effectively, particularly after the murder of a young girl, Sarah Payne, in the south of England in July 2000.

Local Road Safety

As the MF approach would lead us to expect, regime content involved substantial regulatory size for behaviour modification in this risk domain. Indeed, many road safety experts argue that behaviour-modification activity in terms of state spending on risk reduction is lower than would be justified on MF grounds. Behaviour-modification activity ranged from general consciousness-raising efforts—about the risks of speed or drunken driving, or safe road crossing for children—to direct and targeted measures like modification of road layouts to change driving behaviour or segregate different road users. Whether the size of regulatory effort applying to information gathering in this domain was consistent with MF expectations is debatable. Earlier we suggested information costs to individuals in assessing risks of this type were variable. In some cases those costs involved no more than simple lay observation by an able-bodied person, but in others they approached the sort of costs associated with paedophile risks, notably in identifying rogue drivers. The state approached the latter problem both by licensing drivers and by police-patrol activities, together with measures like random breath testing of motorists.

Such activities appear broadly in line with MF expectations. Consistency with MF logic is not, however, so clear in the case of the elaborate investment by UK public authorities in statistical information-gathering on road risks. That activity included extensive attitude surveys as well as 'hard' accident data, sharply contrasting with the approach taken to dog attack and other risks. Perhaps much of the information-gathering activity was needed to direct state investment in highway engineering—the key instrument for risk reduction, as noted earlier—and much of it may have been driven by insurance considerations. Or perhaps the information-gathering activity applied to many of the other risks in our set could be considered 'too low' compared with this case, since public attitude surveying was rare or non-existent in most other cases, and even 'hard' accident data was not always systematically collected.

Pesticide Residues in Food and Water

What seemed surprising about risk regulation in these domains from an MF perspective were the differences between the arrangements for control of residues in food and water. For pesticide residues in food, there were official health-based—albeit non-comprehensive—standards for residues, as might have been expected from an MF perspective. But the behaviour-modification activity could be considered low from an MF viewpoint, given that opt-out costs from risks of pesticide residues in food are fairly high. Sporadic state enforcement activities, varying from one local authority to another, and relying largely on compliance by retailers, might be considered relatively consistent with the MF hypothesis. But retailers were not obliged to disclose the contamination levels of the products they sold to enable consumers to make informed choices about risk. Nor did central government monitors and local authority inspectors identify specific retailers and producers in routine published information to inform consumers about the riskiest sources of food. The only exception to that practice took the form of a limited 'name and shame' policy introduced in 1999, and we shall look further at that development in Chapter 9.

The approach taken for pesticide residue risks in drinking water was quite different. As explained earlier, standards for drinking water were set at 'precautionary' levels so rigorous that they went beyond the limits of what was measurable at the time of their introduction. In addition, suppliers were obliged to provide publicly details of pesticide concentrations in drinking water and enforcement was centralized in a national—for England and Wales—inspectorate. If the restrictive assumption discussed earlier is adopted—that opt-out costs for pesticide contamination risks in water are affordable on a private basis for most individuals in an affluent society—regulatory size was surprisingly large for standard-setting and behaviour-modification in this regime compared with MF expectations. It was particularly surprising that regulatory size for these control components was higher than in the case of pesticide residues in food, for which opt-out costs seemed to be higher in absolute terms. Even if the restrictive assumption about individuals' capacity to opt out of such risks is relaxed, it is not clear from an MF perspective why drinking water should have been exposed to a regime so different from the one employed by the state for pesticide contamination in food. Regulators tended to account for those differences in terms of the working of EU politics and the institutional history of the water industry in England and Wales rather than by MF logic.

5. Conclusion: How Far Can Market Failure Explain Regime Content?

The discussion above suggests that an MF account is consistent with a number of our observations of regime content in nine different risk domains, particularly for information-gathering. It also shows, however, that the approach has at least three limitations as an explanation of regime content.

First, the approach is not always determinate as a predictor, even with the restrictive assumptions set out earlier. The practical definition of market failure in terms of information and opt-out costs, to say nothing of distributional impacts, is to a substantial degree a matter of judgement. Examples of such indeterminacy from our cases include whether collective risk-prevention arrangements are more cost-efficient than individual approaches, as in the case of water, and more generally whether we take a minimal or maximal approach to market failure, as in the case of information-gathering over roads and dogs.

Second, and relatedly, the MF approach is geared to explaining only some aspects of regime content as described in Chapters 2 and 3. It is mainly suited to explaining regulatory size—the degree and aggressiveness of state intervention—and some parts of regulatory structure. But it is less obviously geared to explaining other aspects of structure—notably organizational complexity—and regulatory style. So it seems hard to argue that MF is even in principle an all-purpose explanation of risk regulation.

Third, even for that aspect of regime content that the MF approach seems best suited to explain—namely, regulatory size—that approach did not fit all cases or all dimensions of regulatory control. In principle the approach offers a way of going beyond 'risk society' generalities to specific predictions of variety in regulation. In practice, however, it explained only about half of the observed regulatory regime size in the cases we examined. Examples of observations that could not readily be explained by that approach include the difference in regulatory standards between ambient and occupational benzene, the exceptionally high risk toleration for occupational radon, and the breed-specific features of dangerous dog regulation. Not only did observed regulatory size often deviate from MF expectations, but it differed in both directions. In some cases, as Fig. 5.2 (b) showed, the state seemed to be doing 'too much' and indulged in greater than MF-expected regulation, for instance in its information-gathering activity on domestic radon. In other cases, however, it seemed to be doing 'too little' in MF-expected terms, for instance its behaviour-modification activity on ambient benzene.

Moreover, even for the size of regulatory effort, MF expectations seemed rather better at predicting the information-gathering dimension of regulation than the standard-setting or behaviour-modification dimension. Even here there were deviations, notably over radon. This finding reinforces the point made in Chapters 2 and 3 that different dimensions of regulatory control may be shaped by different factors rather than a single one.

The size of regulatory effort seemed most closely to fit the pattern expected by the MF hypothesis in one or both of two circumstances. One is when there were few entrenched lobbies in the policy community, whether in the form of professional groups within the state apparatus or major business lobbies pressing regulators. The other is when historical and technological change was limited, since in those conditions the risks involved appear less likely to be perceived as 'dread' by the public at large. Out of the nine risk regulation regimes we observed, the dogs regime—except for the element of 'technological change' in the form of new or foreign breeds whose riskiness was hard to assess by the lay public—most closely approached these conditions.[12]

The limited predictive power of the MF hypothesis may surprise those who stress the inexorable forces of global capitalism playing on modern liberal democracies. They might expect such forces to prevent the state from intervening where the market can provide, and to induce it to intervene only at the minimal level needed to correct specific market imperfections. The nine cases observed here suggests the MF approach is valuable as an analytic benchmark, but only moderate in its capacity to explain variations in regulatory content. That suggests we need to look at additional explanations for an adequate account of what shapes the content of risk regulation regimes. Accordingly the next two chapters turn to the other two elements of the 'triangle' of risk regulation regime shapers that we identified in Chapter 4.

[12] It may be a case of the 'simpler' health-based risks that Blaxter (1999: 22) sees as needing more investigation to balance popular and academic preoccuptions with high-tech and complex risks.

6

Opinion-Responsive Government and Risk Regulation

Vox populi, vox Dei

Old saying, used by Alcuin in a letter to Charlemagne c. AD 800[1]

1. Public Attitudes as a Shaper of Regulatory Regime Content

This chapter explores how far public preferences and attitudes can account for variety of regime content. An 'opinion-responsive government' explanation of regime content suggests risk regulation is the way it is because that is how those affected by the risks, or the cost of reducing the risks, want it to be. Regulatory size, and possibly elements of structure and style too, might be expected to reflect measures of those preferences and attitudes, including public opinion salience and the general drift of public opinion. Such an outcome would also be consistent with the normative preferences of those like the early opinion pollster George Gallup (Gallup and Rae 1940), who believed democracy means giving voters at large what they want rather than responding to organized interests, élite opinion, experts, or those who shout loudest in policy debate.[2]

Even though survey evidence of public preferences and attitudes is patchy for the UK and Europe, we can readily demonstrate that risk domains vary widely in public salience and in the apparent policy preferences of the general public. Nevertheless, this chapter argues that 'opinion-responsiveness' is little if any more definite or reliable as a predictor of the content of regulatory regimes than the market failure hypothesis, for at least two reasons. First,

---

[1] See *Oxford Dictionary of Quotations* (3rd edn), London, Guild Publishing 1988: 3.

[2] This doctrine has been advanced in different forms by many other thinkers, including Jeremy Bentham's (1983) idea of a 'Public Opinion Tribunal', the nineteenth-century British Liberal politician Joseph Chamberlain who shocked the young Beatrice Webb by arguing voters should be given the policies they wanted (Letwin 1965: 369), Kirstin Shrader-Frechette's (1991) 'populist' approach to risk regulation, and contemporary enthusiasts for the idea of using information-age technology to conduct public policy by continuous referendum (Laver 1983: 186–7).

there is no single way of listening to *vox populi*. As students of 'deliberative democracy' stress (see Dryzek 1990; Fishkin 1995), there can be marked differences between unreflective snap judgements based on limited information—the normal basis of public opinion polls—and views based on fuller information in a deliberative context.[3] So the 'opinion-responsiveness' or otherwise of risk regulation may depend on how opinion is sought.

Second, even allowing for the different ways that public preferences might be gauged, much of the risk regulation we observed seemed only partially opinion-responsive both in outcome and process. General public opinion seemed sometimes to work as a constraint on regulatory content, but the George Gallup doctrine that government should seek to discover and then follow the preferences of the public at large seemed to be more the exception than the rule in the government of risk. Regulators commissioned systematic polls and surveys in only a minority of the cases we investigated, and much more often left it to others—or no one—to conduct such inquiries. Even the use of focus groups, as a more interactive and in-depth way of probing public opinion than conventional opinion polling, was limited and selective. Indeed, many regulators we interviewed thought opinion-responsiveness meant listening to protestors and organized critics, not discovering and following the preferences of the public at large *à la* George Gallup.

Morever, regulators' approaches to public opinion often contained elements of 'spinocracy', attempting to shape public attitudes—in what Key (1961: 423) termed 'government of public opinion rather than government by public opinion'. Indeed, as we shall see later, when general public preferences appeared to be out of line with the preferences of policy experts or other organized interests, a number of management strategies by regulators were observable. Those strategies included 'don't ask' or 'Nelson's eye' approaches, 'selective attention syndrome' where there were different sources of information about public preferences and attitudes with different policy implications, attempts at 'opinion-shaping' or 'preference-shaping', and doctrines of 'balance' that cast regulators in the role of arbiters of contradictory opinions or policy considerations.

2. Variations in Public Salience and Public Policy Preferences Across Risk Domains

Figure 6.1 compares the media salience of six cases selected from the nine risk domains introduced earlier. It is based on a survey of selected UK national

---

[3] For example, an in-depth qualitative study following a UK train disaster suggested the public did not demand as much money to be spent on rail safety as would be suggested by media headlines and opinion polls (Burton *et al.* 2000).

Low Profile

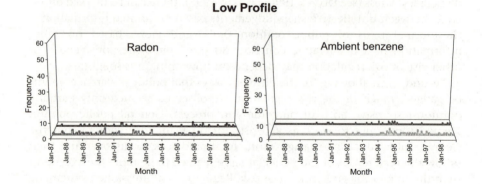

Intermediate Profile

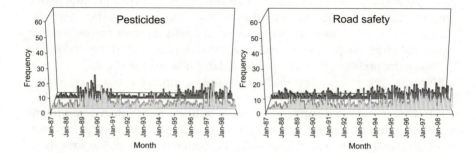

High Profile

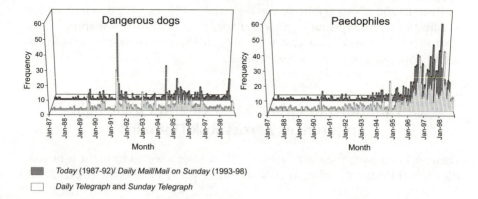

FIGURE 6.1: Media profile analysis of six risk domains: frequency of articles/month, 1987–98

newspaper sources from 1987 to 1998, including tabloid as well as broadsheet newspapers.[4] While this analysis has major limitations—it did not include any local newspaper sources or broadcast media, and any keyword-based search is vulnerable to shifts and nuances in linguistic usage—it suffices to show up major differences in media salience among risk domains and reveals three or four different patterns. One is an 'out of sight, out of mind' pattern, for which the clearest examples are domestic radon and ambient benzene. For these two risk domains we see low and stable media profile scores and a fairly passive style of press reporting, largely consisting of 'agenda-taking' coverage of official reports and government news releases, rather than 'agenda-making' coverage by independent investigative reporting and the like.

At the other end of the media profile spectrum are risk domains with high media salience and substantial independent 'agenda-making' press coverage. This pattern is illustrated in our set by dangerous dog risks and release of paedophile offenders. Within that category, we can distinguish two subtypes. One is a classic 'issue-attention-cycle' pattern (Downs 1972) applying to dangerous dog risks, with periodic high peaks interspersed with troughs indicating volatile press coverage. The other subtype is a pattern of exponential growth in press coverage, applying to the regulation of risks posed by paedophiles.[5]

Between the high and low ends of the media profile spectrum are cases of medium and fairly steady media salience, with occasional independent 'agenda-making' coverage as well as passive coverage of official reports and press releases. Among our cases, pesticide residue risks and road traffic risks had intermediate media profiles. The pesticide residue media profile score is surprisingly low given that pesticides are often regarded as a 'dread risk', as noted in Chapter 3, and the road traffic risk score is surprisingly high given that some of the professionals we interviewed in the field tended to portray the risk as practically invisible to the media and general public.[6] As with much of the other variations in risk regulation discussed in this book, the

---

[4] Articles containing chosen keywords—'radon', 'pesticide(s)', 'paedophile(s)', 'benzene', 'road safety', and 'dangerous dog(s)'—were downloaded from the FT-Profile online archive from selected UK newspapers between 1987 and 1998. Variation among domains was smaller for editorials than total stories. The newspapers chosen included broadsheets—the *Daily Telegraph*, with the highest UK broadsheet circulation, and its sister paper the *Sunday Telegraph*—and tabloids, represented by the mass-circulation *Daily Mail* and the *Mail on Sunday*. Since the *Daily Mail/Mail on Sunday* were included in the FT-Profile database only from 1993, *Today* was chosen to represent tabloid coverage between 1987 and 1992. All stories were sifted for relevance after initial selection through keyword searches, and then frequency of articles per month were plotted over time. Such an analysis does not assume that high-circulation newspapers reflect public opinion. But it does assume such coverage is likely to reflect the flavour of public debate, not least because opinion leaders read such sources (see Gaskell *et al.* 1999: 385).

[5] To some extent this pattern may reflect changing use of the word 'paedophile', the search term used, which came into popular use only in the mid-1990s. However, it echoes a pattern of media coverage of rape observed by Soothill and Walby (1991).

[6] Pesticides would have scored rather higher if editorial rather than total coverage had been taken as the basis for analysis.

TABLE 6.1. *Public attitudes to risk regulation: six selected patterns*

Pattern	Salience of risk	Opinion polarization or conflict	Opinion stability	Example
1. 'Don't know, don't care'	*	*	*****	Domestic radon
2. Conflicting attitudes	**	*****	*****	Ambient benzene
3. Complex and dynamic attitudes (multiple sources,reactive dynamics	***	*****	**	Road traffic risks
4. Issue-attention cycle	****	***	*	Dangerous dogs
5. General and consistent concern	*****	**	*****	Pesticide residues in food/water
6. High but little-examined concern	*****(?)	*	(unknown)	Paedophile risks

***** = high; * = low

markedly different patterns shown in Fig. 6.1 are not readily explicable from general ideas about 'risk society'. It is not our purpose here to explain those variations, but something other than the general characteristics of 'high modernity' seems to be needed to explain why for some non-trivial risks the press took little interest beyond passive coverage of information released by official sources, while for others it adopted heavy and independent coverage.[7]

We can also observe substantial variations in public views on policy over these different risk domains, using such attitude survey material as can be found for each domain. In most cases public attitudes revealed by such sources seemed to echo the pattern of press coverage and six such patterns are summarized in Table 6.1. At one extreme are 'don't know, don't care' public attitudes, involving widespread ignorance and apathy about risks government experts think to be substantial. For instance, such attitude surveys as have been conducted on radon in the UK indicate little public knowledge or concern about a source of radiation that, as noted in Chapter 3, is said by experts to kill about 2,500 people a year in the UK—about the same as the annual death toll on local roads—and to claim roughly the same number of lives at work—250—each year as all industrial accidents (see Lee 1994).[8]

---

[7] Likely candidates for such an explanation include cultural variety and different 'policy community' characteristics.

[8] See also Weinstein, Klotz, and Sandman (1989), Weinstein and Sandman (1992), Leiss, Massey, and Walker (1998), Michael (1991; 1992).

At the other extreme are cases of high public concern about and awareness of risks. This pattern is commonly believed to apply to paedophile risks, although remarkably little public opinion surveying appeared to have been conducted by any of the established players in that policy community. The single UK opinion poll that we discovered on this topic (MORI 2000) did not ask how aware or worried respondents were about the risk of paedophile attack, though it revealed 67 per cent support for the incarceration of paedophiles for life and 58 per cent in favour of the public naming of paedophiles.[9]

Four other intermediate patterns can be identified, as shown in Table 6.1. One, perhaps closely related to the 'don't know, don't care' pattern, involves public policy preferences that appear to be inchoate, conflicting, or contradictory. Ambient benzene seemed to be a case of this type. Public attitudes to ambient benzene as a specific pollutant and carcinogen had been little investigated by UK government. We identified only one government-commissioned study that specifically covered the issue, and that survey indicated a vanishingly low level of public recognition and concern (Hedges 1993). From a broader perspective, opinion polls revealed high and increasing public concern with general air pollution, including 'traffic fumes'. But there was also strong evidence from attitude surveys of general public disinclination to sacrifice car-based individual mobility to reduce collective pollution risks at 'the point where cost-free environmental attitudes meet the real personal costs of mobility constraints' (SCPR 1991: 120–1).[10] Indeed, in a 1993 survey most respondents thought being a car driver or passenger was less risky—when threat of violence was added to likelihood of accidents—than using public transport (Carthy et al. 1993: 9). Such public attitudes hardly provide clear pointers to policy settings even for risk regulators highly disposed to be 'opinion-responsive'.

A more complex pattern applied to road traffic risks, where there were also multiple sources of attitude data indicating different preferences, but also polarization and some reactive dynamics in public opinion. In this case, local government and other policy players made more active attempts to measure local public opinion on how road transport risks should be managed than in any of the other risk domains we examined. Media salience and broad-brush surveys suggested a low to medium level of public concern about reducing risk, with one review inferring 'a lack of sustained interest in road safety on the part of the public at large' (DoT 1987: 17; Webster 1998). However, some survey evidence by the Association of Chief Police Officers suggested higher and more definite concern—but also more polarization and volatility—over

---

[9] However, only 3 per cent of respondents to this poll thought public naming of paedophiles would reduce risks to children, and this measure rated ninth out of a list of measures, far behind stricter speed limits.

[10] See also International Research Associates (1991); Lex Service Plc (1997: 37); SCPR (1998); MORI (1998: 13).

the specifics of local road traffic management, and that road risks rated as high as crime risks in local responses over police priorities (see BBC News Online 1999). Moreover, central government provided empirically-based values for local authorities to use as measures of public willingness-to-pay for reducing the risks of road accidents.

There are several difficulties for opinion-responsive government in such a case. First, given multiple sources of attitude data indicating different preferences, precisely which *vox populi* is to be taken as *vox Dei*? Different players, as we will see later, varied in the attention and emphasis that they gave to the different sources of information about public preferences and attitudes. Second, opinion could be dynamic and reactive. For instance, specific traffic-calming measures designed to reduce risk to vulnerable road users often seemed to command general support among local residents at the time of their introduction, but later appeared to became unpopular, with disillusionment setting in over side-effects and implementation problems (Webster 1998: 33). This feature makes the path to 'opinion-responsive' government far from smooth, since truly opinion-responsive government in those circumstances would need to abandon or reverse those measures shortly after adopting them.

A third intermediate pattern, exemplified by public attitudes to control of dangerous dog risks, comprises substantial and widespread public concern about risk reduction, but also some polarization and volatility over the specifics of regulation. Such public opinion surveys as had been conducted in the UK over the regulation of dangerous dogs and other dog-related risks indicated substantial support for regulatory measures to reduce those risks, such as general dog registration and a ban on dangerous fighting dogs.[11] However, opinion seemed to be more evenly divided when it came to specific regulatory measures, such as whether all American pit bull terriers should be compulsorily executed, an issue much debated in the UK in 1991 after a spate of attacks by such animals attracted extensive publicity.[12] The experience of the UK's much-criticized 1991 Dangerous Dogs Act, which was introduced in the wave of those attacks but later attracted a great deal of negative press coverage,[13] shows some similarities with local traffic calming measures. Both cases show that measures that are broadly 'opinion-responsive' when first introduced can become increasingly unpopular as public awareness grows of hard cases, side-effects, and shortcomings in implementation and

[11] In 1991, when dog attacks were big news in the UK, national polls on the issue were commissioned by a Sunday broadsheet (*Observer* 1991) and a daily tabloid (*Today* 1991), and several polls were commissioned by local newspapers in England (see *UK Press Gazette* 1991).

[12] While local polls in 1991 all showed overwhelming support for compulsory execution of pit bull terriers, one of the national polls suggested opinion was evenly split on the issue and the other revealed a large minority opposed to such a measure.

[13] Our analysis of coverage in one newspaper stable, the *Daily Telegraph* and *Sunday Telegraph*, reveals that in the seven years following the Dangerous Dogs Act's enactment there were over 35 editorial items that used the Act as an example of bad regulation.

enforcement (see Hood, Baldwin, and Rothstein 2000). However, opinion polling on dangerous dogs regulation was surprisingly rare given the peaks of media salience the issue attracted, as shown in Fig. 6.1.

The fourth intermediate pattern, applying to pesticide risks, consists of substantial and widespread public concern without strong evidence of polarization. As noted earlier, pesticides have been identified as a 'dread risk' in the risk-perception literature (Slovic, Fischoff, and Lichtenstein 1980; Frewer, Howard, and Shepherd 1998) and evidence from UK and European opinion polls also suggested relatively high levels of public concern about this risk.[14] For instance, in the 1998 British Social Attitudes Report, 34 per cent of UK respondents identified pesticides as an 'extremely' or 'very' dangerous threat to themselves and their family, and polls in other European countries revealed higher levels of concern (SCPR 1998: 105). We found no surveys focusing specifically on public attitudes to pesticide residue risks in drinking water,[15] but substantial concerns had been expressed to pollsters about pesticide risks in food, with one Eurobarometer survey finding 56 per cent of European respondents saw the 'total absence of pesticides' as a key feature of food safety (International Research Associates 1998). In contrast to dog or road risks, there was no evidence of a large minority group strongly opposed to risk-reducing regulation, or a public-opinion backlash after the adoption of specific measures. Accordingly, the regulation of pesticide residue risks in food and water seemed to be the most 'critical' case in our set for the view that risk regulation is shaped by general public opinion. To put it differently, if opinion-responsive government was to be found anywhere, it ought to have been observable over the regulation of pesticide residues in food and water, since public opinion seemed to be relatively stable and definite in this case and there was no evidence of strong polarization.

3. Regime Content and Public Preferences and Attitudes

Active Alignment of Regime Content with General Public Opinion

Were the government of risk to be opinion-responsive in the sense advocated by George Gallup, policy-makers would actively seek general public opinion

[14] Numerous opinion polls on pesticide risks had been conducted since the late 1980s, commissioned by newspapers and environmentalist and agribusiness groups, notably the British Agrochemicals Association. But the UK government did not actively commission attitude surveys on this topic, in contrast to its approach to road risks.

[15] Some polls had focused on general drinking water quality (see MORI/Water UK 1998: 5), but it is not easy to interpret what such responses imply for attitudes to risk. The responses seem to be linked to a broader debate about privatization of drinking water supply in England and Wales and the cost of implementing the EU Drinking Water Directive, although pesticide residue risks figured large in both of those debates.

and then align regime content with that opinion. As we have already seen, expectations of what would constitute 'opinion-responsive government' are not always clear because of differences in the preferences revealed by different sources or a lack of evidence on preferences and attitudes; indeed, for occupational benzene and radon, no such evidence could be found at all. However Table 6.2 summarizes the degree of fit between regime content—mainly regulatory size—and what might be expected from opinion-responsive government à la Gallup.

As Table 6.2 shows, observed regulatory size frequently deviated from Gallup-type opinion-responsive expectations. In most cases, as was noted earlier, policy-makers did not commission systematic surveys of public preferences and attitudes. Moreover, observed regulatory size deviated from opinion-responsive expectations in both directions. That is, government sometimes seemed to be doing 'too much' compared with what poll evidence of public attitudes would suggest, and sometimes 'too little'.

A notable case of risk regulation that did 'too much' on a public opinion test was the size of the information-gathering and, to a lesser extent, the behaviour-modification components of the domestic radon regime. The extensive state-financed radon detection and mapping exercise on which we commented in Chapter 5 was no more explicable by the opinion-responsive than the market-failure hypothesis, since the public opinion background was a case of 'don't know, don't care'. The content of that regime looked more like an attempt to shape public opinion than to reflect it.

Notable among cases where risk regulation did 'too little' compared with the stance of public attitudes was that of pesticide residues in food. We noted in Chapter 5 that the regulation of pesticide residue risks differed markedly between drinking water and food, with a more transparent and rigorous approach adopted for water than for food. Whether those differences can be plausibly explained by a market failure approach was, as we saw, doubtful, but they seem no more explicable by the opinion-responsive hypothesis, given the fairly high level of public concern revealed by attitude surveys about the risks of pesticide residues in food that were discussed earlier. Other cases of regulatory size that seemed 'too little' by opinion-responsive standards were the absence of general dog registration despite poll evidence of widespread public support for such a measure,[16] the secrecy of the UK sex offenders register, and the adoption of risk-based approaches to dealing with offenders in the community rather than more draconian methods such as lifetime incarceration.

---

[16] Instead, there was only compulsory registration for a few designated fighting dog types, plus a general registration regime in only one part of the UK (Northern Ireland).

TABLE 6.2. *Expected and observed opinion-responsiveness in selected risk domains*

(1) Risk Domain	(2) Regulatory control component	(3) Method of ascertaining public opinion (if any)	(4) Expected opinion-responsive regulatory regime content	(5) Observed regime content	(6) Degree of alignment between (4) and (5)
Dangerous dogs	IG		General dog registration	Limited registration	*
	SS	Mainly 'scream method'	Precautionary standards	Precautionary but breed-specific standards	****
	BM		Rigorous enforcement	Patchy enforcement	***
Radon	IG			Extensive state-funded testing	*
	SS	Some active attitude surveying		Clear standards	***
	BM		Little or no state activity	Limited remediation campaigns	***
Ambient benzene	IG		Indeterminate/limited information-gathering	Growing monitoring effort	***
	SS	Limited polling polling, mainly consultation and 'scream method'	Indeterminate	Delayed standards	***
	BM		Pain-free approach to behaviour modification	Delay plus technical fix approach	****
Paedophile risks	IG		Transparent offenders register	Secret register	**
	SS	Mainly 'scream method'	Precautionary standards	Rudimentary risk management	**
	BM		Rigorous enforcement by draconian methods	Rudimentary risk based enforcement; some local authority NIMBY-ism	**
Local road risks	IG		Medium activity	Extensive monitoring	***
	SS	Extensive polling and attitude surveying	Significant risk reduction	Less than expected risk reduction	***
	BM		Indeterminate/limited behaviour-modification	Consensus enforcement and opinion-shaping	***
Pesticide residues in food	IG		Active and transparent monitoring	Active but delegated and semi-confidential monitoring	***
	SS	Passive/selective consultation	Precautionary standards	Health-based standards	**
	BM		Rigorous and dedicated enforcement	Limited and delegated	**
Pesticide residues in water	IG		Active and transparent monitoring	Active and transparent monitoring	*****
	SS	Passive/selective consultation	Precautionary standards	Precautionary standards	*****
	BM		Rigorous & dedicated enforcement	Delayed UK enforcement of EC standards, dedicated agency formed later	***

***** = high; * = low
IG = information-gathering; SS = standard-setting; BM = behaviour-modification

Passive Responses to General Public Opinion

In other cases, regime content seemed to be broadly aligned with what polls revealed about public opinion, even if the opinion-responsiveness involved did not derive from surveys actively commissioned by policy-makers. Passive opinion responsiveness of this type applied to many other aspects of sex offender and dangerous dog regulation, apart from the elements noted above. In the case of sex offenders, the Sex Offenders Register was introduced in 1997 against the background of rising media salience shown in Fig. 6.1. That figure also reflects a spate of widely reported attacks by Rottweilers and German Shepherds in 1989, including the killing of a girl by two Rottweilers, which led to the Dangerous Dogs Act 1989, amending the previous nineteenth-century dog laws. Two years later, the restrictions placed on pit bull terrier ownership by the 1991 Dangerous Dogs Act were again aligned with the pattern of media salience, but opinion responsiveness alone cannot explain why pit bulls were singled out in 1991 but not Rottweilers and German Shepherds in 1989.[17] The regulation of pesticides in water was another case where high transparency and precautionary policy settings seemed to be aligned with the 'dread risk' nature of pesticides in public attitudes, although in this case the passive opinion responsiveness seemed to come from the EU rather than the UK government.[18]

We also found cases of passive opinion responsiveness over enforcement and implementation. Several police officers told us that enforcement of road traffic laws was limited by public attitudes and one Whitehall official stated: 'We don't want to criminalize all motorists—9.7 million traffic offences were recorded in 1997. How could you enforce . . . if there wasn't consensus policing?' (RS5). We found similar attitudes towards enforcing dog laws, where police were often reluctant to court negative publicity. Even ambient benzene regulation might be seen as passively opinion-responsive. The slow foot-dragging regulatory response to the risk that relied on an eventual 'technical fix' to limit benzene levels rather than immediate imposition of painful lifestyle changes could be said to chime with the contradictory and inchoate nature of public opinion on the issue. While regime content was actively opinion-responsive in only one of the risk domains we explored—local road safety—a large minority of regime content elements we examined could be considered opinion-responsive in a passive sense.

---

[17] We discuss this issue further in Chapter 7.

[18] The UK government allowed water companies to disregard the precautionary standards before the privatization of drinking water supply in England and Wales in 1989, and subsequently made an unsuccessful attempt to replace precautionary standards with generally less onerous 'science-based standards'.

Interaction with General Public Opinion

A further hybrid took the form of attempts at 'opinion responsiveness', in some sense, that were overtaken by a public-opinion reaction. One form of this dynamic involved a progression in which regulation that started as opinion responsive later became opinion unresponsive because public opinion had turned against the measures chosen. As already noted, this dynamic was observable for local traffic-calming measures to reduce road risks, particularly to vulnerable road users. Such measures typically involved deliberate canvassing of local public attitudes before implementation, which was unusual for risk regulation more generally. A similar dynamic applied to dog regulation, though in that case government made no active attempt to discover public opinion. Indeed, after negative publicity over dogs put on 'death row' for infringements of the 1991 Dangerous Dogs Act, the mandatory death sentence for such animals was removed by the Dangerous Dogs (Amendment) Act 1997.

In such cases attempts at opinion-responsive risk regulation seem self-defeating. How does this effect come about? The purest form of this dynamic, as apparently occurred after the UK government banned beef-on-the bone in 1997, [19] seems to involve a group of opinion poll respondents changing their mind in reaction to regulatory action, with uncertainty turning into condemnation of what, or whatever, government chooses to do. A less pure but probably more common variant occurs when different groups with opposed interests dominate the agenda at different stages in the policy process, as seems to have happened with UK dog risk regulation.

In principle, an opposite dynamic is possible, in the form of regime content that is opinion-unresponsive when introduced but later becomes opinion-responsive as public opinion changes from opposition to support. There were no clear-cut examples of this dynamic in the nine risk domains we investigated, but cases like drink-drive and seat-belt regulation, that appear to have attracted increasing rather than decreasing public support over time in many countries, may illustrate this pattern.

Overall: Semi-Opinion-Responsive Government?

The analysis summarized in Table 6.2 suggests the government of risk is rarely opinion-responsive in the sense envisaged by George Gallup, who thought public opinion polling should outweigh sectional interests in setting public policy. Of the nine risk regulation regimes we studied, only parts of road risk

---

[19] After the UK government banned sales of beef-on-the-bone, such as T-bone steaks and spare ribs, in 1997, following scientific advice that there was a small risk of humans contracting new variant CJD from that source, polls indicated public opinion had turned heavily against the measure (see *Guardian* 1998).

regulation approached active gathering of data about public preferences and attitudes. And the cases we identified as critical for the opinion-responsive hypothesis—the regulation of pesticide residue risks in food and water—certainly did not do so. No attitude surveys were commissioned by regulators in either case, and given relatively high public concern about overall pesticide risks, the difference between regulatory aggression for pesticide residues in water and food cannot plausibly be explained as a reflection of different public attitudes.

However, several forms of semi-opinion-responsive government were detectable. We have already referred to the passive form of opinion responsiveness, when elements of regulatory regime content are aligned with public opinion, even though regulators do not commission attitude surveys. A second, more active form consisted of consultations with groups believed or claimed to represent public opinion, rather than conventional opinion polling. For example, this approach was used by regulators of ambient benzene and pesticide residues in food, and formed the basis of their claim to be 'opinion-responsive'. One senior air pollution scientist said, 'The main way for obtaining public opinion [over benzene] is through consultation . . . reports are put out for scientific peer review and at a broader level the National Air Quality Strategy involves consultations with local authorities, trade groups, NGOs etc. Not the man in the street . . . ' (B1).

A third approach was the traditional civil service approach of taking complaints and organized demonstrations as indicative of public opinion. For many risk regulators we talked to, being 'opinion-responsive' was construed as tailoring policy to orchestrated complaints and loud protests rather than finding out whether those complaints and protests were representative of overall public opinion. For instance, the EU abandoned its proposal to replace the precautionary limit for total pesticide residues in drinking water by a science-based standard after 12,000 protest letters sent in a campaign organized by Greenpeace were said to have made the proposal 'politically unsaleable' (P9). Regulating risk by listening to activists and complainers rather than surveying overall public opinion is a close cousin of the 'scream method' traditionally used in government budgeting, with the allocation of funds based on the volume of screams. It means equating 'public opinion' with the views of activists, zealots, and the volubly disgruntled—just what George Gallup aimed to get away from—and paying more attention to those who hold intense views than to the rest of the population.

Figure 6.2 summarizes some of the variation we observed in opinion responsiveness, distinguishing how actively regulators sought to discover public opinion and how far regime content was aligned with what was known about public attitudes, particularly over regulatory size. If the sort of opinion responsiveness envisaged by George Gallup, which would place risk regulation in the top left hand corner of Fig. 6.2 (see p. 104), was little in evidence, most risk domains contained elements of what was earlier termed semi-opinion responsiveness. But the opinion-responsive hypothesis cannot readily explain why 'opinion responsiveness' was construed in different ways by different risk regulators. And even semi-opinion responsiveness seemed an unreliable predictor of regulatory size across the three control components. Only just over half of the elements of regime content analysed in Table 6.2 seemed to be more or less aligned with general public opinion, with just under half displaying 'low' or 'medium/low' alignment. And risk domains whose regime content was opinion-responsive in some way for some elements or dimensions could be opinion-unresponsive for others, as applied to the regulation of dangerous dogs, road risks, and pesticide residue risks in water.

4. When Public Attitudes and Regulators' Strategies Diverge: Strategies for Managing the Gap

The previous section argued that Gallup-style opinion-responsive government was not typical in the government of risk, and the normal case was at best interactive government, the middle zone represented in Fig. 6.2. Indeed, we found several cases where there seemed to be a gap in attitudes and beliefs between the general public and the policy professionals, and such gaps have been noted by numerous analysts of risk policy (see Breyer 1993). In domains such as domestic radon and road safety, policy professionals viewed the risks as more substantial than the public at large and expressed their frustration to us about the low public and media salience of what they considered to be major risks. For example, one road-risk professional said, 'If there was a crash once a week in which 70 people got killed there would be a massive outcry. But because accidents are dispersed the full enormity of the problem is not . . . apparent' (RS5).

In other cases—of the kind highlighted in the 'risk amplification' literature (see Kasperson 1992)—it was the other way round. An example is the risk of releasing convicted paedophiles into the community. Many professionals in the policy domain thought the public wrongly believed all child sex offenders to conform to the most predatory and murderous profile and underestimated the success with which those professionals managed the overall risk from released ex-offenders. The general public was also believed to overestimate the risks to children from attacks by strangers in the street and to underestimate the risks to children of sexual abuse at home at the hands of parents and close relatives.[20]

---

[20] One central government official told us, ' . . . the reality is that the risk is not as great as people fear it to be. The public needs to understand that there are large numbers of well-managed sex offenders in the community' (CSO1). In similar vein, a police officer with experience of dealing with high-profile offenders told us, 'There is a big difference between the perceived risk and the actual risk—what the media and public choose to pick up on is fairly arbitrary' (CSO5).

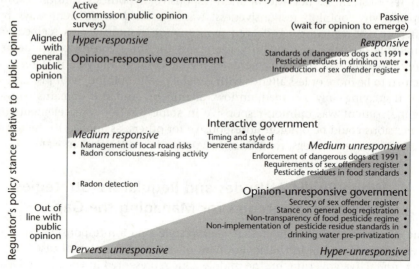

F<small>IGURE</small> 6.2: Observed regime content and opinion responsiveness

We identified four main strategies by which professionals and regulators managed gaps between their perceptions and preferences and those of the public at large, and several intermediate types. We named the four main types the 'Nelson's eye' approach, after the famous English admiral who is said to have put his blind eye to a telescope when he did not want to see a signal from his commander; the 'selective attention syndrome', where there are multiple sources of public opinion with different implications for public policy; the opinion-shaping or 'spinocratic' approach; and the 'high-wire' balancing act. These strategies are not mutually exclusive. We found several cases where they were combined, as well as numerous intermediate strategies.

The 'Nelson's Eye' Approach: Disregarding Signals and Asking No Questions

The strictest form of 'Nelson's Eye' approach consists of studious disregard of survey evidence about public opinion that is inconvenient for policy-makers, locating regulation in the bottom right-hand corner of Fig. 6.2. We found few clear cases of Nelson's Eye, but it did occur sometimes. For instance, UK public opinion polls in the early 1990s indicated broad support for general dog registration, but Kenneth Baker, the minister responsible at that time, refused to adopt such a policy, because in a previous ministerial role he had abolished dog licensing in England and Wales in 1987, presenting that measure as striking a major blow for 'deregulation' (Baker 1993). More common was a less extreme form of 'Nelson's eye', consisting of a failure on the part of policy-makers to produce their public-opinion telescopes at all, in contrast to enthusiasm for opinion polling and attitude surveys in other circumstances.

The purest example of this strategy that we encountered concerned the risks of paedophile release into the community, as mentioned earlier. In a world otherwise awash with opinion polls and attitude surveys, public opinion about what should be done about this issue was sought neither by government nor by other 'third sector' organizations in the policy domain. In sharp contrast with the approach adopted for road risks, none of the state organizations or the various children's NGOs in the field was aware of any surveys of public perceptions of the risk or of public opinion about the management of offenders. It seems likely that this studious avoidance of public opinion testing reflected a belief by such organizations that it was better not to ask, for fear the answers might demonstrate majority support for measures much more draconian than the current policy stance towards such offenders. We observed a variant of the same approach over benzene risks, when an oil company interviewee told us the company did not actively commission public attitude surveys on specific traffic pollutants because it did not wish to be 'associated with benzene and carcinogens in the public mind' (B18). 'Them as asks no questions isn't told a lie', as Kipling's well-known line goes; but 'them as asks no questions' may sometimes be trying to avoid discovering unpalatable truths.

Perhaps it might be argued that active canvassing of public opinion was unnecessary in the case of paedophile risks, since the regulators and policy professionals were exposed to a great deal of unsolicited expressions of views on the matter. We have already commented on the high level of media attention paid to this risk, which dwarfed all the other risk domains we investigated, and the paedophile regulators were highly conscious of media and protest group activity.[21] Other expressions of opinion came in the form of letters, described by one central government bureaucrat we spoke to as 'not vast, more a steady flow', but were particularly important 'when you have serious offenders in the news and MPs get hold of it' (CSO1). In other policy domains, an active approach to surveying public attitudes might have been adopted by regulators to show that the direct-action hotheads were out of line with general public opinion. The apparent choice not to do so over paedophiles may reflect a suspicion that that might not prove to be the case.

---

[21] For instance, several of our interviewees recounted how one tabloid newspaper set up a 'pervert hotline' for readers to call in information about the location of a known offender recently released from prison, and journalists were reputedly offering large sums in cash to people on the street to discover where the offender was living. While this book was being drafted in the summer of 2000, a Sunday tabloid was publishing names and addresses of registered paedophiles, in protest at the failure of the authorities to do so after the murder of a child, which produced widely reported local public protests, including attacks on known or suspected paedophiles (see *Independent* 2000: 3).

The Selective Attention Syndrome

A more complex approach to managing 'gaps' between public opinion and public policy was observable for local road risks. In this case, as has already been noted, there were at least three different sources of information about public preferences and attitudes: general public opinion polling, indicating low to medium levels of concern, in line with media salience; other local polling, indicating higher levels of concern; and willingness-to-pay studies commissioned by central government to calculate, through in-depth focus group work, how much people thought government should spend to reduce risk. The latter studies indicated a value per prevented fatality of about £1 million (DETR 1998c), implying the public would expect up to £1 million to be spent on preventing each road accident death. However, when local authorities prioritized local road safety projects according to the expected number of lives to be saved per project for a given amount of investment, such schemes were in practice funded only if within the first year they could achieve a rate of return on the investment of between 166 and 279 per cent (Toothill and Mackie 1995: 7). That practice meant that, on the assumption that such schemes lasted for five years or so, local authorities would not invest more than £100,000 to prevent one road death.

Such a policy looks wholly opinion-unresponsive on the basis of willingness-to-pay attitudes—almost belonging in the bottom left-hand 'perverse-unresponsive' category of Fig. 6.2, given the care taken to establish public preferences—and could be justified only by ignoring such evidence of public opinion and giving selective attention to general broad-brush polling indicating low-to-medium concern with local road safety. The state was apparently prepared to invest in campaigns to persuade drivers to take more care on the roads, in contrast to the low-to-medium salience of road risks in the press and general public opinion surveys. But when it came to costly highway engineering investment, government in practice seemed to be closer to the low-to-medium salience of the risk as seen through media headlines than the higher risk salience established by its own in-depth willingness-to-pay surveys. Such behaviour suggests a somewhat selective approach to reading and acting upon public opinion.

Opinion-Shaping Strategies: Education and Spinocracy

A third approach included attempts to manage gaps between the attitudes and beliefs of the public at large and the regulators and policy professionals by attempts to inform and shape public preferences and attitudes. For instance, a senior scientist in the benzene policy community sighed, 'There's a huge problem in educating people. The level of awareness and balance in most of the population isn't what it should be' (B1). One local road safety officer insisted that policy was 'driven by statistics, not headlines' and said, 'I see myself as trying to change people's views' (RS10). Another, faced with demands for increasing public consultation over road safety measures, said, 'Consultation rarely helps because you can never find a consensus view' (RS11). Local road safety technocrats aimed to steer decision-making within the boundaries of what they saw as technically feasible and what they anticipated to be publicly acceptable. Sometimes their efforts at opinion-shaping were successful, but sometimes they lost out to political initiatives by local councillors and sometimes their attitude surveys to discover public attitudes to local road safety measures led to those schemes being abandoned shortly after they had been initiated, as was noted earlier.

We found several other cases of interactive attempts to shape public opinion over risk rather than simply to reflect or follow it. A civil servant in the radon policy community said, 'You can't let the public get away with it. If you know something is a risk you should give people information' (R3). A scientist in an environmental agency concerned with pesticide risks told us his agency put out 'regular PR on local radio as well as the national media' to counter criticisms of its work by pressure groups like Greenpeace and Friends of the Earth (P8). Other widely known examples of risk regulators trying to shape public opinion rather than following it include public health campaigns focused on risks from smoking, childhood immunization, and AIDS, including mass advertising and campaigns targeted on particular groups, like crime awareness campaigns focused on the elderly.

Where the professionals saw the risks as more serious than the general public, educational or consciousness-raising strategies were employed to shape public perception. For example, the UK government commissioned attitude research in the 1990s to find out why the public was apparently so apathetic about radon risks (Lee 1994) and adopted a modest, area-specific and relatively low-budget programme of public information about radon risks. Road risk regulators adopted a more vigorous and costly version of the same approach, spending some £5–8 million a year over the 1990s on road safety publicity as exemplified by campaigns on seat-belts, speeding, and Christmas drink-driving (RS2).

High Wire Acts: Doctrines of 'Balance Management'

A fourth approach used by regulators and policy professionals to manage gaps between their strategies and the attitudes and beliefs of the public was to adopt a doctrine of 'balance', casting themselves in the role of maintaining a delicate equipoise among opposed policy considerations, with current public attitudes only one of the items to be balanced.[22]

[22] Raab (1997) has commented on the doctrine of 'balance' as it applies to data protection regulation, and we found analogues to this doctrine in several other risk regulation regimes.

The main example we found concerned domestic radon, where, as noted earlier, the professionals considered the public to be unduly apathetic about the risk. Official doctrine held that government should maintain a subtle balance between a do-nothing policy and a more draconian approach. The do-nothing policy would fit with current public attitudes but might incur blame later if public attitudes changed, while the more draconian approach would educate the public to the risks perceived by the radiation professionals but could create panic if pushed too far. One senior civil servant told us, 'If we [= government] didn't acknowledge the problem there would have been a hoo-ha because we hadn't done anything about it' (R3).

The political dangers of a do-nothing policy that were sensed by this seasoned mandarin were not imaginary. In the UK, radiation professionals urged government to be more active.[23] In France a political storm occurred in 1998 after high radon levels detected in a school built on the site of the former Marie Curie laboratory in Nogent sur Marne led the Ministry of Health to draw politically embarrassing comparisons between the radiation exposure of the school's students and teachers and that of nuclear industry workers (see Massuelle, Pirard, and Hubert 1998). Against the political danger that similar developments might occur in the UK, William Waldegrave, then a minister at the Department of the Environment, set out a conveniently vague official doctrine of 'balance' in a 1987 parliamentary debate. He spoke of walking 'a narrow tightrope' and commented: 'We have the information but if it is wrongly deployed it will unnecessarily scare people'.[24]

Similar doctrines of balance acts could be detected in the regulation of paedophile risks and pesticide residues. The management of particular offenders often reflected public pressure, but regulators—like Alcuin in the epigraph to this chapter—rejected the simple *vox populi, vox Dei* approach and saw themselves as balancing cost and privacy considerations against public pressures for security and transparency. In the case of pesticide residues, a senior water company person told us, 'UK officials like to think of themselves as fixers and there's an element of truth in that they are essentially pragmatic' (P21). Doctrines of balance were also observed at several points in the regulatory content of the road risk regime. For instance, over behaviour modification, as noted earlier, several police officers saw themselves as balancing strict enforcement of the law against what they perceived as public attitudes.

Hybrid Approaches to Public Preferences and Attitudes

In addition to these four ways of managing 'opinion gaps' were several hybrid approaches. One consisted of managed consultation processes that could be

---

[23] See for example Blythe (1997) and Gore (1997: 31–2).
[24] *Hansard* (27 January 1987) Houses (Radon Levels): 191.

said to incorporate public views into the policy process but did not necessarily have any impact on policy substance: for example, 'market research' surveys to anticipate public resistance and aid the implementation of largely pre-determined policy. Sometimes such consultation exercises reinforced the 'balance' approach, if they incorporated parallel consultation of groups with different views. An example is the proliferation of consultation forums on pesticide risks and genetically modified organisms in food in the UK during the 1990s, incorporating representatives of the general public, organized groups, agri-food business, and scientific experts. A second approach, to be discussed further in Chapter 9, consisted of the ability to shift or diffuse responsibility for responding to public demands among a set of regulator organizations in a multi-agency institutional network. Such institutional arrangements may help to make 'opinion gaps' more ambiguous and harder to detect.

5. Conclusion: An Overall Picture of How Public Preferences and Attitudes Shape Regulation

Like the market failure hypothesis, the opinion-responsive hypothesis more readily applies to regulatory size than structure and style. But even for regulatory size, regime content in the cases we investigated was at best semi-opinion-responsive. A wider scan of the literature on risk regulation for the UK did not suggest Gallup-style opinion-responsive government was common in other risk policy domains and there did not seem to be strong grounds for supposing the pattern observed here was unique to the UK. Even for the USA, often said to be dominated by poll-driven politics, Crespi (1989: 6) found federal government agencies rarely used public opinion polling for policy formulation, and Monroe's (1998: 6) study of public opinion and public policy from 1980 to 1993 found policy outcomes were consistent with majority preferences expressed in opinion polls in only 55 per cent of observed cases. In spite—or could it be because?—of the attention paid to lay assessment of risk in the risk perception literature, opinion-responsive government of the kind conceived by George Gallup seemed to be as rare an animal in risk regulation as it is in public policy generally. Those who reject the *vox populi, Vox Dei* doctrine, like Alcuin and Beatrice Webb, would be neither surprised nor dismayed by this finding.

As we have seen, there are several reasons why fully opinion-responsive risk regulation may be hard to achieve even by regulators disposed to seek out public opinion and act on it. Information on what the public thinks about risk policy may be confused or ambiguous, as applies to dog and road risks. General public opinion may be distorted through media or pressure-group lenses. Public preferences and attitudes and beliefs may be polarized or inconsistent between means and ends, as with the desire for safer roads or cleaner air combined with resistance to restrictions on driving, or with the well-known 'not in my backyard' (NIMBY) syndrome, in which some policy is approved in the abstract but there is no agreement on the siting of the necessary facilities in anyone's local area. Public opinion may be changeable and volatile, as applied to traffic calming and dangerous dogs. Such conditions may produce differences between the standard-setting and behaviour-modification components of regulation, since standards are typically set or revised at discrete points in time, while behaviour-modification and information-gathering tend to involve more continuous, ongoing activity, meaning they may be more responsive to public opinion over time than standards. Hence even if one component of regulation is opinion-responsive, another may be less so.

Further, imbalances of information and expertise between regulators, other players, and the lay public may mean that snap survey responses, as opposed to deliberative approaches to discovering public opinion, are unrealistic, simplistic, or tainted with misunderstandings, for example over the speed with which regulators can feasibly respond to an issue. Risks produced or discovered by new technology, such as chemicals used in microchip manufacture or holes in the ozone layer, involve terminology and concepts of which most people have limited knowledge (see Hedges 1993; Lee 1994). Novel developments at the frontiers of science and technology are often contested within the scientific community, making the issues even harder to assess on the basis of the average high-school science education (see Schwarz and Thompson 1990, but contrast Wildavsky 1995). In such circumstances, general public opinion may be too indefinite to form a basis for policy design. Some opinion-shaping or independent activity on the part of policy professionals seems unavoidable in such cases.

While the market failure approach seems as good a predictor of regime content as anything more than the weakest variant of the opinion-responsive hypothesis, a few cases were better explained by some form of opinion-responsiveness than by market failure logic. The most obvious case among our risk domains was the maintenance of a precautionary limit on total pesticide contamination of drinking water during the EU's renegotiation of its Drinking Water Directive in the 1990s. There were also some cases, like dog regulation, that exemplified a policy pattern identified by Marver Bernstein (1955) and later analysts of agenda politics (like Downs 1972 and Kingdon 1984). That is, public attitudes helped to cut through institutional inertia in the aftermath of tragedies, when a 'policy window' opened and public attention was concentrated on a problem normally crowded out of the policy agenda. This well-known 'tombstone' pattern in which risk regulation functions as a monument to public emotions about past tragedies, as in rail safety regulation, was not, however, by any means universal in the cases we examined. On this evidence, any attempt to predict regulatory regime content on the basis of general public opinion seems likely to be wrong or indeterminate at least half of the time. Such a predictor is not much more useful than spinning a coin.

Indeed, even when we combined market failure and opinion responsive explanations of regime content, there were still numerous observations that could not be readily explained. Such observations include the difference in regime content for the regulation of pesticide residues in food and water, differences in the aggressiveness of standards set for radon and benzene risks in the workplace and in other settings, the large regulatory size for information-gathering for radon risks, and several elements of observed regulatory size and style for paedophile, dog, and road risks. Accordingly, Chapter 7 explores whether interest-group pressures can account for such 'hard cases', and whether it can account for the other cases as well as the market-failure or opinion-responsive approaches.

7

Interests, Lobbies, and Experts

> The answer is that there are plenty of vested interests in the risk industry.
>
> Dryzek (1996: 299)

1. Risk Regulation and Interest-Driven Government

This chapter explores the influence of organized interests or 'rent-seeking groups' on regime content, following a central theme in political-science and political-economy accounts of the birth and development of regulatory regimes (see Self 1985; Wilson 1990). It argues that interest-group pressures can explain more elements of regime content than market-failure or opinion-responsiveness and that such pressures are a more reliable predictor of regulatory size. However, there were also some risk regulation regimes in which powerful corporate interests did not emerge victorious and also some domains in which regulators operated in an interest-group vacuum or something approaching it. The chapter starts by looking at the role of organized business interests in shaping risk regulation—groups that ordinarily figure large in 'rent-seeking' analysis—before turning to other types of interest.

2. Business Interests and Risk Regulation Regimes

For understandable reasons, the classic literature on interest groups and regulation focuses heavily on organized producers or business regulatees. Such actors, after all, tend to have strong motives to shape regulation to their preferred patterns, in order to protect or enhance profits or market share. They also possess the opportunity to shape regulation through the various ways organized business can influence government in capitalist democracies, especially through contributions to election campaign funds. They also often form compact groups that are conventionally argued to have a comparative advantage in collective organization (Olson 1965), compared with diffuse groups of consumers or public interest campaigners who may have lower stakes in the regulatory outcome.

In our nine selected risk domains we found many cases where organized business interests sought to shape regulatory regime content. But by no means all the cases we examined exhibited the interest-group pattern stressed by numerous classic writers on regulatory capture (such as Bernstein 1955; Stigler 1971; Peltzman 1976), in which a regulatory regime is dominated and indeed brought into existence by the interests of a single powerful producer group. We did find some cases approximating to this type, but we also identified three other patterns of business interest-group activity. Those other patterns were: cases where there was a near vacuum of organized business interests; cases where such interests existed but were multiple and conflicting; and cases where powerful organized business interests failed to carry the day.

Near Vacuums of Organized Business Interest

Some of our risk regulation regimes involved little or no organized business group activity, even though actual or potential business interests might be at stake over the way regulation was designed. There were at least two variants of this 'vacuum' pattern. One involved no significant organized interests at all other than the regulators or policy professionals, giving free play to those actors. The other involved little or no organized business group activity but a number of other organized groups trying to shape regulatory regime content.

The purest kind of interest-group vacuum comprises cases of 'policies without publics' (May 1991). Here there are no organized business interests seeking to lobby the regulators—and no other significant organized groups in the field outside the state apparatus. Among our cases, domestic radon most closely approximated this pattern. In principle, several business interests stood to gain or lose from the way radon was regulated. Regulation could, for instance, affect the profit or loss of insurers, mortgage lenders, real estate and related firms, and potential private radon testers. Tourist interests, particularly in South-West England, the peak district, and other radon-affected beauty spots, could be affected by increased awareness of radon risks. An interviewee from the Radon Council—a trade association—told us, 'None of the building societies [mortgage lenders] wanted to know [about radon risks]. They wanted to keep it under the carpet. The silence is deafening' (R12). But such business interests seem in the main to have been latent rather than actively organized and engaged in lobbying for or against regulation.[1] Nor were there any campaigning 'cause' groups focusing on domestic radon. Anti-nuclear campaigners took little interest in this risk. There was not even any organized pressure from local public housing authorities or public-health organizations, perhaps surprisingly given the death toll attributed to radon by some government experts, as

---

[1] 'Latent' is Olson's (1965) term for a group that has collective interests but is not collectively organized.

described earlier.[2] That meant the entrenched and cohesive group of nuclear scientists who made up the 'policy community' (Rhodes and Marsh 1992) for radon essentially had the field to itself, particularly given public apathy and lack of media interest in this risk, as noted in Chapter 6.

A different interest-group pattern involved a vacuum of organized business interests but the presence of other organized groups, whether cause groups or organized public-sector interests. The dog and paedophile regimes approximated to this pattern. In these cases too there were latent or potential business interests at stake: for instance, dog breeders, security and custodial-services firms, purveyors of electronic tagging services. Such interests, however, were either not organized or, if they were organized, were not active in the policy domain. Nevertheless, in both cases organized non-business groups, such as dog breed associations, animal welfare groups, human rights lobbies, victim groups, and local NIMBY activists, sought to shape regime content, as we will show later. In both cases too, there were several public-sector professional groups or organizations with interests at stake that were actively engaged in shaping regime content. That produced a more heavily populated policy network than that involving the radon technocrats, as well as higher media salience and public concern over the risks, producing a greater degree of negotiation and inter-organizational interaction in the policy process, and taking the form more of an 'issue network' than a cohesive 'policy community' (*Ibid*).

Fragmented or Multiple Business Interest Organization

While some risk regulation regimes constituted a vacuum, or near-vacuum, of organized business interests, others involved multiple, fragmented, or conflicting business interests. Sometimes business interests pull in opposite directions over regulatory architecture. For instance, some firms may stand to benefit from government-mandated safety enhancements, such as vehicle manufacturers whose markets may be protected or enhanced by such measures, while others stand to lose, such as vehicle fleet operators or truckers whose costs may be raised. 'Traffic calming' measures like road humps that provide work for local contractors may impose extra costs—in delay, extra wear and tear on vehicles—on transport operators. In other cases business interests may be hard to mobilize in conventional ways because the firms involved are small or scattered or illegal—like small builders, fly-by-night businesses, or dog-fighting rings—or the stakes are too low. Where organized business interests are fragmented or multiple, whatever risk regulators do is liable to advance some business interests at the expense of others.

---

[2] The Institution of Environmental Health Officers did take up the issue in the late 1980s, but little came of their activities in the face of local authority and public apathy (see Institution of Environmental Health Officers 1988).

Within our nine risk regulation regimes, the case that best fitted this pattern was local road safety regulation, specifically those measures affecting the balance between in-vehicle and out-of-vehicle risks. Regulatory measures at national or EU level that shaped that balance did involve powerful organized corporate interests. For instance, a local authority road safety officer declared, 'The car and transport companies are powerful actors and have done a lot of wholly self-interested lobbying against progressive strategies' (RS9). Likewise a civil servant in the transport ministry described how brewers 'argued like mad' with the ministry against a lowering of drink-drive alcohol limits (RS2). State-mandated changes in vehicle construction can be, and have been, interpreted from a Chicago-school viewpoint as providing rents to a cartel of powerful motor manufacturers by compelling vehicle buyers to pay for safety enhancements they might not voluntary purchase (Peltzman 1976). Large construction firms and truckers may also have an influence on state investment in motorways and freeways that reduce risk by banning vulnerable road users.

So far, so 'Chicago'. But at the level of local measures governing the balance of risks between vehicle users, pedestrians, and other road users, large corporate organized interests were relatively little engaged. The business interests in play over local traffic calming or pedestrian-control measures included local shopkeepers, construction companies, clamping contractors, and bus, taxi, and truck operators, but these actors did not form a single interest dominating the domain in classic Chicago style. Moreover, the local road risk policy community contained numerous non-business interests. A range of more-or-less organized groups represented users making incompatible demands on road space to reduce their risks: cyclists, local motorists, NIMBY groups battling commuter rat-runs, and the like.

Within the public sector, the standard-setting component of regulation was dominated by local authority budgetary allocation, environment and transport department expenditure control rules, and local road traffic engineers who used these rules, applied to the cost-benefit of competing schemes, to manage and deflect the various interest-group demands.[3] In James Q. Wilson's (1980) four-part typology of interest-group patterns, as discussed in Chapter 4, such risk policy domains look less like 'client politics', with concentrated business interests standing to benefit at the expense of a large diffuse group, than 'interest-group politics', with multiple interest groups, many of them independent or professional-bureaucratic.

---

[3] The enforcement aspect of behaviour-modification, as discussed in Chapter 6, was handled by police responding to a general climate of public opinion.

Defeated Goliaths: Concentrated Business Interests that Fail to Carry the Day

A third pattern consisted of large concentrated business groups that failed to secure the regime content they campaigned for, like tobacco companies subject to increasing restrictions over advertising or sponsorship (contrast Doron 1979). Among our nine risk regulation regimes, the one apparently fitting the 'defeated Goliath' pattern was the regulation of pesticide residues in drinking water. Here the UK's privatized water utilities were subjected to rigorous precautionary residue limits, even though, together with the agrochemical industry, they campaigned hard for less onerous science-based standards in the 1990s during a renegotiation of the 1980 EU Drinking Water Directive. The UK government supported the policy stance preferred by these business interests, and the European Commission itself at one point backed one of the key changes they wanted. Nevertheless, the regulatory standards favoured by these large concentrated business groups were rejected in 1998 in favour of the preferences of larger diffuse groups whose interests were championed by policy entrepreneurs—in this case, green groups orchestrating mass write-ins to the European Commission, as discussed in Chapter 6.

In Wilson's typology this outcome could be considered as a variant of 'entrepreneurial politics'. A senior office-holder in the European Crop Protection Association (ECPA)—the European agrochemical industry lobbying association—told us that the industrial lobby failed to carry the day because of the difficulty of overturning established policy: 'The battle was lost twenty years ago. The MEPs [Members of the European Parliament] said that they agreed with the ECPA but they were not willing to tell their constituents they voted for a relaxation of the standard' (P3).

This 'defeated Goliath' pattern was not, however, a pure case of what Wilson calls 'entrepreneurial politics' because it did not involve concentrated costs being imposed on the defeated corporate interests. Rather, the EU regime governing pesticides in drinking water was mated to the UK's water utility regulation regime such that the water companies could in effect tax their captive consumers for safety improvements at no cost to their profits. That is, the UK price controls over water enabled full pass-through of the heavy compliance costs imposed by EU risk regulation. Before that cost pass-through price control system was set up, at the time when drinking water supply in England and Wales was privatized in 1989, the UK government had simply failed to enforce the EU's precautionary limits and told water authorities they could disregard those limits (Healey and Jones 1989). This pattern is an example of how a complex institutional structure of regulation and the different dimensions of regulatory regimes give concentrated corporate interests an opportunity to gain on the roundabouts what they lose on the swings.

To the extent that this outcome constituted a 'defeated Goliath' pattern—
and, as we have seen, that is only part of a broader swings-and-roundabouts
story—how did it come about? The structure of the regulatory regime was
such that standard-setting operated at EU rather than national-government
level, meaning the British privatized water utilities had to do more than win
the UK government round to their view.[4] Coupled with that was an institutional history in which the EU's precautionary regime first emerged during
an era when drinking water was mainly provided by public or non-profit
enterprises throughout the UK, as well as in the rest of Europe. Perhaps
because of more casual business-risk analysis by such enterprises, the clean-up
costs implied by a rigorous precautionary standard do not seem to have been
appreciated by all member states with high agricultural pesticide use—such as
the French government, which, according to officials involved in negotiations, later changed its position over precautionary standards.

Accordingly, the private business interest was only latent when standards
were first set and the interest of the then public providers were protected by
an enforcement regime controlled by national government—which, as noted
earlier, failed to enforce the precautionary standards and in fact told water
authorities they could ignore those standards. After the water companies were
privatized in 1989 a new approach to behaviour modification was adopted.
The UK government no longer countenanced non-compliance with the EU
precautionary standards, but, as noted above, the price-control regime
allowed all the costs of compliance to be passed to captive consumers. So the
first real defeat of organized business pressures came with the retention of
precautionary standards in the revised EU Drinking Water Directive of 1998,
and even then, as explained earlier, the corporate interests were fully
protected by their ability to place compliance costs on to consumers.

Business-Friendly Regulation: Organized Interests Reflected in Regulatory Design

While 'client politics'—benefits conferred by regulation on a concentrated
business group at the expense of a larger diffuse group—was not the dominant pattern of interest-group activity in the nine risk policy domains we
investigated, elements of client politics could be detected in some of them.
However, client politics often seemed to apply only to parts of regulatory
regime content rather than to all of it. We identified numerous cases where
risk regulation settings and business interests were aligned through business
participation, but the extent of simple 'rent-seeking'—forced property

---

[4] A senior water company interviewee told us his company had 'very good contacts with
government officials. We feed information to government and *vice versa*. We show each other papers
sent to the [European] Commission to check'. But he observed that, 'On pesticides we are just one
stakeholder amongst many, so we have less influence' (P21).

transfer or profit augmentation through state-imposed regulatory requirements—was often ambiguous.

Ambient benzene regulation was a case in point. Chapters 5 and 6 have
shown that this risk domain was one in which public opinion was ambiguous
or contradictory, but also one manifesting major market failures. Readers will
recall that the element of regime content over ambient benzene that was hard
to explain from a market-failure perspective was the 'unpolitics' approach of
decades-long delay in dealing with a known genotoxic carcinogen with high
information and opt-out costs. This feature seems readily explicable from an
interest-driven perspective. After all, risk in this domain arises from the products of giant multinational corporations in 'the great car economy', as Mrs
Thatcher once termed it (*Daily Telegraph* 1990), namely, vehicle and petrochemical corporations with high stakes and considerable practice in dealing
with regulators. One senior health scientist told us, 'Industry have three lines
of defence—we can't do it; we can do it but it will bankrupt the industry; or
finally, we can do it but we need a massive tax rebate . . . ' (B2). In fact, other
lines of defence by vehicle and petrochemical interests were observable too.
For instance, a senior regulatory affairs scientist in an oil company pointed
out that 'smoking presents bigger problems of benzene than cars' (B17).

The EU politics of standard-setting over ambient benzene objectives in the
late 1990s offered plenty of opportunities for interest groups to influence the
final choice of limit between the wide range of upper and lower values recommended by an expert working group. For instance, even after the EU
Commission settled on an objective of 5 μgm^{-3} after much political horse-
trading, Neil Kinnock, the EU Transport Commissioner, was still able to 'put
a spanner in the works', according to an interviewee from a European environmental group. After a failed attempt to stop the Directive 'because it was
seen as an unnecessary burden on transport', he was able to introduce a dero-
gation delaying the implementation date for countries with 'severe socio-
economic problems' (B15).

However, the observed pattern of standard-setting over benzene involved
a staged process, with the interests of the dominant groups changing from
one period to another. The first stage—involving long delay in regulatory
response that could have been expected to be timely and draconian from a
market-failure perspective, given high information and opt-out costs—can in
part be explained by the influence of corporate interests. Such corporations,
particularly vehicle manufacturers, were potentially vulnerable to abrupt
short-term changes, and hence lobbied for delay in implementation time-
tables both for the UK and EU benzene objectives, on the grounds that early
implementation would involve disproportionate cost.[5] But the direction of

[5] Early implementation would also have imposed major costs for the driving public. The year
2010 was apparently chosen as the implementation date for the EU benzene standards because by
then the EU's auto-oil standards on emissions would have taken effect and most older cars would

technological and industrial change was such that ambient benzene levels could be expected to drop over time, even without any regulation. And as time went on, large corporate interests stood to benefit from regulatory 'rents' arising from benzene regulation: that is, the use of state authority to increase the market for 'clean burn' fuels in a market where there was otherwise little differentiation and tight profit margins, and to give vehicle manufacturers the opportunity to develop and sell new engine technologies.

Perhaps surprisingly, independent campaigning groups in the UK seem to have had a minimal role in shaping regulatory standard setting over benzene. Their input into the regime was mainly through the formal and novel incorporation into the EU standard-setting process of the European Environmental Bureau (EEB), an umbrella environmental NGO. But according to our discussions with Friends of the Earth and other green organizations in Britain, benzene was a low priority in their campaigns on air pollution. In fact, it was reported to us that the benzene problem did not come on to the regulatory agenda as a result of agitation by car-hating greens laying siege to gas stations. It came on to the agenda in the mid-1980s during a heated debate over lead in gasoline, because a petrochemical corporation took an action it was possibly later to regret by pointing out that reducing or removing lead in gasoline would increase the risks posed by benzene, an issue which had not previously been generally appreciated. Moreover, organized business, together with companies engaged in technical testing and modelling, were major providers of technical information for the regulatory process. Particularly for the EU's benzene standard-setting process,[6] petrochemical industry representatives were formally incorporated in policy discussions, and through CONCAWE, a body funded by petrochemical companies, provided much of the scientific input into the process.

Regulation of pesticide residues in food also involved close alignment of several elements of regime content with the interests of organized business. Here too there was a range of nationally and internationally organised and coordinated cause groups and green lobbyists such as the UK's Pesticides Trust, World Wildlife Fund for Nature, Greenpeace, and the Pesticide Action Network, as well as victim groups of pesticide exposure whose activities had implications for residues in food. But the concentrated and powerful organized business interests in this policy community—agrochemical companies, food retailers, and organized farmers—constituted a group of risk producers with a common interest in regulation through 'science-based' standards rather than the particularly onerous 'precautionary' standards used for pesticide residues in drinking water.

At one time the UK regime for approvals of pesticide products seems to

have died a natural death. Even so, as noted earlier, some southern European member states managed to secure further derogations beyond 2010.

[6] Though less so for the UK standards, according to our interviewees.

have been a clear case of regulatory capture by agrochemical companies (see Irwin *et al.* 1997). Later, capture became less obvious, but the most powerful corporate interests were accommodated by a tendency to place tighter restrictions on use of pesticides rather than an outright ban. The pressure went on to operators rather than agrochemical producers and on to the fragile, nationally or locally based behaviour-modification dimension of regulation rather than the standard-setting component. For instance, a senior EU official talked about what he saw as the utter unreality of requirements that pesticide operators wear space suits or put buffer zones around toxic pesticides, that is, banning the use of pesticides within a certain distance of water. 'You know that farmers won't observe it' (P11). A UK government scientist also talked about the way the boundary lines between different government agencies—the Ministry of Agriculture, the Health and Safety Executive, and the Environment Agency—made enforcement problematic or ambiguous over issues like disposal of sheep dip or local environmental risk assessments for pesticides (P8). The complexity of the regulatory structure over behaviour-modification made enforcement and compliance weak and opaque, while producing the appearance of regulatory control and taking the heat off multinational pesticide producers.

At the retailing end, the UK food market was increasingly dominated by a handful of giant supermarket chains with highly-developed political savvy and contacts and capable of exerting considerable clout up the food supply chain.[7] So it is hardly surprising that 'commercial confidentiality' considerations apparently prevented transparency in regulatory enforcement of pesticide residue levels in food in the UK until the very end of the 1990s. At that time regulators finally adopted a modest 'naming and shaming' approach, against what one official described to us as a 'vociferous opposition campaign by the supermarkets' (P26). Moreover, in principle a food-safety regime involving costly bureaucratic internal safety checks could help the large established retailers. If, as seems likely, there are economies of scale in operating such checks and strong customer pressures for larger retailers to adopt them anyway, such checks can serve as a barrier to entry to the market and impose relatively heavy costs on smaller operators.

The two occupational regimes—for radon and benzene—in our collection were also relatively business-friendly, with limited interest and pressure by labour unions. For radon, a business-friendly voluntary standard operated until the mid-1980s, and the same threshold was carried over into the UK implementation of the successor standard—the 1985 EU ionising radiation regime (Statutory Instrument No. 1333 1985). While radon was not a problem for the well-ventilated coal mines, the position was different for the

---

[7] In 1996, supermarkets took 53.7 per cent of total UK spending on groceries, and in 1997 had a combined turnover of £34,005 million (DETR 1998a).

economically precarious non-coal mines, so the original standard was chosen in order not to endanger the latter interests. In the words of one inspector, 'The non-coal mining industry determined the original threshold—it was horse-trading between the HSE and the industry' (R6). That may help to explain why the radon Action Level 'kicked-in' at a higher level of risk than applied to other sources of radiation at work, and why enforcement was of a decidedly 'light-touch' character.

Similarly, the early standards for exposure to benzene vapour at work were heavily influenced by industry. Before 1980 the UK exposure limits were taken from the American Conference of Governmental Industrial Hygienists (ACGIH), limits which according to one policy official 'have been criticized because ACGIH are close to industry' (B11) (see HM Factory Inspectorate 1969; see also Salter 1988: Ch. 3). After 1984 the UK set new limits for airborne benzene by a process that included labour union and industrial interests as part of a corporatist institutional balance which one senior oil company representative described as a 'highly consultative process' (B16). When the EU came to tackle the issue in the following decade, the 'corporatist balance' approach was also followed in setting an exposure standard of 1ppm, although the deal was widely considered as more explicitly political than that attending the 1984 UK standard. The oil company representative said, 'The Euro oil industry unanimously came up with the figure of 1ppm and the objective was to stop it going lower,' and a EU official said the European Commission 'considered that 1ppm was high for protecting workers' health, but it was a political not scientific decision' (B10).

Organized Business Pressures and Risk Regulation: An Overview

Figure 7.1 summarizes the discussion above by showing how examples from the cases we studied fitted into Wilson's (1980) four-part typology of interest-group profiles, as described in Chapter 4. As we saw earlier, cases of client politics—the classic Stiglerian picture of regulatory capture (Stigler 1971), in the top right-hand box of Fig. 7.1—tended to be partial and dynamic rather than stable and universal. A maximum of four of our nine regimes could even partially be said to have fitted that picture, and even for three of those there were elements of regulatory regime content that were hard to reconcile with corporate capture.

As the earlier discussion suggests, the influence of organized business interests can explain some observed features of regulatory regime content that seemed hard to square with market-failure and opinion-responsive expectations. But regulation of pesticide residues, the case identified at the outset as 'critical' because business interests appeared to pull in opposite directions from market-failure or opinion-responsive expectations, could only partly be explained by business pressures. For drinking water, a handful of monopoly

Distribution of costs/maleficiaries from regulation	Distribution of benefits/beneficiaries from regulation: *Diffuse*	Distribution of benefits/beneficiaries from regulation: *Concentrated*
	(1) 'Majoritarian politics'	(2) 'Client politics'
Diffuse	'Politics without publics' pattern of domestic radon, and business-interest-free pattern of paedophile release regulation (where organized business interests were only latent)	Ambient benzene standards, introduced on a time-scale accommodated petrochemical and vehicle manufacturing interests as well as motorists by waiting for 'natural' death of old cars UK aspect of EU pesticide residues in drinking water regime(risk-reduction costs paid through ability to tax users plus mark-up) Occupational radon regulation (standards set to accommodate a fragile non-mining industry)
	(3) 'Entrepreneurial politics'	(4) 'Interest group politics'
Concentrated	Aspects of dangerous dogs regulation (with costs concentrated on illegal, mainly drug dealing, business) EU standards for pesticide residues in water (private water companies and agrochemical industry campaigned against precautionary standards)	Aspects of local traffic calming (transport operators, shop-keepersconstruction firms)

FIGURE 7.1: Configuration of organized business interests in risk regulation on Wilson's (1980) typology: selected examples

utility companies had secured a price control regime that enabled full pass-through of the heavy compliance costs imposed by the risk regime, enabling those companies to tax their captive consumers for safety improvement at no cost to their profits. Organized business interests in food were able to ensure they were never subject to the transparency requirements and precautionary standards imposed on drinking water utilities before privatization. Nevertheless, the privatized water producers once established were unable to overturn the more burdensome openness and reporting obligations imposed on them before privatization. So organized business interests cannot explain everything about risk regulation, even if they can account for a number of observed features of regime content.

3. Other Organized Interests

The Stiglerian Chicago-school approach to regulation traditionally focused primarily on organized business, because business was assumed to be the group that ordinarily combined high stakes with a comparative advantage in collective organization to influence regulatory settings. Even from that perspective, however, it need not only be business producer groups that have a comparative advantage in collective organization. Cohesive groups of consumers, such as business users of utility or public services, may form collectivities that have a comparative advantage in organizing. The same may go for compact groups of threatened property-owners, especially if the stakes are high over property values, as with NIMBY organizations formed to fight location of unpopular facilities in their local area.

Moreover, if we go outside the conventional institutional-economics framework for analysing interest-group organization, there are observable cases of organized groups that should be 'latent' according to the expectations of that framework, but are in fact cohesive as a result of cultural characteristics (Douglas 1987) or shared experience of disaster (Showalter 1997). And risk regulation brings in a range of pressure groups other than business producer groups, including labour unions, local amenity groups, consumer or lifestyle groups, and victim groups seeking compensation or policy changes as well as broader 'cause groups' such as green or animal rights campaigners.

As with business interests, we found other organized groups varied in activity and influence from one risk domain to another. Radon, as already noted, seemed to be a near vacuum for interest or pressure groups. We might expect occupational risk regimes to be balanced between business groups, labour unions,[8] and victim organizations, with risk regulators holding the ring. Labour union interest was minimal in the two occupational-risk cases we studied and there were no well-organized victim interest groups either, though in other occupational risk regimes, such as asbestos or organophosphate pesticides, victim organization was stronger.

In other domains, a different 'balancing act' was observable, between business risk producers and risk consumers of other kinds. Examples included the regimes for ambient benzene, pesticide residue levels in water and food, and road risks, with non-business organized groups affecting regime content in

---

[8] Labour unions have high stakes in promoting occupational safety, since risk-reducing regimes can often be used as a means of raising real wages, for instance by shutting out low-wage competitors, as well as simply protecting the lives and limbs of union members.

varying ways. For benzene, environmental and motorist groups exerted little pressure over UK-level standards—environmental groups were mainly concerned with other air pollutants—though environmental groups were more actively engaged over the setting of EU-level standards and successfully pressed for a standard more rigorous than the industry's opening bargaining position. For pesticide residue risks in water, as noted in the previous section, Greenpeace succeeded in preserving the EU's precautionary limits against the less rigorous standards business groups wanted, by orchestrating mass pressure on the European Commission. For road risks, many organized groups other than organized national or local business interests were active at different levels, including groups representing pedestrians and cyclists, national motorist associations, cause groups like Road Peace, and groups seeking to promote children's welfare. Such groups were part of the policy ecosystem, and often part of the pantheon of 'the great and the good' represented on official policy committees, but only occasionally seemed to make a dramatic impact on regime content.[9] Such influence was more visible in the form of local community organization, normally of the NIMBY type, pressuring local authorities to install or remove road layout schemes designed to alter the balance of risk between in-vehicle and out-of-vehicle road users.

Finally, there were cases where organized business interests were absent and other interest groups dominated the policy domain. The two clear cases of this type were the dogs and paedophiles regimes. Organized group pressure explains some of the standards embodied in the UK's 1991 Dangerous Dogs Act that are not readily explicable by the market-failure or opinion-responsive hypotheses. The dog types selected for draconian treatment under the Act were all cases without well-organized breed associations, political connections—for instance in the form of Rottweiler-owning Cabinet ministers—or mainstream cultural location, since they were types either relatively new or not yet introduced to the UK.[10] Those that were given the benefit of the doubt—German Shepherds, Dobermans, Rottweilers—possessed the opposite features. As the then Home Secretary observed in his autobiography, to have treated such dogs in the same way as pit bulls 'would have infuriated the "green welly" brigade' (Baker 1993: 435). While none of the organized groups in this domain commanded the sort of resources normally associated with powerful business groups, they were able to shape the standard-setting component of regulation at the margin.

[9] An exception to this pattern was a threat of litigation by Transport 2000, a public-interest transport group, that caused the Association of Chief Police Officers to abandon a guidance document that drivers on 30 mph roads should not be stopped unless they exceeded 35 mph (*Guardian* 2000).

[10] For example, according to a senior government official we interviewed, the Japanese Tosa and Dogo Argentino were added to the group of dog types subject to the most stringent regulation as a result of pressure by animal-cruelty associations seeking more effective enforcement of the law against dog fighting (D3).

The case of paedophile regulation was another domain from which organized business interests were almost absent. Since private prisons had a limited role in handling sex offenders, business interests were at best latent over the UK's 1997 Sex Offenders Act and, in contrast to the dogs regime, not even the registration of offenders was outsourced to private firms. As noted in the previous section, however, there was a range of organized groups that surrounded the regulators of this risk. These groups included ad hoc local organizations protesting about specific offenders, human rights lobbies representing the rights of ex-offenders to be protected from risks of public attack and double punishment for the same crime, and children's NGOs. Within the latter group, including long-established bodies like the English National Society for Prevention of Cruelty to Children and its Scottish counterpart Children First, child abuse had become 'risk-professionalized', with the development of specialist terminology and a community of professionals concerned to give the issue of general, and not just sexual, child abuse more profile. Such changes interacted with the preferences of some of the key actors in the state structure, to be discussed in the next section. Local community pressures, often working in tandem with media coverage as discussed in Chapter 6, undoubtedly affected the way local police and other regulators handled the release and management of particular offenders. Moreover, the influence of human rights lobbies may explain the confidentiality of the UK's sex offender register, in contrast to its US counterpart, which was a feature of the regime's content that seemed hard to explain by market-failure or opinion-responsive factors.

What this analysis suggests is that interest groups other than organized business could sometimes outgun business interests, as on drinking water standards, and often comprised part of a balance of forces with business and other groups. When organized business was absent from a policy domain, organized non-business interests could shape regulatory regime content in several ways. Several features of regime content that appeared anomalous from other perspectives could be explained by such shaping pressures, and, as we saw in Chapter 6, regulators and bureaucrats often construed public opinion through the activities of such interest groups rather than by commissioning general opinion polls.

4. Bureaucrats and Regulators

In Chapter 6 we examined some of the strategies that risk regulators employed to manage the difficulties that arose when public opinion was out of line with their own policy preferences. Indeed, such bureaucrats are often themselves assumed to constitute an interest group seeking to shape public policy and organization, though what they seek to maximize is much debated. Some in the rational-choice tradition (see Niskanen 1971: 1973) claim that bureaucrats' main interest is to maximize their budgets, especially discretionary budgets that can be spent on bureaucratic welfare. Others see bureaucratic interest as couched more in terms of making their jobs satisfying, for instance by 'bureau-shaping' strategies that help to reduce the exposure of senior bureaucrats to stressful management or front-line work (Dunleavy 1991). Still others have argued the view, heretical for some rational choice theorists, that bureaucrats, public managers, and policy professionals have substantive interest in the policies they administer, functioning as 'zealots' for particular approaches (Downs 1967). If bureaucrats, technocrats, and regulators constitute an interest group, the search for the definitive bureaucratic welfare function remains inconclusive.

Bureaucratic interests approximating to a budget-maximizing approach could be detected in some of the risk regulation regimes we observed. For example, the UK's Pesticides Safety Directorate—which was originally part of the Ministry of Agriculture, Fisheries and Food and in 1993 was constituted as a quasi-independent executive agency responsible for approving pesticide products—was a notable case of a bureaucracy visibly prospering from risk regulation. The organization, which charged for its product approvals on a 'full cost recovery' basis, saw its scientific staff quadruple in the six years to 1992 and adopted an 'entrepreneurial' stance in the EU pesticide approvals market (House of Commons Agriculture Committee 1995: 210). Within the EU's mutual-recognition framework for regulatory approval and licensing, it sought to be the market leader and took an active part in pesticide standard-setting, which was important for marketing purposes given that familiarity with complex requirements could give a competitive edge to such an agency. We also found examples of various EU member state governments seeking to sway the design of test protocols in pesticides to support their national laboratories that specialized in certain tests (see Rothstein et al. 1999). In other cases, as predicted by Dunleavy's (1991) bureau-shaping framework, central bureaucrats seemed to have little interest in expanding their own payroll or budget and were more concerned to craft neat regulatory solutions that added to their reputation as effective fixers or problem-solvers. Such attitudes were held by the architects of the dogs and paedophile standards in our set.

Indeed, our observation of nine risk policy domains suggested three things about the way bureaucrats and regulators functioned as interest groups. First, like private and other interests, bureaucratic and regulatory interests were often multiple and conflicting, not a monolithic bloc. The main exception to this pattern consisted of the group of nuclear scientists who dominated the standard-setting component of the UK regime for domestic radon risks, in the absence of any other organized interests or much interest in domestic radon on the part of other public sector actors. This group seemed to fit the 'zealot'

pattern rather more obviously than the bureau-shaping or budget-maximizing one, though the testing programme described earlier involved a substantial bureaucratic income stream. They formed a relatively cohesive group with
a clear view of radon risks that they sought to propagate in the face of public
apathy. However, their commitment to the view that the public accepted
much higher risks of exposure to natural than to man-made radiation goes
some way to explaining the high risk tolerance built into the radon Action
Level (see International Commission on Radiological Protection 1984: 4ff).
Even on radon, however, bureaucratic interests did not form a complete
monolith. For instance, a senior civil servant we interviewed in the health
ministry was deeply sceptical about the high radon risk estimates coming
from the National Radiation Protection Board (NRPB), the main agency
involved in setting radon standards.[11]

Second, those multiple bureaucrat interests seemed to divide on both vertical and horizontal lines. Vertical divisions were often exposed by a tendency
on the part of national-government regulators to lay responsibilities for regulatory enforcement on police or cash-strapped local authorities, creating the
potential for 'unfunded mandates' unless police and local authorities pressed
for more funding. Examples of this pattern included ambient benzene, where
national-government regulators made local authorities responsible for failures
to meet UK and EU benzene standards; local road risks, where central government's funding of local authorities did not match its own valuations for road
safety, as discussed in Chapter 6; and the paedophile regime, which imposed
substantial extra costs and responsibilities on police, probation services, and
other local actors. Something similar applied to the tendency, noted earlier,
for pesticide regulators to place elaborate restrictions on conditions of use, by
specifying buffer zones and the like. While this approach made standard-
setting regulators' lives easier than the imposition of outright bans on well-
organized producers would have done, it put more pressure on
thinly-stretched organizations at the enforcement end of the regime, notably
the Health and Safety Executive and Environment Agency.

Horizontal divisions were exposed by turf battles, struggles over policy
'ownership', or attempts at blame avoidance. That went for the multiple

---

[11] That senior civil servant said, 'The NRPB is made up of physicists. They like to produce quantitative figures for risk. We should be very careful with such figures', and told us there would need
to be 'good human data', like convincing epidemiological studies, for the department to 'press' the
radon risk issue (G2). This official was also sceptical about the NRPB's motivations, suggesting, 'A
cynical reason for the NRPB taking on radon . . . was because it had evolved to defend the nuclear
industry. Radon offered a useful counterpart to nuclear hazard, because it was natural and probably
more hazardous than nuclear power . . .'. And in the behaviour-modification component of the RRR
the nuclear professionals' view of radon risks came up against different attitudes on the part of local
authorities, ranging from apathy to positive resistance. For instance, according to a senior official in
DETR, some local health chiefs were reluctant to promote radon awareness for fear it might detract
from anti-smoking messages—a feature of radon politics also observed in Canada (see Harrison and
Hoberg 1991: 19).

bureaucratic units with a stake in pesticide policy, both at EU level, where 'ownership' of pesticides policy was divided among three Directorates-General with responsibility for consumer affairs, environment, and agriculture, and at UK central government level, where ownership was also divided among agriculture, environment, and health departments.

A different kind of horizontal division among bureaucratic interests applied over dogs regulation, where police, represented by the Association of Chief Police Officers, were keen to see more aggressive standards that gave them new powers to tackle drug dealers using American pit bull terriers as a weapon: 'Drug dealers used them to put PC Plod off challenging them', as one police interviewee told us (D1). But apart from tackling criminals using dogs as a weapon, police were not otherwise enthusiastic about assuming greater responsibilities over dogs. The 1991 Dangerous Dogs Act regime was therefore constructed to minimize routine police involvement over enforcement, with registration being handled by a private firm. Moreover, after an early burst of active enforcement of the Dangerous Dogs Act, the Metropolitan Police in 1992, so we were told, 'made a conscious decision not to be pro-active in enforcing the Act' (D1). By 1994 they had gone back in effect to the traditional 'one-free-bite' approach to dangerous dogs that the Dangerous Dogs Act had ostensibly replaced, and a low-key reactive style of enforcement reflected a low priority placed by police on dangerous dogs work. As one police officer told us, 'There's an awful lot of aggravation about bringing in a pit bull . . . You don't get many Brownie points for it' (D1).

On the other hand, police developed an elaborate new role for themselves out of the introduction of the Sex Offenders Register in 1997, which, in contrast to the registration system used for dangerous dogs, made police responsible for operating the register. In a rare and not fully intended example of 'joined up government', police drew probation and increasingly even local authority housing representatives into elaborate joint decision arrangements that we will discuss further in Chapter 9. What those two cases suggested was that the same organization might take up different 'bureau-shaping' stances over different risk regulation issues.

Third—to anticipate an issue to which we return in Chapter 9—the specific 'bureau-shaping' interests that tended to animate risk regulators and bureaucrats were concerns to avoid or shift blame and liability, and to find short cuts through complex questions that made their jobs more tractable: both traditional features of bureaucratic behaviour. Short-cuts were reflected in the way technical standards were often borrowed from international bodies or other countries with minimal adaptation, as occurred for domestic radon and occupational benzene—as noted earlier. For the standard-setting dimension of risk regulation, blame-avoidance tactics by regulators typically included attempts to construct 'technocratic shields' or formulae recommended and blessed by experts. An example is the establishment of an EU scientific committee in

1995 to propose a limit value for exposures to occupational benzene, in an attempt by the Commission to avoid a repeat of a political process which had caused a previous proposal to be thrown out ten years earlier.[12]

For the behaviour-modification dimension of risk regulation, blame avoidance was often helped by a complex organizational structure involving indefinite and/or dispersed responsibilities: an oft-observed hierarchist way of diffusing blame (see Thompson, Ellis, and Wildavsky 1990). For instance, the ambiguity and dispersal of responsibilities over enforcement and implementation that was built into the regime for ambient benzene risks seemed to constitute a classic example of blame avoidance by public authorities. The same went for the dispersal of responsibilities over pesticide usage noted above, and we shall comment further in Chapter 9 on the role that blame-avoidance considerations play in regulatory regime dynamics.

Accordingly, bureaucratic interests seem to have often been important in the shaping of regime content, sometimes for regulatory size but also for structure and style. Sometimes they were paramount forces as with domestic radon, sometimes they were 'ringmasters' as with road risks, sometimes they were key players as with paedophile risks. Sometimes they seem to have been important in shaping one element of regime content while external interests shaped another, as in the ambient benzene example. But the values that those bureaucratic and professional 'interests' comprised were far from uniform. Indeed, the worldviews of regulators varied widely and often clashed within and between regimes. Readers will recall that in Table 1.1 we described a quartet of attitudes and beliefs that could be expected to be manifested in risk regulation regimes, and we found examples of each of those four sets of attitudes in the inner worlds of risk regulation that we explored.

Space prevents a lengthy discussion of such variety in regulatory worldviews, but that variety can be demonstrated by comparing two of our cases, namely domestic radon and dangerous dogs, across the different control components. For radon, information gathering followed a 'hierarchist' or expertized view that extensive data gathering should be obtained even in the face of public indifference. Standard setting involved elements of that 'hierarchist' view, with Action Levels set by expert authority, but also accommodated the individualist view that the Action Levels should not be binding on householders and that it should be up to individuals whether to take any notice of those levels. But the behaviour-modification component of the regime was essentially fatalist, with most local authorities and other actors

---

[12] The tactic rebounded on the Commission because, according to an EU official, the expert committee 'did not want to propose a standard for a chemical that had no threshold of safety' (B10). The committee therefore proposed a number of levels associated with different expected rates of cancer, thus leaving the political questions unanswered.

convinced that nothing much could be done in the face of public indifference to the risk and all of the other issues competing for their time and resources.[13]

The dangerous dogs worldview profile was rather different. In that case, the information-gathering component reflected a wholly individualist approach, with no state activity to gather systematic 'expertized' data on the extent of the risk.[14] Standard setting involved a mixture of hierarchist, egalitarian, and individualist attitudes. The 1991 Dangerous Dogs Act singled out 'devil dogs' highlighted by the tabloids, and was directed against 'luxury' dogs that no one needed to own if they simply wanted canine company and affection. The legislative strategy adopted reflected the view that the major source of dog risks—attack by the family pet at home—was a matter for individuals and not for state activity. Perhaps there was even a fatalist element in the dog standard-setting process, in the view that standards could be changed only through political pressure following dog attack tragedies. As one senior official elegantly put it, 'It's catastrophe theory—supercool until you can't bear it' (D3). Behaviour modification on the part of the police largely reflected a fatalist view that every dog is allowed one free bite, in spite of the attempt by the Act to move away from this traditional approach to dog risk regulation.[15]

Figure 7.2 depicts this variety, showing that the different 'worlds' of risk regulation varied in these cases as much across the different components of control as they did across risk domains. Such analysis shows that bureaucratic

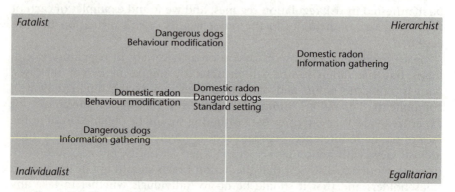

FIGURE 7.2: Types of bureaucratic value amongst the components of two risk regulation regimes

[13] Much the same applied to Health and Safety Executive inspectors' attitudes to enforcement of occupational radon requirements, according to one of our interviewees (R6).

[14] As one Home Office official put it, 'If a pit bull was to bite someone then we would see it in the papers' (D4).

[15] After an initial burst of enthusiasm for enforcement of the 1991 Act by the police which attracted considerable adverse publicity over 'death row dogs'.

'interests' reflected different values and different sets of attitudes and beliefs, entrenched in different parts of the regimes. That variety of worldviews was more obvious than a general drive for budget-maximizing on the part of bureaucrats. It was consistent to some extent with the idea of bureaucrats as 'bureau-shapers', but that idea is relatively empty without an analysis of different 'shaping' values in play in the inner worlds of regulatory regimes.

5. Conclusion: Regimes as Interest-Driven

As was noted earlier, the pressure of organized interests cannot be completely separated from public-opinion pressures, and indeed some risk regulators equated public opinion with the activities of organized groups. Some of the observed features of risk regulation regimes that are explicable from the market-failure and/or opinion-responsive hypotheses are also explicable from the interest-driven standpoint.

Accordingly, following the 'critical case' approach described earlier, Table 7.1 identifies the observations in our nine risk regulation regimes that were 'anomalous' from a market-failure and/or opinion-responsive perspective, and notes the extent to which those anomalies are explicable from an interest-driven perspective. It shows that at least one—perhaps two—of those anomalies can be clearly explained by active business lobbying. Three other anomalies can be at least partly explained by interest-group activity. But to explain up to three of those anomalies we need to stretch the conventional notion of interest-group activity to include the interests of regulators, professionals, and bureaucrats within each regime

Indeed, one advantage of taking a dimensional approach to risk regulation is that we can see that the various components and elements of regimes can be shaped by different organized interests. As noted earlier, regulatory size in standard-setting for ambient benzene had to accommodate powerful corporate interests in its glacial shift from 'unpolitics' to potentially lucrative mandated shifts in vehicle and fuel technologies. But regulatory structure in that risk regulation regime, especially for behaviour modification, seemed to reflect the play more of public-sector interests than private corporate ones.

Similarly, in the case we identified as critical for an interest-driven explanation—the regime for pesticide residues in water compared with food—powerful corporate interests were defeated over water standards but accommodated by a price regime linked to monopoly licences. Such a pattern of 'swings and roundabouts' interest group accommodation is easier to achieve in regulatory regimes that are high in structural complexity, with responsibility for different components of regulation residing in numerous different organizations.

TABLE 7.1. *Organized interests and the explicability of five observed 'anomalies' in regulatory regime content*

Anomaly in observed regulatory regime content from market-failure and opinion-responsive perspective	Extent and manner in which the observed anomaly can be explained by interest-driven pressures
Emphasis on state-financed information gathering and high official action thresholds in domestic radon	Explicable only by preferences of government risk technocrats, not active lobbying by business or other pressures
Selection of dog types for most draconian regulation under 1991 Dangerous Dogs Act	Not explicable by business pressures but reflected police pressures to target pit bull terriers, animal cruelty associations' pressures to target fighting dogs and pressures by breed associations to exempt established breeds
Non-disclosure of 1997 Sex Offenders Register	Not explicable by business pressures but reflected pressure of human rights lobby and bureaucrats concerned with public order
30-year delay in regulatory response to a known genotoxic carcinogen (ambient benzene)	Explicable by active business lobbying from petrochemical and vehicle industries as well as by opinion-responsive factors
More rigorous standards for pesticide residues in water than for food, as maintained in 1998 renegotiation of EU Drinking Water Directive	Not readily explicable by business pressures but explicable by cause group lobbying

This analysis of the play of organized interests further supports the view that much of risk regulation can be understood by the application of fairly well-tried and long-standing forms of explanation rather than searching for some all-pervasive essence of 'high modernity'. It also supports the view that there may be as much variety within different forms of risk regulation as there is between the regulation of risk and other types of policy. Chapter 8 draws together what we have learnt from the analysis of how regime content is shaped by regime context in Part II of the book and sets the stage for Part III.

8

Regime Content and Context Revisited:
An Overall Picture

Even when theorists offer explanations . . . they often turn out to be
elaborate policy stories.

John (1998: 196)

1. Introduction

The previous three chapters explored how far and in what ways differences in
regime content can be explained by variations in the three basic elements of
regime context—type of risk, public preferences and attitudes, and organized
interests—identified earlier. This chapter draws together the earlier analysis
into an overall picture. It summarizes those elements of regime content across
the three regulatory-control components that fitted expectations based on
the hypothetical regime shapers of market-failure, opinion-responsive, and
interest-driven government.

That analysis shows that, when they were taken together, the three
elements of regime context gave us a fairly robust basis for understanding
variety in the size and style elements of regime content across the control
components, although structure was rarely determinate. The number of serious anomalies—elements of observed regime content that were far out of line
with expectations—seemed to be greatest for the market failure approach and
least for the interest-group approach, with serious market failure anomalies
roughly double the number of serious anomalies for the interest-group
approach.

Apart from the indeterminacy of 'structure', such an approach has at least
three limitations. First, as we have seen, the expected impact of the three
elements of regime context overlap, so that elements of observed regime
content may be compatible with more than one contextual explanation.
Second, while there are conceptual 'hard core' features of each of the three
'context' hypotheses that are readily distinguishable, each hypothesis can be
extended beyond those 'hard core' features in a way that blurs the boundaries

between the hypotheses at the margin. Third, unless each contextual approach is extended to the point of indeterminacy, there are a number of observed features of regime content that do not fit what would be expected from the three contextual approaches individually or jointly.

This chapter is divided into three main parts. First, it brings together the analyses of expected and observed elements of regime content from the previous three chapters. Second, it switches the analysis to the other dimension of regime anatomy—the control components—looking at the forces shaping information gathering, standard setting, and behaviour modification. Third, it revisits the discussion of 'non-contextual' explanations of regime content that were not readily explicable by market failure, opinion-responsive or conventional interest-driven logic, either jointly or separately.

2. Putting Together the Analysis of Shaping Elements

Building on the comparison of regimes in Chapter 3 and bringing together the analysis of the previous three chapters, Table 8.1 compares observed and expected elements of regime content for each of the three contextual hypotheses discussed earlier. For simplicity, it depicts only the basic elements of size, structure, and style discussed in Chapter 2,[1] and aggregates them across the three components of regulatory control. It also considers only interest groups external to government, not the interests within the bureaucracy that were discussed at the end of Chapter 7: we revisit those 'inner life' interests later.

Accordingly, the first column of Table 8.1 lists the nine regimes in our study and the second column divides each of those risk regulation regimes into size, structure, and style. The third column summarizes the observed characteristics, relative to other regimes, of each of those elements of regime content. The next three columns summarize the differences between the observed and expected risk regulation regime characteristics of each element of regime content from the perspective of the three contextual hypotheses. The key to the symbols is given at the foot of Tables 8.1 and 8.2.

As the previous three chapters showed, expectations can be ambiguous for some elements of regime content. Expectations about structure are hard to derive from any of the three contextual elements, and deriving determinate expectations from an interest-group perspective can be particularly problematic, as we saw in Chapter 7. The expectation was that overall regulatory size

---

[1] That is, at the top level of aggregation shown in Table 2.3, where 'size' combines regulatory aggression with level of investment, 'structure' (complexity) combines organizational/regime complexity and funding complexity, in the sense of proportion of private investment, and 'style' (intensity) combines rule-orientation and regulatory zeal.

TABLE 8.1. *Three content elements of nine risk regulation regimes observed against three sets of expectations*

Risk regulation regime	Regulatory control component	Observed	Observed vs market-failure expectation	Observed vs opinion-responsive expectation	Observed vs external interest-driven expectation
Dangerous dogs	Size	Small	✔	✔	✔
	Structure	Simple	✔	–	–
	Style	Fairly relaxed	↓	✔	✔
Radon in the home	Size	Small	✔	✔	✔
	Structure	Simple	✔	✔	–
	Style	Relaxed	✔	✔	✔
Radon at work	Size	Small	↓	–	✔
	Structure	Fairly simple	✔	–	✔
	Style	Medium relaxed	↓	–	✔
Ambient benzene	Size	Small	↓	✔	✔
	Structure	Medium complexity	✔	–	✔
	Style	Fairly formal	✔	✔	✔
Benzene at work	Size	Medium	✔	–	✔
	Structure	Fairly complex	✔	–	–
	Style	Formal	✔	–	✔
Paedophile risks	Size	Fairly small	↓	↓	✔
	Structure	Medium complexity	–	–	–
	Style	Fairly formal	↓	✔	✔
Local road risks	Size	Fairly big	✔	✔	–
	Structure	Fairly complex	✔	–	✔
	Style	Medium formality	↓	✔	–
Pesticide residues in food	Size	Medium	✔	↓	✔
	Structure	Complex	✔	–	✔
	Style	Formal	✔	↓	✔
Pesticide resides in drinking water	Size	Big	↑	✔	↑
	Structure	Complex	–	✔	✔
	Style	Formal	✔	✔	✔

See Appendix C for notes on methodology.

✔= in line with expectations; ↑, ↓ = greater (less) than expectations; – = indeterminate.

and style—intensity—would reflect the degree of market failure, the extent of public concern, or the degree and nature of lobbying pressure from outside government. The expectation was that structure—complexity—would reflect scale or degree of market failure and the existence of other complementary— upstream or downstream—regimes, the nature of public opinion,[2] and the interest-group structure: for example, whether it comprised predominantly localized enterprises or multinational corporations interested in 'owning' particular regulatory sectors.

The analysis depicted in Table 8.1 suggests three conclusions about regulatory regime context and content. First, the interest-driven explanation was the most accurate overall predictor of regime size and the market-failure and opinion-responsive explanations were roughly equal in explanatory power. When concentrated business interests were in the field, the position they could be expected to prefer over regime content was normally adopted, whatever the logic of general opinion responsiveness and minimum feasible response might suggest. The main exception, discussed in Chapter 7, was the defeat of UK privatized water utility interests over the maintenance of precautionary standards in EU drinking water regulation. But, as we saw, what those interests lost on the EU swings they gained on the UK roundabouts, having established a price control regime that allowed monopoly drinking water suppliers to pass through their full clean-up costs, plus a profit mark-up.

That outcome accords with the casual observation that, in risk regulation, victories by cause groups over powerful corporate interests occur occasionally, but that the latter interests, if thwarted over standard-setting, can often find compensatory strategies. And such interests are often especially well placed to influence elements of regime content that may be more detached from general public opinion pressures and require close-in knowledge of institutional procedures. One example, noted in Chapter 7, is the way corporate interests secured delays in the deadline for implementation of controls over ambient benzene, after haggles over the rigour of standards. Another is the way, according to one official, that some member states secured a delay in implementation until 2003 for the EU rules applying to workplace benzene, to protect the interests of their national industries (B10).

Second, regulatory style was largely consistent with external pressures but somewhat less so than size. In some cases style was modified, at least to some extent, to fit with those pressures, as in the case of paedophiles, which we discuss further in Chapter 9. In others, 'inner life' features of regimes meant that style was out of line with some external pressures, such as police 'one-free-bite' practices over dangerous dogs—in spite of the 1991 Dangerous Dogs Act—or technocratic cost-benefit rules for road safety investment clashing with local public pressures.

---

[2] Where any public views could be found or imputed on the subject of structure.

Third, structure, taken in terms of organizational and financial complexity for this analysis, was the element of regime content that was hardest to explain by any of the three contextual elements. Such an observation is perhaps not surprising. Like style, structure might be expected to be highly susceptible to 'inner life' forces like institutional inertia or 'inside' bureaucratic manoeuvring, and of least interest to outside interests or general public opinion.

Overall, the three contextual elements predicted size and style better than tossing a coin, in the sense that only about a third of observations were far from expectations. Structure was harder to predict. Moreover, in most cases observed regime content deviated from expectations in both directions, that is, both more and less than would be predicted. Even allowing for the possibility that some of those errors might be put down to data limitations or coder bias, it seems that we would need either other contextual factors or non-contextual explanations to account for a non-trivial minority of regulatory regime features.

2. Regime Component Characteristics

Our observations also suggest that the three components of regulatory control may to some extent be differentially shaped by the various elements of regime context. Table 8.2 compares the observed and expected features of standard-setting, information-gathering, and behaviour-modification for each of the three contextual hypotheses. For simplicity, paralleling Table 8.1 and following a similar layout, Table 8.2 aggregates the control components across the regime content elements of size, structure, and style.

For the nine risk regulation regimes, the market-failure hypothesis was as good a predictor of the information-gathering component of regulation as the interest-driven hypothesis. The opinion-responsive hypothesis was consistent with substantially fewer cases, and our interview material suggested public opinion in most cases had mainly indirect influence over information-gathering in risk regulation.[3] Business interests, however, often figured larger in information-gathering arrangements. After all, corporations involved in hazardous processes or products were often the repository of technical know-how and risk data—for instance on ambient benzene and pesticides—and often provided the first line of control in risk regulation, with state officials

[3] That is not to say public opinion never plays any part in shaping information-gathering arrangements. The case of paedophile registration involved public opinion at least working in tandem with professional opinion and interests. Public concern also seems to have worked in the same direction as market-failure logic, and against business pressure, to move governments to engage in further research before approving genetically modified food and crops (see Gaskell *et al.* 1999).

TABLE 8.2. *Three control components of nine risk regulation regimes observed against three sets of expectations*

Risk Regulation Regime	Regulatory control component	Observed	Observed vs market-failure expectation	Observed vs opinion-responsive expectation	Observed vs interest-driven expectation
Dangerous dogs	IG	Little activity except fighting dogs	✔	↓	✔
	SS	General behaviour standards with exception of fighting dogs	↑	✔	✔
	BM	Reactive and low key	✔	↓	✔
Radon in the home	IG	Voluntary combined with state funded testing	↑	↑	↑
	SS	Voluntary and entailing high risk tolerance	↓	✔	✔
	BM	Voluntary with low key campaigns	✔	✔	✔
Radon at work	IG	Little activity	↓	–	✔
	SS	High Action Level	↓	–	✔
	BM	Little activity	↓	–	✔
Ambient benzene	IG	Medium sized monitoring programme	↓	✔	↑
	SS	'Achievable' but long delayed standards aimed at risk reduction	↓	✔	✔
	BM	'With the grain' enforcement	↓	✔	✔
Benzene at work	IG	State monitoring	✔	–	✔
	SS	Aimed at risk reduction	↓	–	✔
	BM	'Compliance' enforcement	✔	–	✔
Paedophile risks	IG	Compulsory registration of ex-offenders	↓	✔	✔
	SS	Aimed at risk reduction through better 'intelligence'	↓	↓	✔
	BM	Limited information, 'risk based' surveillance and enforcement	↓	↓	✔
Local road risks	IG	Extensive data-gathering	↑	↑	–
	SS	Aimed at risk reduction using CBA	✔	↓	–
	BM	Traffic law enforcement and highway investment	✔	✔	–
Pesticide residues in food	IG	State monitoring	✔	↓	✔
	SS	Health-based limits for individual pesticides	✔	↓	✔
	BM	Ad hoc enforcement in largely confidential style	↓	↓	✔
Pesticide residues in drinking water	IG	State monitoring	✔	✔	↑
	SS	Very low limit for total pesticides	↑	✔	↑
	BM	'Compliance' enforcement and freedom of information	✔	✔	↑

See Appendix C for notes on methodology.
✔= in line with expectations; ↑, ↓ = greater (less) than expectations; – = indeterminate.

playing the role of 'super-controllers'. In some cases too, commercial testing organizations were prominent in the information-gathering dimensions of risk regulation, for example on pesticide safety. Even so, we observed few cases of information-gathering activity that was markedly out of line with market-failure logic because of business pressure.

If market-failure was as good a predictor of information-gathering activity as interest-groups, the same did not apply to standard-setting. For this component of control, market-failure was a less accurate predictor of observed placings than opinion-responsiveness, but interest-driven approaches offered the most accurate predictions. For instance, the science-based rather than precautionary nature of food pesticide residue standards was compatible with organized business preferences, but out of line with the apparent public perception of pesticides as a 'dread' risk. As noted in Chapter 7, standard- setting for the occupational regimes was dominated by interest-driven bargaining, with public opinion playing little role. General public opinion is evidently not the source of detailed standards over product risks, since such standards necessarily build on specialized knowledge and analytic techniques available only to bureaucrats, policy analysts, or business corporations. Even so, the way technical standards incorporated rigour or laxity, precautionary or science-based approaches, a balance of risk against cost versus 'zero tolerance' of risk, or timely versus delayed responses, could be expected to be shaped by general public opinion.

When it came to behaviour-modification activity, there was little difference between the capacity of market-failure and public opinion to predict observed placings, but interest groups again offered the best predictor. This observation is not surprising since, as was noted earlier, behaviour-modification might be expected to be at least as amenable to interest-group influence as standard-setting activity. The scientific professionals who are often involved in risk standard-setting are frequently detached from the details of implementation and enforcement, and mastery of such details requires time, knowledge, application, and resources of a sort that organized interest groups outside and inside government have both motive and opportunity to command. The main observation that went against that expectation was a transparent 'naming and shaming' approach applied to breaches of pesticide residue limits by water companies. That approach seems to have been more draconian than would be served by the narrow interests of the concentrated group of producers involved.[4]

This discussion shows that separating risk regulation into different dimensions of control and different elements of regime content can help us to see

---

[4] As noted earlier, a pale imitation of the same approach was eventually adopted for supermarket chains over pesticide residues in food. The water regime is explicable to some degree by the fact that it emerged before the water utility companies were privatized, and hence it was harder for profit-seeking companies to oppose it. What is less easy to explain from an interest-group perspective is why subsequent lobbying activity did not overturn this historical legacy.

more clearly what shapes such regulation, than viewing regulatory regimes in aggregated forms. Not only did contextual elements better predict regulatory size and style than structure, but those contextual elements varied in their capacity to predict the various dimensions of regulatory control. The market-failure approach worked best as a predictor of information-gathering and worst as a predictor of standard-setting. As expected, the force of opinion-responsive government seemed to be felt more strongly in the standard-setting dimension of risk regulation than in the other dimensions, though even in an age when public policy is alleged to be driven by public opinion it was still a notably less accurate predictor of observed placings than interest-driven activity.

3. Outside the Triangle of Contextual Shapers: Regimes' 'Inner Lives' Revisited

As shown earlier, a minority of our observations of regulatory regime content could not be readily explained by the three contextual elements. So even with an 'Occam's razor' bias, other forms of explanation may be called for. One possibility is to add other contextual elements to the trio. For instance, what was earlier termed 'tombstone-ability'—the capacity of a risk to produce deaths or suffering victims through dramatic catastrophes that command media coverage and thus focus public attention—seems likely to augment the force of public opinion in shaping regime content. Only one of the observed elements of regime content that was way out of line with the opinion-responsive hypothesis involved a 'tombstone-able' risk. That example—the case of dangerous dogs—shows, however, that 'tombstone-ability' does not always override all other pressures. In that case, widespread media agitation over dog attacks, following a number of much-publicized tragedies in Britain in the early 1990s, did not lead to regulation requiring all large and fierce dogs implicated in attacks causing serious injury or death to be muzzled, neutered, and kept on a lead in public. Rather, it led to special provisions for pit bull terriers, which had no powerful lobby group behind them and which the police, particularly in London, wanted to target in their attempts to control drug dealers and other dog-using criminals.

Further, as historical institutionalists would expect, interest-group activity was shaped by historical points of departure. Even without a headline-grabbing disaster, strict standards once introduced tended to be hard for interest groups to shift, as was shown by the case of pesticide residues in water, discussed earlier.[5] The cost in time and effort of introducing radically new

---

[5] Instances of relaxation of standards occur occasionally, as in the case of EU boron standard in drinking water, but they are rare.

legislation or standards meant that incremental adjustment and patching was commonplace. Even when a regime moved in a new direction from the historical pattern, residues of the past often remained. An example is the 1991 Dangerous Dogs Act. In some ways an attempt to radically modernize dog safety regulation, it nevertheless left large parts of its Victorian predecessor— the 1871 Dogs Act—in place because it would simply have taken too long to make the 1991 legislation a comprehensive replacement for the 1871 Act.

Such familiar features of the regulatory policy process could be considered as adjustments or refinements to a contextual account of what shapes regimes, particularly for those such as Peter John (1998: 57) who think 'institutions' are best understood as constraints on policy choices, rather than as a real alternative to interest-based or other accounts of public policy. However, several elements of regime content, and particularly the elusive element of structure, seemed to be as plausibly explicable by the inner working of the professional-bureaucratic policy communities involved as by contextual elements. As Chapter 7 showed, much of the detail of regime content was easier to understand when we stretched the notion of interest-group activity to include the politics of professional-technocratic interests in and around the state structure as well as business lobbies and cause groups. Indeed, the more we disaggregate regime content, the more we have to refer to the 'inner life' of the regulatory policy community.

Three examples of 'inner life' affecting regime content from our set are the extensive state monitoring activity for domestic radon in the UK, the secrecy of the UK sex offenders' register, and the extent of state activity on ambient benzene. As discussed in Chapter 5, the first involves a hazard that is capable of being detected at relatively low cost to individuals, meaning that the 'information cost' rationale for state testing seems weak on market-failure grounds. The second contrasts with arrangements in the USA, from which British policy-makers originally took the idea of compulsory registration of sex offenders, and has been maintained up to the time of writing against legal challenge, tabloid newspaper campaigns, and mass public protest. The third involved state activity over a specific risk that is little recognized by the public, was not a key campaigning issue for environmental cause groups, and was raised by business groups only incidentally during the lead-in-gasoline debate, as discussed earlier.

To explain the first observation we have to move away from considering interest groups outside the government structure, and focus on the activity of a compact international group of public-sector radiation professionals with a relatively common view of the seriousness of radon risks. The state testing programme that developed in the UK reflected the technocrats' agenda and their ability to persuade politicians that to do nothing, even in the face of public apathy over the risk, might be to court political blame in the future if radon victims found a way to hold government liable for sins of omission.

To explain the second observation—the secrecy of the sex offenders register—we also have to go beyond a view of interest groups as external to government. The development of a professional community concerned with paedophile risks seems to have been just as important as mass public opinion in creating pressure for a paedophile register and associated risk-management regimes for released offenders. But while substantial elements of media and public opinion, distrustful of the competence of the criminal-law authorities to 'manage' paedophile risks behind a veil of secrecy, pulled in the direction of an open register, other institutional forces worked against that outcome. In contrast to the position in the 'legalistic' USA, British and European jurists interpreted the international, and specifically European, human rights legal framework to convey a right of privacy to ex-offenders who had served their sentence. Politicians of all stripes seem to have avoided taking up a strongly 'populist' position, side-stepping responsibility by deferring to the professionals in the classic blame-avoiding manner. Police and probation service professionals, for their part, seem to have strongly favoured a secret register. This combination of institutional and 'inner' forces shaped the content of the regime, and the professional community even managed to regroup and maintain the secrecy of the register in the face of substantial public challenge in the summer of 2000 after a child-murder tragedy that commanded sustained public and media attention.

To explain the third observation—the extent of state activity over ambient benzene—we also need to refer to the 'inner life' of the regulatory technocrats within the state apparatus. Air pollution in general was a major focus of public concern, but it was effectively left up to the regulators to determine what to count as priority pollutants to tackle. Their choice of benzene partly reflected a scientific concern with a genotoxic carcinogen—though the setting of the target involved keen debate within government, as noted in Chapter 7—but also reflected a desire to influence the shape of the EU regime for ambient benzene by setting up air pollution controls in the UK first.

Such observations about the 'inner life' of regulatory institutions and the role 'risk bureaucracies', regulatory scientists, and public policy professionals can play in shaping regulatory regime content would not surprise those rational-choice analysts who see institutional structures as shaped by the self-interest of key state officials (such as Niskanen 1971 or Dunleavy 1991), students of policy networks (such as Rhodes and Marsh 1992) or those in the Weberian tradition (such as Page 1992) who stress the power of bureaucrats and technocrats to shape public policy. In the absence of a single dominant private business interest, which applied to several of the regimes we investigated, the preferences of risk bureaucracies may be crucial in fashioning the shape of regulation, as those who advance the idea of 'risk society' might expect. Many of the technocrats we interviewed portrayed their worlds as domains seldom entered by politicians, either from lack of interest or for blame-avoidance reasons. Tragedies or upsurges of public and media interest may provide the 'policy windows' of politician attention in which the professionals roll out new approaches or regulatory developments, as those who follow John Kingdon's (1984) approach to understanding public policy or the simpler 'tombstone theory' of risk regulation would expect. When we look inside risk regulation regimes, however, we may often find professionals 'incubating' those approaches and developments before the window opened.

Even the UK's Dangerous Dogs Act of 1991, often interpreted as a 'knee-jerk' political response to a spate of highly-publicized dog attacks,[6] could in part be understood in this way (see Hood, Baldwin, and Rothstein 2000). It reflected a view by the policy professionals that the then existing nineteenth-century legislative framework had become outdated and unworkable, and that a criminal-law approach needed to be taken for the control of dogs. We shall return to the issue of policy incubation inside professional regulatory communities in Chapter 10.

Such observations fit with well-established accounts of the policy process in political science and show the value of paying close attention to the 'inner lives' of regulatory regimes. Another reason why those 'inner lives' need to be understood, however, is that the preferences of those technocrats and policy insiders were relatively diverse. That diversity in preferences is less easy to explain from conventional accounts of the policy process, and it relates to the cultural rather than 'rule' dimension of institutions, as we showed in Chapter 7. It directs attention to the way professional cultures or conventions evolve and the way policy domains are settled or captured by particular 'tribes' over time.

Our analysis suggests that, even at a relatively high level of aggregation of elements of regime content, some observations are not readily explicable by the three elements of regime context considered in this part of the book and need to be explained in terms of the regimes' 'inner lives'. Even for those observations that are compatible with the contextual explanations, an 'inner life' account offers an alternative or complementary way of understanding the patterns. Explaining structure by reference to 'inner life' elements may come close to tautology, but the more we move down the scale of disaggregation of regime content that was discussed in Chapter 2, the more we need to refer to 'inner life' explanations.

4. Conclusions

This chapter has discussed how far regime content can be explained by the three elements of regime context that were introduced earlier under the headings

---

[6] By a Conservative Home Secretary, Kenneth Baker, facing criticism from his party over a major prison riot, at Manchester Strangeways prison, in the summer of 1991.

'type of risk', 'public attitudes', and 'organized interests'. As the discussion has shown, prediction of variety in regime content is an inexact science. While we share the bias of those who favour parsimony in analysis, with as few 'moving parts' as possible, a few observations of regime content were out of line with what would be predicted from the trio of contextual elements. In principle we could increase the predictive power of the trio by combining them, for instance, by taking the interest-driven approach as the first predictor and then turning to market-failure and opinion-responsive accounts as alternative predictors; but there would still be some surprises over placings.

To explain those surprises we need to add in 'inner-life' elements of regulatory regimes as discussed in the previous section and at the end of Chapter 7. Some anomalies disappear when we allow for the force of historical or institutional inertia. Others disappear when we go beyond the contextual elements to look into the inner institutional life of regulatory regimes, notably the organizational micro-politics and the culture and activity of risk bureaucrats or technocrats.

Such an analysis suggests that contextual and non-contextual explanations of what shapes regulatory regimes can offer complementary rather than rival accounts. Even the three orthodox contextual shapers considered in the last three chapters frequently overlapped, with only a few critical cases where they pointed in different directions. But this analysis can help us to identify the elements of regime content that can be dominated by technocrats and professionals—a central theme of the 'risk society' literature—and those that cannot. It can help to make 'risk society' ideas more precise by putting them in a conventional policy analysis framework and identifying the contextual conditions in which 'risk society' characteristics are most likely to be found, as against those involving conventional forms of interest-group activity and capitalist democracy. We began this book by arguing that 'risk society' was the wrong place to start in seeking to account for variety in risk regulation regimes, but a dimensional analysis linking regime context to regime content can help us to put 'risk society' in its place using fairly conventional analytic tools.

As this chapter has shown, there are some parts of regime content in risk regulation that a first-order contextual analysis does not seem to be able to reach, and some aspects of regime content, particularly over organization and structure, that seem to stem from the inner life of regulatory organizations. In Part III of the book, we delve deeper into this aspect of regulation. We put the spotlight on the workings of institutional and professional-bureaucratic forces, and turn from a comparative analysis of the relatively enduring aspects of regulatory regimes to explore their dynamics and the policy issues arising from our analysis. How do risk regulation regimes respond to pressures for change, particularly in the form of demands for greater transparency and openness on the part of public and private organizations? And what, if anything, are the policy implications of a dimensional approach to risk regulation?

III

Exploring the Dynamics of Risk Regulation Regimes

9

Regime Development Under Pressure: Staged Retreats and Lateral Mutations

'Using less paper is one of the ways we show our support for the environment'—New World Telephone spokesman on why the company uses 0.63mm type for contract terms.

Quotes of the Week, *South China Sunday Morning Post* (9 January 2000)

1. Transparency as a Test of Institutional Adaptation in Risk Regulation

This chapter turns away from considering regulation 'regimes' as relatively enduring phenomena—the focus of the earlier parts of this book—to put the spotlight on regime change. How do institutions engaged in risk regulation and management respond to pressures for change? To what extent, or in what conditions, do they seek to contain such pressures, alter what they do, or just roll with the punch?

There are plenty of bar-room anecdotes about the way organizations respond to changes in their environment, as the epigraph to this chapter reminds us. Scholars of organization and management have tried to go beyond the anecdotes to identify what organizational characteristics are linked to the degree of change in the environment, mainly drawing on studies of business firms (Lawrence and Lorsch 1967; Mintzberg 1983). A limited number of behavioural studies have also been conducted into the response of public-sector organizations to changes in their environment, such as cutbacks, managerial changes, or broader changes in state structure. This chapter belongs in the latter tradition, and aims to use our analysis of risk regulation regimes to explore some conventional accounts of how organizations respond to pressures for change. It focuses particularly on pressures for change in the direction of greater openness or transparency. We place the emphasis on this feature of change for two reasons. One is that greater transparency is a central and recurring recipe for 'better regulation', both in the regulation of risk and for regulation more generally.[1] Such pressures come from egalitarians distrustful of backdoor machinations in big public and private organizations and from courts and lawyers for whom transparency is a key entailment of the rule of law (see Fuller 1964). They also come from various kinds of 'rationalist' reformers seeking to expose hidden subsidies and other cosy and unexamined institutional processes (see Hood 2001). Openness and transparency come as close as any other contemporary doctrine to being an all-purpose remedy for misgovernment, because of its claimed ability to reduce corruption and transaction costs, increase legitimacy and legality, and improve policy quality through enhanced intelligence and learning.

The other reason for focusing on pressures for change in the direction of greater transparency is that such change poses a particularly interesting test for institutional adaptation. The great sociologist Max Weber wrote of bureaucracies as neutral machines, able to be reprogrammed for different tasks (Gerth and Mills 1948: 229), and certainly that is the official ideology of bureaucracies in democratic states. But Weber also wrote that secrecy and control of information was central to the power-position of bureaucracies (Gerth and Mills 1948: 233–5; Page 1992: 9), contributing to his claim that 'Under normal conditions, the power position of a fully developed bureaucracy is always overtowering' (Gerth and Mills 1948: 232). Accordingly, pressure for greater transparency constitutes a—arguably *the*—key test for institutional neutrality or distortion in risk regulation.

To frame such a test, we begin this chapter with three hypotheses about how institutions respond to pressures for increased transparency. We then put the hypotheses to the proof by examining how well they describe the dynamics of seven of the risk regulation regimes we observed. On the basis of those observations we advance a modified system-environment interpretation of processes of lateral mutation.

2. Three Hypotheses about Institutional Responses to Pressures for Increased Transparency

One theme running through much institutional analysis is a vision of human organizations as relatively closed systems that adapt selectively to environmental disturbance. By 'selective adaptation' is meant that institutions have

---

[1] For instance, in the recipe for 'better regulation' produced by the UK Government's Better Regulation Task Force (Better Regulation Task Force 1998) and the 'populist' recipe for better risk regulation advanced by Shrader-Frechette (1991). It is a theme that goes back at least to Bentham's (1843) maxim that 'secrecy, being an instrument of conspiracy, ought never to be a system of regular government'.

their own purposes and imperatives, and adopt strategies for survival that seek to reconcile those purposes and imperatives with environmental conditions or external demands. Institutions are thus seen as filters or distorting lenses in their dealings with the outside world. An example is the 'bureaucratic paradox or irony' noted by Clay and Schaffer (1984: 10), in which organizations focus on what is readily doable whether or not it contributes to some larger purpose (see also Schaffer and Lamb 1981). Numerous observers of bureaucracy have commented on the phenomenon of bureaucratic inertia (see Rourke 1976: 29) and Richard Hall (1972: 343) argues: 'Organizations operate conservatively regardless of whether they are viewed as radical or reactionary by the general population'. In similar vein is the idea of 'autopoiesis' advanced by Teubner (1987) and others, which focuses on the limits of direct external control of complex systems of discourse programmed towards 'self-reproduction'. The theme of institutional distortion in law and policy is sometimes linked with biological ideas about evolutionary strategy, but similar conclusions can be reached from independent propositions about individual and social behaviour.

As suggested in the previous section, demands for increased openness in risk regulation seems to offer an especially good test for such views of institutions. There are good reasons to expect institutional filtering or distortion in response to pressures for greater transparency, participation, and accountability, because such changes are often likely to be seen as increasing the threat of blame and liability for failures or to make work more stressful and conflict-laden. Indeed, one of the key reasons why institutions limit openness in risk regulation in the first place is to limit or deflect blame or liability, in line with standard advice from lawyers and insurers to 'never admit fault'. So there are strong grounds from an institutional perspective for expecting a filtering response to demands for increased openness in risk regulation, whether in the form of privacy protection (Brin 1998), official secrecy, or commercial confidentiality. So if institutional filtering or distortion processes of the kind mentioned above can be expected to be observable anywhere, pressures for increased openness in risk regulation should bring those processes out. Many different detailed hypotheses could be explored about institutional responses to demands for increased openness in risk regulation, but we begin here with three selected hypotheses.

The first is a hypothesis that institutions neutrally comply with external demands for increased openness without perceptible filtration or distortion. This hypothesis posits that institutions react to pressures for greater transparency by simple compliance with such pressures to the limit of their organizational ability. Full compliance can be seen as a null hypothesis because it goes against the central tenet of institutionalist analysis, as noted earlier, that institutions have their own inbuilt agendas and imperatives that cause them to act as filters rather than echoes or relays of environmental demands.

At the opposite extreme is a hypothesis of strong institutional 'self-closure'. As noted earlier, the most extreme form of this way of looking at institutions is the idea of 'autopoiesis', that is, the idea of institutions as bounded systems that exhibit tendencies towards self-closure that are so strong that it is impossible to exert direct control over them from the outside. One school of thought about complex systems of law and organization sees such systems as tending to be 'autopoietic' because they embody distinct patterns of 'discourse' that requires laborious translation in dealings with the world outside those systems (see Brans and Rossbach 1997: 432ff). The strongest conditions for autopoiesis seem likely to apply in recondite inward-looking professional discourse communities, such as law, medicine, or natural science. Accordingly, an 'autopoiesis' hypothesis holds that institutions will tend to respond to outside pressures for greater openness in ways that repro-duce their basic modes of operation with minimal disturbance. To the extent that organizations or professional communities have autopoietic tendencies, compliance with external demands for change can be expected to be prob-lematic and full of unexpected side-effects.

A third hypothesis, coming somewhere between the hypothesis of neutral compliance and the autopoietic dynamic-conservatism hypothesis, is what we call a 'staged retreat' hypothesis. This idea posits that institutions respond to pressures for environmental change in a series of phases or steps that amount to a staged rearguard action away from some initially-preferred posi-tion. The idea is encapsulated in numerous 'style-phase models' identifying processes of staged-retreat from an initial inertia preference.[2] In this vein, it is common to distinguish, following Levy (1986: 8–9), between 'first-order' and 'second-order' responses by organizations to environmental disturbance. This distinction comes originally from biology and cybernetics, differentiating changes that have elements of 'dynamic conservatism' from those that alter the genetic code in some fundamental and permanent way. As applied to human organizations, first-order responses have been variously defined, but broadly involve shifts in managerial arrangements and other organizational systems that leave core value systems or deeper structures unchanged. Second-order responses involve changes in those value systems.

Richard Laughlin and Jane Broadbent (1995; see also Laughlin 1991) have further differentiated first-order and second-order institutional responses to environmental disturbance.[3] They divide first-order responses into 'rebuttal'—attempts to resist the disturbance and maintain the organization relatively

[2] For instance, style-phase models have been used to depict bureaucratic responses to continued pressures for cutbacks (Beck Jørgensen 1985; 1987) or state responses to continued demands for welfare interventions (Joo 1999).

[3] Laughlin (1991) views organizations as a combination of sub-systems, design archetypes, and interpretive schemes, and sees first-order responses as affecting only sub-systems and the more tangible aspects of design archetypes, while second-order changes affect interpretive schemes and associated elements of design archetypes.

unchanged—and 'reorientation'—dynamic-conservatism involving organizations changing in ways designed to protect their core values. Similarly, second-order responses involving changes in core values are divided into 'colonization' and 'evolution'. In 'colonization', external pressures force change in an organization's 'design archetype' which in turn changes the organization's 'interpretive scheme' towards new core values. In 'evolution', organizations move to new 'interpretive schemes' in a way that 'is chosen and accepted by all the organizational participants freely and without coercion' (Laughlin 1991: 219). That is, evolution comes when all stakeholders have absorbed new values.

Laughlin is careful not to present these types in style-phase terms; although he argues that the first three types are 'progressive' in some sense (Laughlin 1991: 200), he sees 'evolution' as likely to be reached by a social pathway different from the others and argues that attempts to provoke 'colonization' change in organizations by progressive application of external financial pressure may not succeed. However, for the purpose of framing a third hypothesis, we modify Laughlin's approach by representing the four types of change as progressive forms of 'staged retreat', going from the least to the most radical kind of adaptation as external pressure for change continues. The expectation is that organizations shift from first-order to second-order responses on some approximation of the pattern depicted in Fig. 9.1 if they are exposed to continuing outside pressure for increasing openness. This hypothesis is a mixture of the null hypothesis and the autopoietic hypothesis in that it leads us to expect first-stage responses to new environmental demands that involve some attempts at autopoiesis, to be followed later by responses that are closer to the null hypothesis.

3. Observed Changes in Openness in Risk Regulation Regimes

We can define increasing openness as involving some or all of three types of change across the central components:

(1) greater transparency in procedures for information-gathering, standard-setting, and behaviour-modification;
(2) wider public participation in some or all of theses components of risk regulation regimes; and
(3) heightened accountability across these components in terms of increased obligations on the part of those responsible for regulating and managing risks to explain and justify their actions to others.

Over the past decade or so, strong pressures for increased openness have been experienced in the UK and elsewhere in some much-discussed domains

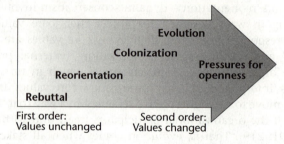

FIGURE 9.1: Institutional responses to environmental disturbance: Laughlin's four change types conceived as a progressive set of responses

of risk regulation, such as food safety, health care, and nuclear power. Indeed, some have claimed or implied that all risk regulation has been exposed to such pressures (see Health and Safety Executive 1998: 6; Royal Commission on Environmental Pollution 1998). But such accounts of pressures for openness in risk regulation may be over-generalized. Our study of risk regulation regimes led us to conclude that pressures for openness as defined above were far from universal in risk regulation. Readers will recall from Chapter 6 that general public interest and media salience were low and stable for several of our regimes, particularly radon.

Scoring overall regime openness is a far from exact science. But when we compared regime content in Table 9.1 for seven risk domains—the nine cases considered earlier less the two occupational-safety regimes—we drew four general conclusions.[4]

First, pressures for increasing openness were by no means observable everywhere. Regimes can vary widely both in the degree of openness they have displayed in the past and in the degree of change to which they have been exposed over recent decades. Second, regimes that began from a low level of openness were not necessarily exposed to strong catching-up pressures towards high openness. Our domestic radon case, discussed in earlier chapters, shows it is possible for there to be a low degree of movement from initially low openness (Leiss, Massey, and Walker 1998).

Third, the four regimes we identified as experiencing continuing pressures for increased openness all began from a position of high professional cohesion in the relevant policy communities, but observation of the changes suggested that regimes could move to greater openness in different ways and in response to different pressures. The four regimes that were subject to pressures for increased openness were the regulation of release of paedophile offenders from custody, the regulation of pesticide residues in food and drinking water, and

---

[4] We focused on information rules and conventions, participation or scrutiny rules, and the extent of de facto accountability by decision-makers to public scrutiny, as shown in Table 9.1.

TABLE 9.1. *Changes in openness and seven United Kingdom risk regulation regimes*
(a) Three cases with little general increase in pressures for openness over 20 years

Domain	Enduring features		Public, media and business pressure	Overall openness
	Information rules	Participation and scrutiny rules		
Radon in homes	*Reporting or collecting obligations*: No obligation on property owners to undergo or undertake tests; no obligation on government to assess radon levels, apart from a 1990 EC recommendation that Member States assess radon levels; UK govt. by convention has conducted a UK-wide survey of radon levels by area *Publication/disclosure obligations*: *Caveat emptor* rule on disclosure for property vendors; govt. by convention publishes radon levels by area but not house by house	*Consultation obligations*: By convention only with international policy community of radon experts and UK radiation professionals *Exposure of regulators to public accountability*: Limited, with responsibility located in an expert UK-wide quango relatively detached from government departments	*Public pressure*: None *Media pressure*: Minimal *Business Pressure*: Minimal	*Low* Low salience and 'expertized' but with official risk data base providing general information
Dangerous dogs	*Reporting or collecting obligations*: No general obligation to register dogs (except N. Ireland) after demise of dog licence in 1988 (except for four types specified in 1991); no obligation on citizens to report dog attacks and no international obligations or conventions for state authorities to collect or collate dog accident statistics (except N. Ireland) *Publication/disclosure obligations*: No general obligation for dogs to carry ID (by chips/collar tags etc.) except for four types specified under 1991 Act; and no obligation on regulators to publish or disclose any specific risk information	*Consultation obligations*: Ministers obliged to consult domestic dog experts but little international consultation *Exposure of regulators to public accountability*: Parliamentary scrutiny/questions to ministers and accountability through local councillors and police	*Public pressure*: Broad popular concern about dangerous dogs and activism by dog owners *Media pressure*: Periodically high at national and local level *Business Pressure*: None	*Medium* Occasional high salience but no official risk database

TABLE 9.1. (continued)
(a) Three cases with little general increase in pressures for openness over 20 years

Domain	Enduring features			Overall openness
	Information rules	Participation and scrutiny rules	Public, media and business pressure	
Road accident risks	*Reporting or collecting obligations:* Statutory obligation to report all accidents involving vehicles causing human injury and since 1974 for local authorities (LAs) to assess and reduce road risks. Obligation on vehicle manufacturers to undergo tests for passenger and general safety, and by convention a new EU programme is assessing safety performance of cars	*Consultation obligations:* LAs obliged to consult local residents for traffic management schemes requiring Road Traffic Orders. Safety standard setting for vehicles expertized	*Public pressure:* Mainly localized but facilitated by green groups etc.	*Medium to high* Mainly localized salience and largely 'expertized' but with official 'expertized' but with official risk data base providing general information, and slowly increasing information on car safety performance
			Media pressure: Low at national level except for occasional 'big news tragedy' but occasionally high at local level	
	Publication/disclosure obligations: By convention national government publishes aggregated road accident data and value of life figures for local road safety engineering, and by convention and discretion LAs and police disclose local road accident statistics (subject to Data Protection Act). Results of detailed tests of vehicle safety subject to commercial confidentiality but by convention EU publishes results of car safety performance programme	*Exposure of regulators to public accountability:* Mainly through local councillors for local road safety engineering but limited by professionalized and 'protocolized' nature of road traffic engineering	*Business pressure:* Low at local level on road safety engineering but high at national policy level on road and vehicle safety	

TABLE 9.1. (Continued)
(b) Four cases subject to increasing pressures for openness over 20 years

Domain	Status quo features				Post-status quo features			
	Information rules	Participation and scrutiny rules	Public, media and business pressure	Overall openness	Information rules	Participation and scrutiny rules	Public, media, and business pressure	Overall change
Ambient benzene	*Reporting or collecting obligations*: No legal obligation to collect information on ambient benzene until 1997 *Publication/disclosure obligations*: No legal obligation to disclose	*Consultation obligations*: By convention restricted to professionals *Exposure of regulators to public accountability*: No defined regulator responsibility apart from general ministerial responsibility	*Public pressure*: Minimal on benzene specifically but more on general air pollution *Media pressure*: As public *Business. Pressure*: Minimal until late 1980s	*Low*	*Reporting or collecting obligations*: Statutory obligations on LAs to assess and manage ambient air quality together with other quangos *Publication/disclosure obligations*: Statutory disclosure of ambient benzene levels under EU FOI rules and dissemination via CEEFAX and Internet	*Consultation obligations*: Ministers legally obliged to hold wide consultations on ambient air quality policy. EU obligations and consultation with Euro business and public interest groups by convention *Exposure of regulators to public accountability*: Overlapping LA, quango and cent. govt. responsibility	*Public pressure*: Persistent pressure *Media pressure*: Persistent interest *Business pressure*: Strong push for transparency in face of tight restrictions	*High to medium* Move to more transparent standards and info. on ambient air quality from a low base
Paedo-philes	*Reporting or collecting obligations*: No general duty on govt. to collect information on offenders and	*Consultation obligations*: No obligation to consult and little/no consultation by convention	*Public pressure*: Incident-specific until mid 1980s	*Low*	*Reporting or collecting obligations*: Police duty to keep record of released offenders and offenders' duty to report	*Consultation obligations*: Convention of consultation and exchange of information across public agencies, extending to other	*Public pressure*: Appears to move from incident-specific to more generalized concern	*Low* Creation of official database consulta- tion across govt. but limited or

TABLE 9.1.b (Continued)

Domain	Status quo features				Post-status quo features			Overall change
	Information rules	Participation and scrutiny rules	Public, media and business pressure	Overall openness	Information rules	Participation and scrutiny rules	Public, media, and business pressure	
	no general duty on offenders to report *Publication/disclosure obligations:* No duty or convention to disclose	*Exposure of regulators to public accountability:* Orthodox ministerial and police accountability	*Media pressure:* As public *Business pressure:* None		organizations on discretionary basis *Publication/disclosure obligations:* No change	*Exposure of regulators to public accountability:* No change	*Media pressure:* Significantly growing *Business etc. pressure:* Increasing concern of organizations with duties to children	no general disclosure
Pesticide residues in food and drinking water	*Reporting or collecting obligations:* General duty on food and drinking water suppliers to test for fitness for human consumption *Publication/disclosure obligations:* None until late 1980s for both water and food suppliers	*Consultation obligations:* No general consultation outside professional community *Exposure of regulators to public accountability:* Mix of LAs and cent. govt for food; minimal for water providers	*Public pressure:* Long-term growth of concern since 1960s *Media etc. pressure:* As public *Business pressure:* Low	Low	*Reporting or collecting obligations:* Obligation on food and drinking water suppliers to test *Publication/disclosure obligations:* Water regulators obliged to publish residue data. Food regulators introducing 'name and shame' policy by convention	*Consultation obligations:* By convention more general consultation beyond a narrow professional group (except for approvals) *Exposure of regulators to public accountability:* No change for food; specific regulators for water since 1988	*Public pressure:* High but some evidence of peaking/declining general concern *Media etc pressure:* As above *Business pressure:* Increasing pressure on decision-makers	*Medium* Starting from low base, more transparency on water and to a lesser extent on food

the arrangements for control of ambient benzene. These regimes have been discussed in earlier chapters, so we will comment only briefly on their dynamics in response to pressures for transparency here.

Fourth, pressures for openness may vary across different control components within and across regimes. We will see below that, in some risk regulation regimes, the call was for transparency over information-gathering activities, while in other regimes demands centred on openness and access over standard-setting or enforcement activities. Nor can it be assumed that pressures and responses must centre on the same control components.

Paedophile Release Risks

As noted earlier, professional and public concern about the risks of paedophiles at large in the community grew in the 1990s in the UK, as in many other countries. Until then, the state had no duty to collect systematic information on the whereabouts and risk posed by ex-offenders in the community, and the information that did exist was limited and ad hoc, rarely shared among the relevant state organizations and never relayed to the general public. As was also noted earlier, the UK government's response to the increased public salience of paedophile risks was to be seen mainly in the information-gathering component of the regime. The government introduced a statutory requirement in 1997 that police record the names and addresses of certain types of sex offenders, thus creating a Sex Offenders Register. In contrast to the transparent arrangements adopted by some US States under the 1994 'Megan's Law' (Brin 1998: 19), the cultural bias of the professionals managing this register was heavily against public disclosure of information about ex-offenders, and the State authorities committed substantial resources to preventing leaks and defending a no-disclosure policy. They avoided the use of court-imposed restrictions on offenders that would reveal identity and fought off pressures for disclosure from courts,[5] tabloid newspapers, and public protests.[6]

The simple legal requirement that police compile the information for the register, however, potentially increased the 'blameability' of police, probation, and other welfare bureaucracies—notably, if re-offending by released paedophiles led to accusations of inept risk management by those organizations. Accordingly, three observable changes in institutional behaviour in managing the release of ex-offenders accompanied the introduction of the registration requirement.

[5] In a 1997 test case, a court upheld the non-disclosure policy, holding that disclosure should be only on a need-to-know basis (*R v. Chief Constable for the North Wales Police Area Authority et al.*, 10 July 1997).

[6] Their argument was that reducing the risk of child sexual abuse by publicly identifying paedophiles would increase the risk of vigilante activity and mitigate the effectiveness of paedophile risk management by sending offenders underground.

One blame-limiting strategy was the adoption of more collegial behaviour among the various bureaucracies involved in the management of risk from released offenders, to share blame and minimize the ability of organizations to blame one another after a tragedy for not passing on crucial information. This information sharing and lock-in approach was not confined to the core public bureaucracies involved. It also extended to 'third sector' voluntary organizations and even to MPs.[7] Second, and linked to the collegial information-sharing strategy, was the adoption by the paedophile bureaucracies of more formal written procedures or checklists for risk assessment and management of ex-offenders. The ostensible purpose of these procedures was to improve decision-making, particularly in allocating scarce resources. They also served the important purpose, as noted by many of our interviewees, of limiting blame, giving the paedophile bureaucracies a procedural excuse if registered offenders committed further offences.

A third change relating more to behaviour-modification was the classic NIMBY response, in the form of refusal by a few local authorities to take any responsibilities for resettling offenders in their communities, particularly in providing housing. In some other cases, a bias towards conservative risk assessment by police and probation officers, seeking to protect themselves to blame in the event of reoffence, meant a large number of released offenders were classed as 'high-risk'. The rising numbers of 'high-risk' offenders in turn led local authority and other housing organizations to become increasingly concerned about the potential blame they were incurring in assuming responsibility for housing such offenders.

Ambient Benzene

As we have seen earlier, ambient benzene has been known to be a genotoxic carcinogen for decades, but systematic monitoring of ambient benzene levels and the development of specific standards for ambient benzene developed in the UK only in the 1990s.[8] In contrast to the approach taken to the paedophile register, however, UK government began to post the results on CEEFAX and the Internet once that monitoring began. This response constituted high initial transparency over information gathering. This strategy followed the line of least resistance and was designed to avoid the need for bespoke responses to green lobby groups and others demanding data under

---

[7] UK central government adopted a policy of confidentially informing MPs of high-risk ex-offenders being released in their constituencies—a policy which may have unintentionally contributed to generating local 'resettlement refusal'.

[8] In 1997 the UK government set an 'objective' of not more than 5 ppb as an air quality standard, to take effect in 2004 (Statutory Instrument No. 928 2000); whether that 'objective' was a justiciable limit was highly ambiguous. In a parallel process the EU set a more stringent European objective of just over 1.5 ppb to be achieved by 2010, accompanied by mandatory monitoring by member states (see Commission of the European Communities 2000).

EU rules on freedom of access to environmental information (Statutory Instrument No. 3240 1992).

The UK's ambient benzene targets, involving as they did a new methodology and a controversial justification, provoked pressures for more transparency in decision-making over standards (EPAQS/DOE 1994; ILGRA 1997). That pressure came not from green lobbyists but from the petrochemical industry, fearful that its interests might be threatened by the new standards. The government department responsible responded to that pressure by making only marginal changes,[9] but two substantial institutional changes accompanied the advent of transparent monitoring and quantified standards for air quality. One was legislation laying responsibility on local authorities for assessing and reviewing air quality in their areas. This legislation could be interpreted as a strategy by central government to shift or share blame, though the division of responsibilities over roads between central and local government could create fertile opportunities for mutual blame avoidance. A second development concerned behaviour modification, involving the preparation of procedural defences against blame for failure to achieve objectives, at both local and central government level. That is, if local authorities failed to achieve the UK targets set to take effect in 2004, their defence would consist of putting together an action plan to reduce benzene levels as part of an Air Quality Management Zone.

Pesticide Residues in Food and Drinking Water

The introduction of statutory maximum residue levels (MRLs)[10] in the 1980s for pesticide residue levels in drinking water and food replaced less formal approaches to regulation. The regulatory response to these limits was different in the cases of water and food, though in both cases the first response was one of minimal transparency. For food, 'commercial confidentiality' arguments, not accepted for the commercial water companies after privatization of water supply in England and Wales in 1989, at first prevailed. That meant low transparency on information gathering: food retailers and suppliers were not obliged to disclose the results of their monitoring to consumers, and the same went for local authorities, the bodies responsible for enforcement of food-safety regulations. Some ad hoc monitoring of pesticide residue levels in food had been carried out by UK central government since 1957, and from 1988 this monitoring developed into a systematic testing programme with

[9] Arguing that full openness in the standard-setting process might inhibit candid discussion among expert advisers, the department proposed to publish non-verbatim minutes of meetings or not to attribute remarks to named individuals: 'Chatham House rules' (DETR 1998b: 11).

[10] The 1980 EC Drinking Water Directive (80/778/EEC) limited drinking water pesticide residue levels to 'precautionary' levels of 0.1 ppb. And from 1988, also in response to EC concerns with harmonization over product approval, the UK government began to introduce statutory MRLs in food for some pesticides (Pesticides (MRLs in Food) Regulations 1988).

aggregated results published annually, though anonymizing the retailers and suppliers of the food tested.

However, as pressure continued for more openness over pesticide residue regulation, government responded in two ways. First, it extended participation in debates over pesticides by establishing a Pesticides Forum in 1996, which included established and trusted consumer and green groups, and extended the 'stakeholders' to be consulted beyond a formerly narrow circle of expert insiders and agribusiness consultees. Second, as noted in Chapter 7, central government in 1997 took a modest step away from the previous aggregated and anonymized pattern of residue reporting to a limited 'name and shame' approach in which all retailers and suppliers of food tested were identified—a strategy combining information gathering and behaviour modification (MAFF *et al.* 1999). Perhaps predictably, this move led to greater scrutiny of the adequacy of the government's sampling and testing methodologies by supermarkets, putting more pressure on the transparency of those arrangements.

A more substantial shift towards transparency over information-gathering and behaviour-modification took place for drinking water, which perhaps offered the clearest case of a move from a 'first-order' to a 'second-order' response in the face of demands for more openness. The initial response to the imposition of the very low Maximum Admissible Concentration (MAC) for pesticides by the 1980 EC Directive was far from transparent in the UK or in other EC countries. Most EC states undertook no monitoring at all in response to the 1980 Directive and, even after monitoring became mandatory across the EU after the Directive was renegotiated in 1998, member states' response to EU requests for information tended to be one of delay. The UK government at first simply assumed the targets were being met, conveniently meaning no monitoring was needed; but that assumption was shown to be unfounded when research revealed substantial breaches of the MAC. The UK government responded by claiming those breaches represented no threat to health and campaigned, unsuccessfully, for the replacement of the MAC with generally less restrictive health-based limits for individual pesticides. Indeed, as we noted in Chapter 7, British ministers formally told water companies they need take no action over breaches of the EU standards as long as they stayed within health-based limits specified by the UK government.

However, a major step towards transparency in the UK regime—one seen across all three regime control components—came with the privatization of drinking water supply in England and Wales in 1989. This privatization conveniently removed direct public responsibility for water supply in those parts of the country, specifically England, where pesticide contamination of drinking water was a real issue. Part of the privatization settlement was an enhanced regulatory system that embodied freedom of information requirements over pesticide residue levels along with mandatory monitoring, such that breaches of the limit were openly established. Water companies had to put forward plans to deal with pesticide residues and from privatization to the time of writing water companies spent about £2 billion on compliance with EU drinking water rules, with the costs fully borne by captive consumers, following the 'swings and roundabouts' pattern discussed in Chapter 7.

4. Evaluating The Initial Hypotheses

Table 9.2 summarizes the institutional responses to pressures for increased openness within each of four regimes exposed to high pressures for increased openness. It seeks to identify those features of the institutional responses that are consistent with each of the three hypotheses we set out earlier. Our focus here rests on the general consistency of responses with the three hypotheses, not variations of approach across the three different components of regulatory control. The preceding section showed that responses may differ across control components: for instance, it is conceivable that an institution may fully comply with calls for open information gathering but act autopoietically in response to transparency demands over behaviour modification. Such issues, however, are put aside here and we look at regulators' overall responses to pressures for greater openness.

Contrary to the expectations of much institutional analysis, there were elements of institutional behaviour in each of the four high-pressure regimes that were consistent with the hypothesis of straightforward non-distorting responses. Those observations are summarized in Table 9.2. But this null hypothesis *alone* cannot account for all the observed responses; and several observations fitted the institutionalists' expectation of organizational distortion or filtration. For paedophile risks, for instance, a simple statutory requirement that the names and addresses of ex-offenders be recorded triggered major changes in institutional behaviour that were not mandated by the UK's 1997 Sex Offenders Act. For pesticide residues, different responses were observable in the cases of food and drinking water, with the more radical move to transparency in water seemingly shaped by the institutional history of water in the UK as it passed from public enterprise to privatization. For ambient benzene, the history was telescoped, but even there institutional responses to specific targets and monitoring included reshuffling of responsibilities and an 'inertia compliance' approach to targeting.

Some responses to demands for transparency also approximated to autopoiesis, as noted in Table 9.2. The professional communities involved in the management of paedophile release moved towards internal transparency in the sense of sharing information across professional and bureaucratic boundaries, but closed ranks to maintain their traditional approach of

TABLE 9.2. *Institutional responses to pressures for increased openness in four risk regulation regimes*

	Risk regulation regime domain		
	Release of paedophile ex-offenders	Control of pesticide residues in (1) food and (2) drinking water	Control of ambient benzene
Degree and type of pressure for openness	Strong public and media pressure for public disclosure of registration data but counter-pressures on privacy from human rights lobbies and institutions	General public and media concern for more information over pesticide residues; business concern with commercial confidentiality and regulatory requirements	General public and green lobby pressure for more information on general air pollution, rather than benzene in particular; strong business pressure for transparency over standards
	Features of regulator response		
Fitting null hypothesis	Substantial resources committed by police to collection of information on released ex-offenders	Post-1989 privatized water companies generally met EC limits, after public disclosure at first revealed breaches of those limits	Many local authorities adopted a 'get on with it' approach and central government took line of least resistance in publishing monitoring data under EU monitoring rules
Fitting autopoietic hypothesis	Alteration of procedures to keep public disclosure to the minimum	Pre-1989 state-owned water suppliers simply ignored EC limits, but on ministerial advice	Flexible approach to national targets and objectives: goalposts movable in the event of non-compliance
Fitting stage-response hypothesis	Little more than 'first-order' responses discernible: e.g. more resources committed to explaining policy of non-disclosure; alteration of procedures to limit possibility of blame shifting by 'hang-together' approaches; extension of checklist approach and written procedures to provide procedural defence against blame; NIMBY approach of refusal to house by some local authorities	Little more than 'first-order' responses discernible in food, with reorientation of regulators to 'control of control' but limited and delayed disclosure policy over non-compliance Apparently clearer case of progression to 'second-order' in drinking water, with eventual move to 'transparent compliance' approach after earlier delay and regulatory collusion over evasion	Little more than 'first-order' responses discernible, with developing 'inertia compliance' approach of delaying onset of targets until long-term techno-logical changes could be expected to deliver compliance without 'hard choices', linked with re-orientation of formal responsibility to make culpability ambiguous in the event of non-compliance

minimal disclosure to the public at large, in the face of multiple pressures for openness and legislation that could have been interpreted to mean greater transparency. Water regulators allowed the water companies to tax their way out of the problem presented by the combination of freedom of information and stringent EU residue limits. For ambient benzene, state authorities adopted an inertia compliance strategy, mixing a 20-year delay in effective monitoring with a flexible approach to standards that avoided the need for hard choices in the short term. Again, however, none of the risk domains seems to have been a pure case of autopoiesis, in the sense of 'self-reproduction' by the policy communities. Substantial changes in behaviour and the distribution of power among the players took place in the paedophile release regime. Water companies and regulators had to get used to a transparency system that would have been unthinkable 20 years before. The benzene regime, moreover, set the stage for an attempt by central government to shift at least part of the blame—or glory—over compliance to local authorities.

By a process of elimination we might conclude that the 'staged retreat' hypothesis fitted observed institutional behaviour in these four cases better than the other two hypotheses. But, as with Laughlin's (1991: 229) observation of responses to radical financial change by the Church of England, we found little evidence of a clear progression at regime level from a first stage in which institutional values remained unchanged to a later stage when those values had changed. The only fairly clear-cut case of such a progression seemed to be the drinking water regime, which moved from an initial pattern of see-no-evil denial and regulatory collusion over evasion in the public-enterprise era to a substantially transparent regime after privatization. Arguably something similar happened with publication of monitoring data for ambient benzene, but in that case before the onset of target standards. From the observed institutional responses, it seems hard to argue that there was a clear shift between first-order institutional responses to disturbances to a second-order when very different values come into play.

Indeed, as Chapter 7 suggested, the institutional value that seems most consistently to have underlain the various responses we observed was that of limiting blame and liability. Institutions facing demands for increased openness tended to engage in 'blame prevention re-engineering',[11] seeking to transfer or dissipate the increased blame or liability that increased transparency might bring. So a hypothesis that would best fit with these observations seems to be a mixture of the second and third hypotheses set out earlier. Accordingly, in the next section we briefly develop an analysis that combines elements of a very weak form of autopoiesis with a modified form of the first stage of the staged-retreat approach stressing lateral mutation.

[11] The acronym 'BPR' in the language of management science conventionally denotes 'business process re-engineering'. But BPR as 'blame prevention re-engineering' seems equally important in institutional behaviour.

5. Modifying the Initial Hypothesis: From Staged Retreat to Lateral Mutation

As suggested above, much, but not all, of the behaviour observed in the 'high-pressure' regimes was consistent with a hypothesis that institutions faced with demands for greater openness and transparency in risk regulation tend to adopt 'blame prevention re-engineering' responses. But what is the repertoire of such responses?

Readers will recall from Fig. 9.1 that Laughlin and his colleagues divided first-order institutional responses to environmental disturbance into 'rebuttal' and 'reorientation' strategies. Both types of response were readily observable in the high-pressure regimes. As we have seen, 'problem denial' and resistance to demands for transparent operation occurred in some form in all of them, often but not always at an early stage of policy development. 'Reorientation' also figured prominently in institutional behaviour, in modification of the regulatory structure element of regime content. Such reorientation in several cases took the form of increased complexity of regulatory structure, for instance in the redistribution of responsibilities, through modification of 'design archetypes', with the aim of reducing blame or liability.

However, rebuttal and reorientation are categories that have to be stretched to cover the whole range of observed institutional behaviour. Those cases showed at least six different types of institutional response to pressures for openness, of which rebuttal and reorientation in the simple sense of those terms are only two forms. Those responses, summarized in Table 9.3, overlapped and were not always distinct.

Of the four responses other than the two basic types mentioned above, 'delay' was observable in some form in two of the four cases. Delay in responding to requests for information has been observed as a common bureaucratic response to freedom of information regimes.[12] Perhaps the best example here is that when EU member states were asked by the European Commission to provide information on levels of pesticide residues in drinking water in the mid-1990s, responses involved substantial delay, in some cases involving several years.[13] Several variants on the theme could also be detected. They included 'planned obsolescence' in the reporting of violations in standards—pesticides in food—and delaying the onset of targets when monitoring information became available—ambient benzene.

A more problematic response from the viewpoint of Laughlin's schema is the well-known contemporary phenomenon of 'pre-buttal': attempts by organizations, public officeholders, and their spin-doctors to respond to

---

[12] For example, by Roberts (1998: 3–6) in his analysis of responses to Canadian FOI legislation.
[13] Partly in consequence, the EC summary report was itself published much later than was intended.

TABLE 9.3. *Six varieties of institutional response*

	Risk regulation regime domain		
Institutional response	Management of paedophile release	Pesticide residues in food and drinking water	Ambient benzene
Delay	Public disclosure of information about paedophiles only as final resort	Heavy emphasis in drinking water, e.g. delay by some EU Member States in reporting levels of pesticide residues in drinking water, and built-in delay in 'naming and shaming' policy over food	Heavy emphasis: 20-year delay in developing monitoring after discovery of benzene as a genotoxic pollutant; delay in EU Member States' response to Commission demands for information; delay of onset of targets until techno-logical change makes them likely to be achievable without pain
Simple rebuttal	Rejection and legal contestation of demands for greater public disclosure	Original denial of compliance problem over drinking water, followed by assertion that no health hazard involved in breach of EC precautionary limits; use of commercial confidentiality to limit public disclosure over food	
Organizational reorientation	Pooling information to share blame for management of risks of registered paedophiles	Privatization of water in England and Wales creating greater ambiguity over blame in failure to meet standards	Assignment of manage-ment responsibilities to local authorities, creating a structure of studied ambiguity through organizational complexifica-tion over blame for non-achievement of targets
Service abandonment	Some local authorities refusing to house registered paedophiles		
Protocolization	Checklist approach as a procedural defence against blame	'Due diligence' checklist defence developed in food after 1990 Food Safety Act, and in water	'Management plan' as potential defence against blame by local authorities not in compliance with targets
Prebuttal	Increasing effort of agencies to explain management of offenders in the com-munity to local residents without disclosing specific information	'Control of control' approach in food to limit regulator exposure to blame	

anticipated criticisms or demands for information before they materialize. The key feature of rebuttal is the manufacture of excuses in advance, such that attempts to blame an organization in the light of increased transparency will fail to hit their target. At the least this response involves an increase in organizational sophistication or capacity to cope with a goldfish-bowl existence: more flak-catchers and environmental scanners to get the organization's retaliation in first, as with the increased emphasis adopted by the police in dealing with the media over paedophiles after 1997.

If delay and some types of prebuttal could be considered a variant of 'rebuttal', at least two variants of 'reorientation', involving change in 'design archetypes', were also observable. One is the 'protocolization', or formalization of organizational operations, which is a standard bureaucratic approach to minimizing blame and liability problems (see Lawton and Parker 1998). Following transparent rules potentially provides 'due diligence' defences when an organization's risk management comes to be questioned, and produces a verifiable 'audit trail' for regulators to link to (see Power 1997). Protocolization in some form appeared in all of the change cases we observed and particularly in the paedophile regime, where it was central to the defensive blame-prevention re-engineering strategy of the public organizations concerned.

The other and perhaps most drastic 'reorientation' response to pressures for openness is the abandonment of some types of service or activity altogether. 'Service abandonment' is more commonly observable among regulatees, particularly small or marginal operators faced with increasing regulatory burdens, than among regulators or public authorities. Public agencies, however, can make similar responses, for instance when they stop issuing advice or information for fear of blame, legal liability, or other adverse risks.[14] Among our cases, the clearest case of service abandonment was observable in the management of paedophile risks. That was the refusal of some local authorities to resettle ex-offenders classified as 'high-risk' by the risk assessment process, putting pressure on central government to create a national back-stop facility for settling ex-offenders.

While we did not directly observe other responses in our cases, a seventh type of response can be observed elsewhere: that of outright 'data fabrication'. As we noted in Chapter 2, that response to pressures for transparent information is commonly reported or alleged, for instance by those responsible for providing test data for hazardous products (see *Independent* 1999; Millstone 1986: 99). Data fabrication seems likely to be a response to pressures for increased openness where there is little recognition that information is being demanded for valid or legitimate reasons—for example, professionals versus

---

[14] For example, the Malaysian government was reported to have stopped publication of air pollution levels in 1999 amid fears that media reports of smog levels might scare tourists away (*Guardian* 1999).

managers in educational or health-care organizations; where stakes are high; and where the cost of producing honest data is substantial. The latter feature obviously makes checking or enforcement costly too.

Expanding Laughlin's two first-order responses into the six to seven types of 'blame prevention re-engineering' response summarized in Table 9.3 suggests a 'lateral mutation' interpretation of many institutional responses to pressures for transparency rather than a staged response leading to 'evolution'. While rebuttal can often be expected to come at an early stage in the sequence of responses, the cases we examined suggested that rebuttal may precede, follow, or accompany a delay response, and rebuttal's 'cousin' prebuttal may come later in the sequence of responses. Service abandonment, protocolization, and reorganization of organizational boundaries, procedures, or responsibilities likewise need not take place in any particular order.

Second, as noted earlier, many of the institutional blame prevention reengineering responses discussed here are hard to fit into Laughlins' and others' distinction between first- and second-order responses. Many if not all of them could be responses to both types. For instance, 'prebuttal' might be a sophisticated first-order response, representing a high point of anticipation and manipulative capacity. But it could also be a second-order response by an organization that has so thoroughly absorbed openness values that its public-information base constitutes a way of nipping demands for release of data or decisions in the bud. Protocolization also seems ambiguous for any distinction between first-order and second-order responses, since it could either be a symptom of an organization that has adopted new values or simply function as an official screen against prying outsiders, offering a procedural defence that established routines have been followed. Service abandonment too might be an extreme form of first-order response—perhaps the only way to keep underlying values unchanged—or it could be the ultimate expression of change in values.

A modified 'lateral mutation' hypothesis, summarized in Fig. 9.2, can accordingly fit the observations here. Such a hypothesis is that institutional blame-prevention re-engineering responses to demands for increased openness and transparency in risk regulation may take any of the seven forms we have discussed above—others might well be revealed by other cases—but downplays 'second-order' responses. Expressed pictorially, this hypothesis looks less like the ladder or set of stages which we depicted in Fig. 9.1 than a 'Catherine wheel': a type of rotating firework. It conceives of a 'problem space', constituted by demands for increased openness and accountability over risk management, to which institutions can respond in any of the ways discussed above. If those responses relieve the 'openness pressure', the system moves out of the 'problem space'. But if the response fails to relieve the pressure, the system can be expected to return to the 'problem space' for another iteration. There is no automatic sequence of response and no necessary

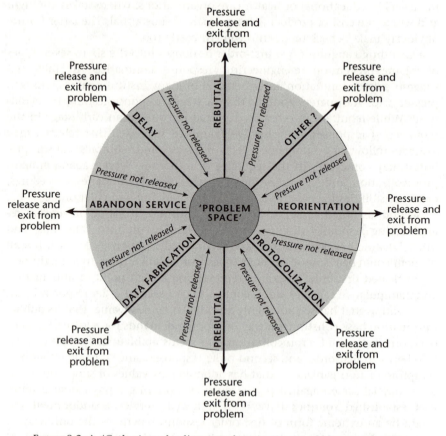

FIGURE 9.2: A 'Catherine wheel' approach to institutional blame prevention re-engineering

'ladder' process. And apart from simple rebuttal—but not 'prebuttal'—each of the organizational responses depicted in Fig. 9.2 could be linked with both value change and value stasis.

6. Conclusion

The analysis in this chapter has been based on only a few cases, so conclusions must be tentative. We can, nevertheless, draw seven main conclusions. First, not all risk domains are exposed equally, or at all, to long-term pressures for greater transparency and openness. Only some of the cases we examined fell into that category. Second, institutional filtering or distortion processes were readily be detectable in the four high-pressure regimes. The null hypothesis, of full, undistorted compliance with demands for openness, was compatible with only a minority of observations. Third, much of what was observed in the four high-pressure regimes we studied was compatible with a lateral-mutation process, portrayed in Fig. 9.2, in which institutional responses were dominated by blame prevention re-engineering considerations, and a varied repertoire of blame prevention re-engineering responses was available. We have argued in earlier chapters that society-wide generalizations about risk regulation have little power to explain why risk regulation regimes differ from one another. The same point seems to apply to the analysis of regulatory dynamics. Those dynamics appear to be variable, and to predict or explain them in detail we need to pay close attention to differences in historical context and the way institutional filters work.

Fourth, not all control components within individual regimes are exposed equally to pressures for openness; demands may target information-gathering, standard-setting, or behaviour-modification differentially or in varying combinations. Similarly, institutional responses relating to different control components may vary and not necessarily correspond to the pressures exerted from outside; for example, calls for openness on standards may be met with greater transparency on information-gathering. It may be that responses relating to one control component are not independent of, but are linked to, responses in other components. In other words, institutions may react to transparency pressures by offering 'packages' of procedural reform involving varying concessions, or resistance, to transparency across different control components.

A fifth conclusion, related to the fourth, is that what happens in relation to transparency and openness at the regime level of risk regulation can be different from what happens at the level of individual organizations. For example, in some risk domains, such as the regulation of pesticide levels in food, numerous organizations may move to higher levels of openness, but the regime as a whole remains only partially open, because a key group of players whose information is needed to complete the loop in some way stay at the level of first-state responses. Alternatively, even if the various regulator organizations within a risk regulation regime respond to pressures for openness by organizational complexification, as in sub-contracting or decoupling of risk regulation regimes, the upshot may be a regime that is even harder for ordinary consumers, workers, or citizens to understand, hence substantively more opaque even if each component organization is procedurally more open.

Sixth, in some domains all that is needed for the regime as a whole to move to greater transparency and openness is for one powerful organizational player to change its position, as happened with the change in the UK government's position over compliance with the EU Drinking Water Directive when drinking water supply was privatized in England and Wales.

A final conclusion is that strategies intended to avoid blame will not necessarily achieve that effect in practice—which is why Fig. 9.2 incorporates itera-
tive search—and may still produce effects incorporating some of the policy
consequences conventionally associated with increased openness, as noted at
the outset. For example, even if the police response to the UK's 1997 Sex
Offenders Act was dominated by blame prevention re-engineering considerations of locking all the other public-sector players into collective deliberation,
the effect of that strategy was nevertheless to enhance intelligence and shared
information across the regime. Similarly, even if blame-shifting was a key
factor in the UK central government's response of assigning responsibility to
local authorities for ambient benzene in the face of openness pressures, those
authorities nevertheless had to compile explicit and locally oriented plans
against a background of published benzene monitoring data. While responses
to pressures for increased openness dominated by blame prevention re-engineering may in some conditions detract from policy effectiveness through the
side-effects they produce—for instance, in service abandonment or goal-
displacement through protocolization, one of the classic sources of bureaucratic dysfunction identified by Merton *et al.* (1952)—they can also in some
conditions contribute to greater policy capacity and intelligence.

We can accordingly add an 'institutional-distortion' element to the well-
known debate about applying the 'precautionary principle' or a default
assumption of no harm in risk policy. Adding the institutional element to the
precautionary principle debate would be to suggest that it is dangerous for
those seeking to change the informational architecture of risk regulation
regimes to base their interventions on the 'null hypothesis' assumption of no
filtering or distortion. Rather, they would be well advised to follow a precautionary principle in their anticipation of institutional responses. Chapter 10
looks at the overall policy implications of our analysis of risk regulation
regimes.

10

The Regime Perspective in Risk Regulation: Implications for Policy and Institutional Design

> Politicians can never free themselves from the hope that better information or improved administrative machinery can prevent the policy dilemmas which they so much dislike from emerging.
>
> Brittan (1964: 251)

1. Reprise

Comparing risk regulation regimes in different policy domains enables us to draw some conclusions about how such regulation works and reflect on the implications for regulatory theory, policy, and institutional design. Readers will by now be familiar with our 'discoveries', but we begin this chapter by briefly rehearsing them. Those empirical findings can be summarized under three main headings: the ways in which risk regulation regimes differ from one another; what explains those differences; and how regimes change.

First, although 'risk society' literature draws attention to general features held to make today's society different from those of the past in the way it conceives and handles risk—as noted in Chapter 1—we have instead sought to spotlight variety in the way different risks are regulated. Margaret Thatcher once famously declared, 'There is no such thing as society . . .' (Cohen and Cohen 1993: 367–8) and in a similar vein we came close to the conclusion that there is no such thing as *risk* society, only different risk regulation regimes. The analytic method developed in Part I of this book can be used to show that risk regulation regimes vary substantially across policy domains in a way that the generalist tone of risk society-type analysis obscures and cannot explain. Acceptable risk levels varied by orders of magnitude among different policy domains, and the evidence on which standards of acceptable risk were based varied widely in rigour and style. Official information gathering varied from non-existent or minimal activity to the sponsorship of careful willingness-to-pay surveys and imposition of statutory obligations to notify or register. Behaviour modification or enforcement activity ranged from half-hearted efforts at consciousness-raising to criminalization of some types of behaviour. Observers in other countries (such as Breyer 1993) have also noted that risk regulation varies sharply across policy domains in terms of the risk tolerance built into standards and the administrative effort and public spending devoted to dealing with different risks.

Second, although the literature on 'risk society' claims to identify a number of epoch-making changes that render risk in today's society different from previous ones (Beck 1992: 22ff), we can explain some key differences in the ways risks are regulated by three fairly conventional shaping factors, discussed in Chapters 4–8, operating singly and in combination. We found that much of the variety of *regime content*, particularly the size of regulatory effort, could be adequately explained by features of *regime context* that are well-known in the analysis of public policy. It will be recalled from Chapters 5, 6, and 7 that these shaping factors were the technical problems posed by different sorts of risk to market or tort-law processes, the force of public preferences and attitudes, and the pressure exerted by interest groups. At the very least, this analysis enabled us to explore 'risk society' from a more conventional—and falsifiable—policy-analytic standpoint. The observed characteristics of risk regulation regimes that were not readily explicable by the conventional trio of policy shapers seemed to be explained by variations in bureaucratic or technocratic culture linked to the forces of historical institutionalism—the way the point of departure shapes subsequent development.

Third, the risk regulation regimes we observed changed over time, but again—and also contrary to the tenor of some of the 'risk society' literature—the institutional dynamics seemed to be variable. Some of the differences related mainly to the pace of change, with some regimes more hare-like and others more tortoise-like in the speed of transformation. Some regimes, more like the sleeping hare than the plodding tortoise in Aesop's fable, did not seem to be changing at all. Nor did the various runners always seem to be headed for the same destination, even at different speeds. Chapter 9 showed that pressures for greater transparency were far from uniform across policy domains. In several cases there was low pressure or little change, or both. In others pressure for change did seem to be building up over time, while in still others there was a cyclical 'issue-attention-cycle' pattern in public and regulator attention to the risk.

Each of these conclusions raises questions for further investigation. We do not claim to have developed the risk regimes analysis beyond first principles and the process undeniably involves difficult judgements. We need more refined ways of mapping differences in regimes and tracing institutional dynamics. The cases examined in this book are intended to take the comparative study of risk regulation beyond the stage of anecdotes or commercial travellers' tales. But they are only a starting point. Only examination of many more cases could help to identify more clearly the relative force of different shaping factors. Moreover, several paradoxes or surprising findings merit more investigation. One of those paradoxes is the limited degree to which a quasi-functional market-failure approach can explain policy stances in what is said to be an age of economic rationalism. Another is the weakness or indeterminacy of an 'opinion-responsive government' approach in explaining policy in what is said to be an age of focus groups and poll-shaped public policy. As we showed in Chapter 6, 'selective attention' by government and regulators to evidence about public preferences and attitudes could take a number of forms.

Such findings have at least two implications for regulatory theory. First, explanations of regulatory evolution or development may vary in their force or relevance across different components and elements of regimes. For instance, we noted in Chapter 7 that the various parts of a regime can be shaped by different organized interests. So causal accounts of what shapes regulation may need to be more precisely targeted towards the different components of regulation, and no single factor, like 'capture' or 'tombstone' effects, should be expected to explain everything. We may need multi-causal theories directed at different components of regulatory regimes or at the various 'spaces' that regimes embody. Second, a key challenge for regulatory theory is to account for the linkages among the different components of regimes. How can we explain the relationship or lack of it among the different elements of regime content and context or among the different components of control? In what ways, for instance, is the behaviour-modification dimension of regulation shaped by standard-setting and information-gathering strategies and practices? Such questions have hardly been asked in the analysis of risk regulation to date, let alone answered.

The main aim of this final chapter, however, is to move away from the analytic-descriptive focus of earlier chapters in this book and briefly to draw some conclusions from our study that relate to issues of policy and institutional design. We have three interrelated sets of conclusions, and devote a section to each of them. One concerns how coherently the various components of regulatory control—information-gathering, standard-setting, and behaviour-modification or enforcement—need to be combined into overall regimes. A second has to do with the implications of institutional blame-avoidance imperatives for broader regulatory outcomes. The third conclusion concerns the particular challenges posed by risk regulation for the development of well-founded principles of regulatory assessment.

2. Regulatory Regimes and Regulatory Coherence

As earlier chapters have shown, limited institutional or system coherence seemed to be a feature of many of the regulation regimes we observed, though some occupational safety risk regulation was an exception to this pattern. If, as was suggested in Chapter 2, a viable control system must possess information-gathering, standard-setting and behaviour-modification components with clear linkages among them, many of the regulatory regimes we looked at could hardly be considered as viable control systems. In some cases one or more of those components was nearly or altogether absent, as with those cases where parliaments and governments enact laws with penalties for non-compliance but police in practice devote no resources to enforcing the laws. The linkage between those components, moreover, was often problematic. It was common and even typical for there to be substantial underlap or disconnection between the standard-setting and the behaviour-modification dimensions, with a sharp separation of institutions, professions, and cultures and very different values and priorities in play for different components of regulation.

But does institutional coherence, or the lack of it, really matter? It might be objected that what really matters is policy coherence, not coherence in institutions. Perhaps, like over-anxious parents faced with their untidy teenagers' bedrooms, we should not be too obsessed with institutional neatness and learn to relax about an element of apparent disorder—even if, unlike the teenage-bedroom problem, the prospects of that disorder lessening in the future seem distinctly low. Indeed, it may be more than a case of accepting the inevitable. The apparent disorder could even be beneficial. After all, polycentricity, institutional overlap, and diversity are often claimed to be positive virtues by policy analysts who are opposed to apparently rationalistic and comprehensive institutional forms (see Ostrom 1974).

There are at least seven related ways in which the virtues of such diversity can be portrayed. First, redundancy—the multiplication and apparently wasteful duplication of facilities—is often said to be desirable in institutional arrangements to protect a system against disablement of any one of its parts or from capture by any one interest or mind-set (see Landau 1969; George 1972). Second, in an argument that goes back at least to Montesquieu, an institutional system composed of multiple units is commonly said to be more conducive to learning and experimentation than uniform arrangements. Third, the 'multi-tasking' of public organizations across different policy domains may reflect successful cost-saving and effectiveness rather than mere muddle (see Hood 1986). Fourth, capable policy entrepreneurs or politicians can transcend administrative boundary lines, using system skills to link up the parts and thereby create public value (see Ostrom 1965; Ioannou 1992). Fifth, setting up special-purpose institutionally integrated control systems for every policy problem may lead to excessive separation among issues that would be better handled 'holistically' by the same institutions.[1] Sixth and

---

[1] The classic 'vertical silos' problem that arises whenever policy space is carved up into functionally separate bureaucratic or professional fiefdoms.

relatedly, considerations of specialization and division of labour—for instance, by the police as specialists in how to enforce the law on the streets and how to gain the necessary intelligence—may often be more telling than integration of functions for any particular policy purpose. Finally, the much-discussed, if seldom defined, principle of 'subsidiarity' also tends to imply a separation of monitoring and enforcement from policy-setting.[2] Any geographically extended political system can set standards from the centre, but diversity in law enforcement is often seen as both necessary and desirable. Only a certain, and contestable, kind of administrative tidy-mindedness points to uniform and neat arrangements for every policy issue.

But while we do not deny the force that such well-known doctrines can sometimes carry in institutional design, the risk regulation regimes we observed did not in all cases possess the positive qualities that are often lauded by defenders of institutional polycentricity and diversity. Lack of coherence came in several forms. One was variations in enforcement activity over common standards, across different EU member states, police forces, or local authorities, and in some cases variations in information-gathering activity too. Separating enforcement or information gathering from standard setting and locating these components at different administrative levels may produce diversity, but that diversity did not seem in all cases to be associated with the desirable consequences that the celebrators of polycentricity emphasize. There is a well-known local-democracy case for making local law enforcement responsive to local public opinion, but the variety we observed often seemed to reflect the attitudes of different police forces or police chiefs rather than to be obviously rooted in local public opinion. Moreover, against the local-democracy argument, some degree of uniformity in law enforcement across a jurisdiction is often taken to be a basic requirement of the rule of law (see Fuller 1964).

Second, in many cases the disconnection between standard setting and other parts of the regulatory process made transparency difficult or impossible to achieve. Transparency is another element that is typically identified as a key requisite for the rule of law, and is also held by 'safety culture' theorists to be a precondition for learning from experience, both in response to failure and in assessing varied approaches (see Sagan 1993: 14–28). In many of the regimes we observed, only established players—sometimes not even those—knew exactly who did what in the fragmented institutional setting. Particularly where regimes built on complex linkages to other regimes, as with benzene and pesticides, there was substantial scope for haziness about what

---

[2] 'Subsidiarity' originated as a quasi-theological doctrine and still has that character. Broadly, it denotes the idea of locating administrative functions at the lowest geographical or organizational level compatible with policy effectiveness. The idea is to bring administration as 'close to the people' as it can be and to employ the least amount of the special legal powers of the state compatible with the task to be performed (Hood and Schuppert 1988: 19).

was going on, who was responsible for what, and what the effect of any one piece of regulatory machinery was intended to be. Moreover, far from open sharing of experience to identify 'best practice', enforcement practices were typically opaque, with variety often unacknowledged and covert. That pattern applied to several cases we observed of enforcement of EU Directives by member states, but it also applied to some domestic UK regimes.

Third, the division of monitoring, standard setting, and enforcement typically produced functional underlaps rather than redundancy in the strict cybernetic sense of multiple independent back-up systems capable of operating as defences against partial failure through regulatory capture or other routes. In many cases there seemed to be too little genuine redundancy, not too much, and the separated elements operated like bottlenecks, not substitutable system elements. And policy entrepreneurs or other actors, like trade unions, spanning the divide among the different regulatory components also seemed to be more the exception than the rule. Indeed, it was often in the interest of the established institutional players in risk regulation to keep those functional components separate—a point to which we turn in the next section—rather than to bring them together.

In short, the institutional pattern we observed in many risk regulation regimes seemed to achieve neither the virtues of polycentricity briefly sketched out earlier nor those of comprehensive uniformity. So even if the abstract policy logic was coherent, the system for operating and delivering that policy was not. The task of integrating the culturally and institutionally plural elements of the administrative jigsaw into a coherent overall regime constitutes a challenge for policy entrepreneurship and public management that in few, if any, cases was even recognized, let alone met.

3. The Implications of Institutional Blame-Avoidance Imperatives for Regulatory Outcomes

The issue of overall system coherence, or the lack of it, that we discussed in the previous section was related to another feature of the government of risk. Much of the administrative architecture and dynamics of the risk regulation regimes we observed seemed to stem from institutional imperatives—on the part of regulators and regulatees alike—to avoid blame and liability. That blame-avoidance imperative seemed to shape risk regulation just as much as, if not more than, the sort of 'functional' considerations attending the technical characteristics of different risks that were discussed in Chapter 5. It will be recalled from Chapter 9 that we termed this institutional imperative 'blame prevention re-engineering' and it often seemed to be a more important influence on the shaping of regime structures than 'business process re-engineering' in management theory.

Blame prevention re-engineering is a theme that links to the contemporary emphasis on 'business risk management' in the private and public sectors. Business risk management—the development of various institutional routines and decision aids to assess and control elements that can affect the survival, reputation, or shareholder value of an enterprise, linking to general corporate strategy—is a notable growth point in contemporary corporate practice (see Anderson 1999; Power 1999; ICAEW 1999). The growth of risk management language and routines in the private corporate sector in the recent past is a phenomenon that has been much discussed, though as yet there is no authoritative explanation for this development.

Private-sector management fashions are not usually slow to transfer to the public sector in some form; predictably, at the time of writing, government organizations are subject to pressure from consultants, public audit offices, and others to adopt similar routines to manage their 'business risks'. Indeed, some of the countries known for their 'managerial' emphasis in public services have already developed standards for public sector risk management (see Management Advisory Board (Commonwealth of Australia) 1995). In principle, there is much to be said for such a development, not so much as a knee-jerk imitation of private corporate practice but rather as a means of systematically debating and balancing the contradictory pressures on regulators and other public-sector organizations to be 'entrepreneurial' and to avoid rash mistakes. To the extent that risk regulators and public organizations generally are exposed to undiscussed 'double-bind' pressures over risk (Hennestad 1990), business risk management approaches offer the prospect of bringing that double bind into the open in discussion of planning and strategy.

On the other hand, it can be argued that bringing business risk management approaches to government could easily be used to augment the 'blame prevention re-engineering' approach that is already all too well established in public sector organizations generally and risk regulation in particular (see Hood and Rothstein 2001).[3] Without an alteration of that culture, encouraging public sector organizations to pay more attention to business risks could easily be more like giving an alcoholic another drink than a real lifestyle reform for public management. To avoid that result, business risk management would need to be a way of engendering intelligent deliberation about the handling of risk in the public interest rather than mechanistic blame shifting. It would need to be a way of bringing together multiple public and private sector organizations responsible for managing risk rather than dividing them. It would need to be a way of opening up policy debate rather than of giving corporate managers yet more reasons for limiting information to

---

[3] As suggested above, blame prevention engineering could even be considered as a covert form of 'business risk management' *avant la lettre*.

protect their organization's liability. But few public bureaucracies anywhere, still less private firms involved in the management of risk, are geared to working in those ways. The inertia bias of bureaucratic and organizational behaviour runs the other way.

The broader policy-design question is how far 'business risk management', particularly if it is construed as blame prevention re-engineering, by public organizations seeking to limit liability and protect their institutional position is compatible with effective risk regulation for society at large. How far do the requirements for effective social risk management by government run together with business risk management considerations for particular organizations, and how far does the one exclude the other? In principle, a similar issue is faced by private-sector corporations. Typically, however, business risk management by private firms takes no account of the so-called systemic risks that affect whole industries rather than those affecting single enterprises. Government's central *raison d'être* is indeed often held to include 'system risk' roles such as risk-taker of last resort and the regulation of collective or public risk, so the issue is perhaps more salient for the public sector.

It is in principle possible for risk management to be pursued at both the level of individual organizations and the 'systemic' or social-system level without contradiction. We could even imagine circumstances where the two could be mutually reinforcing in a positive way, for instance where high mutual trust among different levels of government means that one organization's risk management information feeds into a larger-scale risk management calculus by central-level organizations. For instance, central government organizations' assessment and management of major social events like epidemics could be shaped and reinforced by the risk management plans of individual hospitals and *vice versa*. But logical possibility is one thing, typical institutional behaviour another. The requirement of high mutual trust across different organizations is far from universally achieved in government, and indeed the 'corporate' thrust of 1980s thinking about public sector management reform was designed to make public organizations go in exactly the opposite direction.

Indeed, there are reasons for thinking that compatibility between business risk management by government organizations and management of overall social risks may often be highly problematic. As we saw in Chapter 9, institutional blame-prevention concerns often seem to make risk-related public services more precarious and can even lead those services to be withdrawn altogether for fear of litigation or because of insurance problems. Blame prevention re-engineering could also reinforce existing tendencies to fragment risk regulation regimes into unconnected institutional pieces. The underlaps and overlaps could give each player an excuse for denying responsibility and passing the blame to other organizations. And the logic of blame prevention could augment the tendency to restrict potentially incriminating information on grounds of commercial confidentiality. Similar concerns for blame prevention in other contexts seemed to be leading to protocolization and risk assessment inflation to establish procedural alibis as a form of bureaucratic insurance.

At a time when public sector organizations are being urged to take on board private-sector-sourced business risk-management ideas, some of the basic policy trade-offs between collective and organizational risk management merit more attention. Indiscriminate or inappropriate application of corporate risk management approaches could detract from, rather than augment, the quality of the government of risk by putting more emphasis on existing bureaucratic tendencies to blame-avoidance. What seems to be needed is an approach to business risk management in government that is neither an unreflective adoption of private business practice nor based on an unrealistic view of organizational behaviour in the public sector. Such an approach would need to include several ways of regulating the regulators of risk, including provisions of transparency rather than the commercial confidentiality that typically governs private-sector risk management. That point takes us on to the final issue to be considered in this chapter.

4. Challenges Posed by Risk Regulation for Principles of Regulatory Assessment

Third—and this conclusion is also related to the other two—the government of risk seems to pose a particular challenge to contemporary efforts by governments and the OECD to develop effective principles of regulatory assessment. 'Better regulation' and the development of new ways to assess regulation and to think about regulatory alternatives has been a notable theme in public policy in the EU, OECD, and USA over the past 15 years. The increased emphasis placed on regulatory policy analysis and evaluation seems to stem from several developments, including privatization of formerly state-owned public utilities, increasing recognition of regulation as a potential 'non-tariff barrier to trade' within and across countries, and interest by economists and policy analysts in identifying alternatives to traditional 'command-and-control' regulation. Against this background, the 'principles' that have been advanced for regulatory assessment typically comprise some mix of 'economic rationalist' cost-effectiveness criteria together with rule-of-law criteria—such as proportionality and transparency—and policy evaluation to identify regulatory impacts and alternatives.

'So far, so bland', as Lewis Gunn (1987: 35) put it in another context. But the regulation of risk poses several challenges for principles of regulatory assessment. Some of these challenges are no doubt shared by other domains of regulation. The approach developed in this book suggests that any serious attempt to evaluate regulation has to include an assessment of how regulation works at the level of *regimes*, and that, as we have suggested earlier, often involves putting together hard-won knowledge that is scattered among multiple organizations and levels of government. Regulatory assessment that focuses exclusively on standards but not on the effect of enforcement or behaviour-modification activity may be easier to do against tight deadlines but will fail to capture how the regime works. Moreover, such an analysis has to take account of the extent to which specific regimes are nested in or connected with other regimes. A 'stand-alone' regime is far easier to assess for its effectiveness than a regime which is part of a complex of regimes intended to be complementary, as with the case of ambient benzene.

A 'regime' perspective is applicable to the assessment of any type of regulation, but three challenges to regulatory assessment seem especially sharp for risk regulation. They are the problem of how to go beyond the stage of 'proverbs and platitudes' in regulatory design principles, how to distinguish regulatory skill from the tractability of the material regulators face, and how to accommodate a broadly rationalist approach to regulatory appraisal with the political realities of regulatory development. We briefly discuss each of these issues below.

Where the Proverbs and Platitudes of 'Better Regulation' Meet Policy Dilemmas in Risk Regulation: Type I and Type II Errors

The first difficulty highlighted by risk regulation is the problem that 'better regulation' principles often turn out to be a set of 'contradictory proverbs'— as the Nobel laureate Herbert Simon (1946) portrayed administrative theory in the 1940s—without any practical guidance on what to do when one proverb clashes with another. By that we mean the tendency to enumerate a wish-list of regulatory desiderata, each of which is perhaps unexceptionable on its own, but which in practice can only be achieved at the expense of one of the other principles. The 'principles of better regulation' announced with a fanfare by the UK Blair Labour Government's Better Regulation Task Force (BRTF) in 1998 are a clear example of this tendency. The Task Force's 'New Labour' eminences set out five principles and various other properties of better regulation. But those eminences showed no sign of even recognizing that their principles were in many cases mutually incompatible, let alone offering any practical guidance on what regulatory designers should do when they were faced with making unavoidable tradeoffs among the principles (see Hood, Baldwin, and Rothstein 2000).

Of course risk regulation is by no means alone in posing ineluctable tradeoffs among design principles—as the epigraph to this chapter, taken from observation of the economic policy process 30 years ago, reminds us—and the

Blair government's Better Regulation Task Force is hardly the first set of reformers that has sought to play down such tradeoffs. Inherent dilemmas are ubiquitous in public policy and administration (Hood 1976). But the regulation of risk does pose one special and generic policy dilemma on which the UK Better Regulation Task Force's 'principles' were altogether silent. That is the issue, much discussed in the literature on risk regulation, of how to trade off the risk of making Type I and Type II errors (see Shrader-Frechette 1991: Ch. 9; Raiffa 1968; Baldwin, Scott, and Hood 1998: 15–16).

Type I errors are normally taken to be errors of imposing regulatory restrictions on items that turn out to be harmless, like evacuating a local population on the basis of an earthquake warning that turns out to be false. Type II errors denote the errors of failing to regulate substances or behaviour that turn out to be harmful. In responding to risk, especially when it is revealed or created by new scientific developments, regulators commonly and even typically have to trade off the two types of error. The standard example is the approval of new drugs, in which the Type I error consists of banning drugs that could be beneficial and the Type II error consists of approving drugs that turn out to have serious adverse effects. So a central and much-debated policy question for 'better regulation' is when to prefer which type of regulatory error. If principles of regulatory assessment are to have any effective 'purchase' on the design of risk regulation, they must go beyond the BRTF's proverbs and platitudes to offer guidance on how to handle that issue, or how to structure the policy-deliberation process to do so.

Separating Regulatory Craft from Inherent Policy Problems

A second challenge for 'better regulation' principles that is posed by many types of risk regulation is the issue of how to separate the quality of regulatory skill or craft applied to a particular problem from the inherent tractability of the problem the regulators are trying to deal with. This problem was also entirely ignored by the BRTF in setting out its assessment principles in 1998. Again, the issue of how to assess 'value added' is not unique to risk regulation or even to regulation in general: it arises in many public policy domains. For instance, it is a well-known problem in assessing the quality of teaching. The unqualified use of exam grades to assess schools does not distinguish between the poor school with good exam grades because its students are able and/or privileged, and the excellent school that does much more to bring on underprivileged students but achieves less good exam grades. Exactly the same problem arises with regulatory quality. The regulatory equivalent of the poor school with good exam grades is the uncreative regulator operating in a high-compliance culture and with favourable conditions for ready enforcement, such as plenty of intermediate organizations available as first-line enforcers. The equivalent of the good school with worse exam grades is the creative regulator working with less tractable material, for instance in dealing with phenomena that are inherently difficult to identify unambiguously.

However, many types of risk regulation pose especially sharp 'value-added' issues of evaluation. Any form of regulation that requires a shift in attitudes or behaviour of the population at large or large sections of it away from established habits—for instance, over driving, smoking, drinking, or eating—is likely to constitute a severe test of regulatory capacity. Compare, for example, the order of difficulty involved in imposing tighter controls over dogs and in making drivers drive on the customary side of the road—right or left. The latter case goes with the grain of established habits in the population at large—other than those from countries that drive on the opposite side of the road—and a compliance culture linked with direct self-preservation impulses. But the former has none of those characteristics. Any form of regulation that is hotly contended, which applies to some but not all risk regulation, is not likely to encounter a culture of compliance. And when there are would-be martyrs seeking to create maximum embarrassment by well-publicized suffering and lawyers looking for every loophole, a standard of regulatory craftsmanship that would amply suffice in more consensual circumstances is likely to be severely tested.

Moreover, regulation at the frontier of scientific research, in conditions where knowledge is tentative and its significance has to be translated among different specialist communities—the features stressed by theorists of 'risk society', though not applicable to all risk regulation—will present inherent difficulties for aspirations to evidence-based policy. That makes it all the more important for a serious evaluation of policy to be based on a careful analysis of the initial conditions and constraints faced by regulators and of the difference the regulators' actions made. But to do that properly requires a labour-intensive effort, involving patient and systematic historical evaluation from the 'inside', rather than snap judgements based on superficial scrutiny of whether regulatory policies ran into difficulties or encountered a bad press.

Factoring Policy Windows and Policy Entrepreneurship into Regulatory Assessment

A third and related challenge for principles of better regulation that is posed by risk regulation is the issue of how to evaluate regulation that emerges or changes in the wake of media agitation and responses to tragedy. The issue is whether the sort of unexceptionable sentiments and econocratic principles that make up so many of today's 'better regulation' principles are compatible with processes of policy development that appear far removed from a technocratic image of rational choice involving cool deliberation over pre-stated objectives and alternatives. Again, this challenge is far from unique to risk regulation. Many generic accounts of policy development stress the relatively unpredictable forces that cause policy 'windows' to open or close, creating or destroying opportunities for new initiatives or policy development.[4]

However, the challenge of accommodating such empirically observable features of regulatory politics to rational evaluation systems is posed by risk regulation in a particularly acute way. That is because, as we have seen earlier, risk regulation regimes commonly develop and change as part of a process of public reaction to unexpected tragedies and disasters. Sometimes, as we have seen, risk regulation is anticipative or precautionary, but just as common is the 'tombstone' pattern of policy development that has been recognized by analysts of regulatory politics at least as far back as Marver Bernstein's (1955) famous life-cycle theory of nearly 50 years ago. Rather than systematic scanning by legislatures or Cabinets of the regulatory landscape, new issues for risk regulation often literally crash or explode on to the policy agenda as a result of media-attention-grabbing disasters like rail accidents, earthquakes, or food poisoning tragedies.

Given these commonly observable features of the policy process, should a sophisticated assessment of risk regulation simply dismiss 'tombstone' processes as indefensibly irrational? The UK's BRTF (1998) pointedly condemned 'knee-jerk responses' in regulatory policy, and used one of the cases we have discussed earlier—dangerous dogs regulation—as a prime example of inappropriate 'knee-jerk' policy. But condemning regulation simply because it is hastily introduced in the aftermath of disasters also runs the risk of arriving at policy judgements that are both superficial and at odds with the principle of opinion responsiveness in democratic government. So it could be argued that a more appropriate and sophisticated test is to examine how creatively 'policy entrepreneurs' and public officials use policy windows constituted by public, media, and legislative attention focused on problems revealed by tragedies or disasters. If policy entrepreneurs use such windows to launch proposals for regulatory reform that have been carefully thought out in advance, the process may only superficially resemble a 'knee-jerk response'.

To assess how far changes in risk regulation truly consist of unreflective or panic reactions to disasters that come out of the blue, it is necessary to do more than simply inspect the time-scale and media salience in which those changes are introduced. We need to know whether changes in regime content have been well-thought-out and incubated well in advance of the policy window that created the legislative or policy-change opportunity, or whether

---

[4] Those accounts include Kingdon's (1984) well-known account of the confluence of different 'streams' in the policy process and the 'garbage-can' theory of organizational decision-making (Cohen, March, and Olsen 1972) from which Kingdon's analysis stems. The management theorist Henry Mintzberg (1983) makes a similar point, albeit without citing the 'garbage-can' model, in his analysis of 'adhocracy'.

they are a truly unthinking reflex response.[5] Speed of introduction is not always incompatible with quality in public policy. But again, what is needed for a proper assessment is to go beyond a mechanistic application of middle-level routine to a careful examination of where risk regulation proposals come from and how they are developed.

These three issues show only some of the challenges posed by the government of risk to the assessment of regulation, by indicating some of the difficulties of going beyond unexceptionable sentiment and superficial judgement. We make three tentative suggestions on the basis of the discussion above. One is that a mechanistic painting-by-numbers approach to assessing risk regulation may have its value as a political fig leaf but may do more harm than good in contributing to improvement of policy quality. Good policy analysis, of which regulatory assessment is only a sub-type, takes time and painstaking immersion in the details and history of the policy process.

A second conclusion is that transparency in the process of regulatory assessment is as important as the transparency that assessors demand of regulators themselves, because such assessment involves weighing principles that are mutually incompatible in regulatory design. Concealing those tradeoffs and keeping judgements about the relative priority of different principles implicit makes regulatory assessment just another forum for exercise of covert political judgement by those who claim some sort of technocratic expertise or non-political authority. What are needed are public statements of how assessors reasoned about the issues, to avoid the impression of ad hoc political judgements masquerading as technocratic expertise.

Third, to the extent that ideas about 'better regulation' involve contradictory values, there is a case for building those rival values into the administrative architecture, so that they are constantly being juxtaposed in an open process of institutionalized debate. Instead of trying to encompass all regulatory values in a single *numéraire* or institution trying to exercise the wisdom of Solomon, we could entrench the contradictory values into rival regulators or institutional routines constantly vying for priority. The implication is to put responsibility for rival goals such as promoting 'entrepreneurialism' and avoiding egregious risk-taking into separate hands, and to encourage their champions to compete (see Dunsire 1975; Hood 1996). Such a strategy would at least ensure that managers and regulators engaged in some reasoned public debate about rival values such as the avoidance of regulatory sins of commission and omission, as discussed earlier, even if there is no final and definitive way of setting the balance among them.

---

[5] How far that applied to the dog-risk case condemned by the BRTF is debatable, but at least some of that regulation was 'incubated' well before the media feeding frenzy over dog bites that launched the legislative opportunity (see Hood, Baldwin, and Rothstein 2000).

Overall

Our overall conclusion is that the 'regime' approach that we have begun to develop in this book can earn its keep in the analysis of risk regulation in three related ways: descriptive, explanatory, and prescriptive.

The descriptive value of this approach, which we sought to demonstrate in Part I of this book, is to produce a more systematic way of mapping and describing how risks are managed and regulated, to identify the commonalities and differences. As we explained in the opening chapter, comparison of regimes can help to fill the gap between incommensurable single-case studies and aggregated statements about how modern societies regulate risks. Dimensional comparison aims to do for risk regulation what a new generation of sociologists did for organizational analysis in the 1960s, but the focus rests on the collection of organizations that make up the regulatory system rather than on the operation of any one of them in isolation. In that sense it is a method that fits with the emphasis on policy networks and 'governance' rather than particular organizations that has developed in public management and administration over the past decade or so (see Rhodes 1997).

The explanatory value of the approach is to contribute to a better middle-level debate about how and why risk regulation varies across public policy domains, by separating different elements of regulatory regimes and exploring their interrelationship. It is a way of bringing better evidence to bear to the debate about how risk is handled by organizations and institutions and what if anything makes risk regulation special or different from other types of politics. Again a parallel can be drawn with the contingency approach that developed in organization theory from the 1960s, because it has the potential to move us away from over-generalized world-historical claims about the social handling of risk to more differentiated forms of explanation. Just as we can show that there seems to be as much variation in the way contemporary society regulates risk as in what some claim to differentiate historical from current risk management, we can show those variations are shaped by a mixture of forces familiar in the public-policy literature. Similarly, it seems possible to show that risk regulation shows a number of different dynamics, not a single one, and that many of those dynamics can be accounted for by relatively conventional system-environment models and attention to the 'inner life' of regulatory regimes.

The third potential payoff of the 'regime' approach, as discussed in this chapter, is as a policy-analytic tool to make a contribution to the assessment of institutional and policy design. Debates about institutional design bring together discussion of value, context, and instrumental alternatives and many different disciplines and analytic approaches can evidently contribute to such debates (see Goodin 1996). What the regime perspective developed in this book can offer to such discussion is a way of analysing all the dimensions of institutional control systems, and a way of looking at the context of risk regulation that parallels the 'strategic triangle' developed by Moore (1995) for public management. Both of those analytic lenses can be used to look across the boundary lines of organizational geography in government and in the private or independent sector.

However, the analysis of risk regulation regimes remains in its infancy. It needs to be developed and explored further in several ways. We need more debate about alternative ways to capture similarities and differences among regulatory regimes. We need to extend the range of comparisons well beyond the limited number of cases examined in depth in this book. And we also need to develop the approach in a cross-national comparative context, cutting across different institutional traditions and regulatory cultures and including developing countries as well as the affluent democracies.

Appendix A
FURTHER READING ON LAW AND POLICY IN NINE RISK REGULATION REGIMES

Dangerous Dogs

At the time of writing, the main statute on dangerous dog risks in the UK was the Dangerous Dogs Act 1991 amended by the Dangerous Dogs (Amendment) Act 1997 (not extended to Northern Ireland). This legislation was concurrent with Dogs Act 1871, the Dangerous Dogs Act 1989 (for Great Britain), the Town Police Clauses Act 1847 (for England and Wales) and the Civic Government (Scotland) Act 1982 (for Scotland) and the Dogs (Northern Ireland) Order 1983 (No.764 (NI.8)).

For background on the development of UK policy on dangerous dogs, see the series of government consultation papers: Department of the Environment (1976), Department of Environment and Welsh Office (1989), Scottish Office (1989), Home Office *et al.* (1990). See also Hughes (1998) and the Hansard Society for Parliamentary Government (1993: App. 6).

Radon in the Home and Workplace

Voluntary radon Action Levels for UK homes were introduced in 1987, and after 1990 a single Action Level was set at 200 Bqm^{-3} (National Radiological Protection Board 1987; *Hansard*, 27.1.1987: 189–97; National Radiological Protection Board 1990; Department of the Environment 1990; Gore 1997). For new-build homes in high-risk regions, building regulations required precautions to be taken to avoid danger to health and safety from radon. For England and Wales see Building Regulations (Statutory Instrument No. 2531 2000) and broadly equivalent Building Standards Regulations for Scotland and Building Regulations for Northern Ireland).

Radon in the workplace and public buildings was subject to a voluntary regime until the implementation in Great Britain in 1985 of the Ionising Radiation Regulations (No. 1333), implemented in Northern Ireland in 1985 (No. 273). These regulations implemented Directive 80/836/Euratom, itself influenced by recommendations of the International Commission on Radiological Protection (ICRP 26 1977). Directive 96/29/Euratom implemented revised ICRP recommendations (ICRP 60 1991) and was implemented in Great Britain in 1999 by the Ionising Radiation Regulations (Statutory Instrument No. 3232 1999), still to be implemented in Northern Ireland at the time of writing.

For background on the development of UK radon policy, see Royal Commission on Environmental Pollution (1984), NRPB (1990), House of Commons Environment Committee (1991), O'Riordan and Miles (1992) and Gore (1997). For discussion of radon policy in North America, see Esau and Beattie (1990), Nero (1992), Cole (1993) and Edelstein and Makofske (1998).

Ambient Benzene and Benzene at Work

There were no specific powers in the UK for setting statutory ambient air quality standards prior to the Environment Protection Act 1990 (Haigh 1992: 6.1–3). Under the Environment Act 1995, an ambient benzene objective of 5bb was first set for Great Britain in 1997 by the Air Quality Regulations (Statutory Instrument 1997, No. 3043), subsequently revised, for England, by the Air Quality Regulations (England) (Statutory Instrument 2000, No. 928). At the time of writing a regulatory framework for local air quality management was yet to be established for Northern Ireland. Also at the time of writing the EU was in the process of finalizing a limit for ambient benzene (Commission of the European Communities 2000), under EU Directive on Ambient Air Quality Assessment and Management 96/62/EC (Council of the European Communities 1996a).

For occupational safety, from 1969 to 1989 in the UK airborne benzene at work was covered by a recommended limit, reduced in 1977. In 1989, the limit was made statutory in the UK under the Control of Substances Hazardous to Health Regulations (Statutory Instrument 1988 No. 1657) and COSHH Regulations (Northern Ireland) 1990, and the limit was further reduced in 1991 and 2000 (Health and Safety Executive 1989; 1991; 2000). EU Directive 97/42/EEC—an amendment to the EU Carcinogens (Framework) Directive 90/394/EEC—specified an occupational airborne limit for benzene of 1 ppm to be implemented by 2003.

For policy background on ambient benzene, see OECD (1986), IPCS/WHO (1993), EPAQS/DoE (1994), DoE/SO (1997), and Commission of the European Communities DGXI (1999). For policy background on occupational limits see, Commission of the European Communities (1993), Health and Safety Commission (1995), Health and Safety Executive Advisory Committee on Toxic Substances (1997), and ILGRA (1997).

Paedophile Ex-offenders Released from Custody

The registration of certain sex offenders in the UK was first required by the Sex Offenders Act 1997, and the release of offenders was governed by the Criminal Justice Act 1991 (Chapter 53), and the Crime and Disorder Act 1998 (Chapter 37, Part IV).

For background on policy, see Hughes, Parker, and Gallagher (1996), Hebenton and Thomas (1996), Grubin (1998), Kemshall (1998), 'Working with Sex Offenders': a special issue of *Child Abuse Review*, 17/6 (1998), and HM Inspectorate of Probation (1998). For a discussion of housing issues, see Chartered Institute of Housing (1998). For a discussion of the US regime, see Hebenton and Thomas (1997).

Local Road Safety

At the time of writing, responsibilities of government and local authorities for highway engineering, education, and enforcement in Great Britain were governed by the Road Traffic Act 1974, re-enacted in 1988, the Highways Act 1980 (for England and Wales), the Roads (Scotland) Act 1984, the Road Traffic Regulation Act 1984, the Road Traffic Offenders Act 1988, and the Traffic Calming Act 1992, as well as secondary legislation provided for under these Acts. For Northern Ireland, the relevant legislation was: the Road Traffic Northern Ireland Order 1981 No. 154 (NI 1); the Roads Northern Ireland Order 1993 No. 3160 (NI 15); the Road Traffic Northern Ireland Order 1995 No. 2994 (NI 18); the Road Traffic Offenders Road Northern Ireland Order 1996 No. 1320 (NI10); and the Road Traffic Regulation Northern Ireland Order 1997 No. 276 (NI 2). In addition, long-term targets for reducing casualties were set by UK government since 1987 (see Department of Transport 1987; DETR 2000).

For further background on road safety policy, see DETR (1997; 2000), Department of Transport (1987), Ogilvie-Smith, Downey, and Ransom (1994), and HMIC (1998).

Pesticide Residues in Food and Water

Before 1989, water undertakers in the UK were under a statutory duty to supply 'wholesome water', but wholesomeness was not statutorily defined (see Ward, Buller, and Lowe 1995: 97). The European Drinking Water Directive 80/778/EEC limited residue levels in drinking water to 0.1ppb for any one pesticide and 0.5ppb for total pesticides. This limit was applied to England and Wales by the Water Supply (Water Quality) Regulations 1989 (Statutory Instrument No.1147 1989) issued under the 1989 Water Act, consolidated by the Water Industry Act 1991 and the Water Resources Act 1991, which privatized the regional Water Authorities in England and Wales. The Directive was implemented in Scotland by the Water Supply (Water Quality) (Scotland) Regulations 1990 (No.119 (S.11)), and was implemented in Northern Ireland by the Water Quality Regulations (Northern Ireland) 1994. The EU Directive was revised in 1998 (Directive 98/83/EC) and was expected to be implemented in the UK by the end of 2000.

Statutory pesticide residue levels in food were first introduced in the UK in 1988 and at the time of writing were prescribed by the 'Pesticides (Maximum Levels in Crops, Food and Feedingstuffs) (England and Wales) Regulations' (Statutory Instrument No. 3483 1999), the 'Pesticides (Maximum Levels in Crops, Food and Feedingstuffs) (Scotland) Regulations' (Statutory Instrument No. 22 2000), and 'Pesticides (Maximum Residue Levels in Crops, Food and Feeding Stuffs) (National Limits) Regulations (Northern Ireland)' (Statutory Instrument No. 32 1995) (and No. 33 for EEC limits).

For policy background on pesticide residues in food and drinking water see Gillespie (1979), Gilbert and Macrory (1989), Beaumont (1993), Lang and Clutterbuck (1991), Sheail (1991), Tait, Brown, and Carr (1991), Parliamentary Office of Science and Technology (1993), and Ward, Buller, and Lowe (1995).

Appendix B
CODED LIST OF INTERVIEWEES

Interviewee code	Organization	Official capacity
Radon		
R1	National Radiological Protection Board	Scientist
R2	National Radiological Protection Board	Scientist
R3	Department of the Environment, Transport and the Regions	Policy official
R4	Department of Health	Policy official
R5	Environment DG, European Commission	Policy official
R6	Health and Safety Executive	Inspector
R7	Health and Safety Executive	Policy official
R8	Midlands Local Authority 1	Chief Environmental Health Officer
R9	Midlands Local Authority 1	Environmental Health Officer
R10	Midlands Local Authority 2	Environmental Health Officer
R11	Scottish Office	Policy official
R12	Radon Council	Director
Child sex offenders		
CSO1	Home Office	Policy official
CSO2	Home Office	Policy official
CSO3	Childline	Senior official
CSO4	Police	Chief Constable
CSO5	Police	Chief Superintendent
CSO6	Police	Chief Superintendent
CSO7	Police	Detective Inspector
CSO8	Probation Service	Chief Probation Officer
CSO9	Probation Service	Chief Probation Officer
CSO10	Home Office	Senior Civil Servant in the Probation Inspectorate
CSO11	Probation Service	Senior Probation Officer
CSO12	Probation Service	Probation Officer
CSO13	Department of Health	Senior Civil Servant with responsibilities for child protection

CSO14	Southern City Council	Director of Social Services
CSO15	University of Newcastle	Forensic psychiatrist
CSO16	Local Government Association	Policy official
CSO17	University of Bristol	Lecturer
CSO18	De Montfort University	University researcher

Road safety

RS1	Police	Chief Constable
RS2	Department of the Environment, Transport and the Regions	Policy official
RS3	Department of the Environment, Transport and the Regions	Senior policy official
RS4	Department of Health	Policy official
RS5	Home Office	Policy official
RS6	Scottish Office, Development Department, Transport Division	Policy official
RS7	Scottish Office, Development Department, Transport Division	Policy official
RS8	Midlands County Council	County Surveyor
RS9	Northern City Council 1	Road safety official
RS10	Northern City Council 2	Road safety official
RS11	South East County Council	Road safety official
RS12	Local Government Association	Senior official
RS13	Transport Research Laboratory	Road safety expert
RS14	University College London	Road safety expert

Dogs

D1	Police	Sergeant with specialist dog expertise
D2	Home Office	Policy official
D3	Home Office	Policy official
D4	Home Office	Policy official
D5	Department of Health	Policy official
D6	Northern City Council	Dog warden
D7	West Country County Council	Dog warden
D8	North West County Council	Dog warden
D9	N. Ireland City Council	Dog warden
D10	Royal Society of Medicine	President
D11	Royal College of Veterinary Surgeons	Official
D12	Independent Veterinary Surgeon	Expert witness

Benzene

B1	Department of the Environment, Transport and the Regions	Policy official
B2	Department of Health	Senior scientist
B3	Scottish Office	Policy official
B4	Scottish Office	Specialist advisor

B5	Scottish Office	Policy official
B6	Expert Panel on Air Quality Standards	Chairman
B7	Environment Agency	Retired inspector
B8	Environment Agency	Policy official
B9	Technical Consultancy	Scientist
B10	Employment and Social Affairs DG, European Commission	Policy official
B11	Health and Safety Executive	Policy official
B12	Scottish District Council	Senior Environmental Health Officer
B13	Scottish District Council	Environmental Health Officer
B14	Central London Borough Council	Chief Environmental Health Officer
B15	European Environment Bureau	Policy officer
B16	Multi-national Petrochemical Corporation 1	Chief Medical Officer
B17	Multi-national Petrochemical Corporation 2	Expert on environmental health and human toxicology
B18	Multi-national Petrochemical Corporation 1	Senior Manager

Pesticides

P1	Supermarket	Company chemist
P2	Supermarket	Public Relations Executive
P3	European Crop Protection Association	Director General
P4	Department of the Environment, Transport and the Regions	Policy official
P5	Department of Health	Senior scientist
P6	Drinking Water Inspectorate	Senior official
P7	Drinking Water Inspectorate	Inspector
P8	Environment Agency	Scientist
P9	Environment DG, European Commission	Policy official
P10	Agriculture DG, European Commission	Policy official
P11	Health and Consumer Protection DG, European Commission	Policy official
P12	Environment DG, European Commission	Policy official
P13	European Environment Agency	Official
P14	Health and Safety Executive	Policy official
P15	Pesticides Trust	Senior representative
P16	Consultant to European Environmental NGOs	Consultant
P17	Pesticides Safety Directorate, Ministry of Agriculture Fisheries and Food	Senior official

P18	Pesticides Safety Directorate,	Senior official
	Ministry of Agriculture Fisheries and Food	
P19	Pesticides Safety Directorate,	Director (Policy)
	Ministry of Agriculture Fisheries and Food	
P20	Scottish Office	Policy official
P21	Water Company 1	Head of Environmental Quality
P22	Water Company 2	Environment Officer
P23	Local Authorities Coordinating Body on	Senior official
	Food and Trading Standards	
P24	De Montfort University	Professor
P25	Edinburgh University	Professor
P26	Pesticides Safety Directorate,	Official
	Ministry of Agriculture Fisheries and Food	

General

G1	Department of Health	Senior official
G2	Department of Health	Senior official
G3	Royal Commission on Environmental	Official
	Pollution	

Appendix C
METHODOLOGICAL NOTES FOR SELECTED FIGURES AND TABLES

This Appendix sets out the methodological basis on which risk regulation regimes were arrayed in Fig. 3.1 and Tables 3.1, 3.4, 8.1, and 8.2. The Figure and Tables and have been reproduced below, but methodological notes have been inserted to replace the specific placings of individual regimes.

Aggregated score of 'regime content' elements:
overall rating on regulatory size, structure, and style

Aggregated score of 'regime context' elements: overall rating on type of risk, public preferences and attitudes and interest group organization

Regimes arrayed by mapping the combined regime 'content' ratings for the size, structure, and style of each regime as set out in Table 3.4, against the combined regime 'context' ratings for the overall risk, opinion salience, and interest group pressure characterizing each regime as set out in Table 3.4.

FIGURE 3.1: Nine risk regulation regimes

TABLE 3.1: *A dimensional comparison of nine European Union and United Kingdom risk regulation regimes*

Regime context		Method
Type of risk	Degree of risk without relevant regime	Regimes ranked according to the likely number of deaths and serious injuries that would occur in the absence of each specific regulatory regime, but not in the absence of other potentially related regimes that may impact upon the risk. Where there were serious information deficits or controversies, assumptions made by government regulators were used as the default categorization.
	Degree of market and tort law failure re above risk	Regimes ranked according to the extent to which the risks were characterized by serious market failures as set out in Chapter 5, second section. Failure in either dimension of 'opt-out' or 'information' costs was taken as sufficient to warrant complete market failure.
Nature of public and media opinion	Media/public salience	Regimes ranked according to the profile of the public and media salience of each risk as set out in Chapter 6, second section.
	Degree of uniformity or coherence of opinion	Regimes ranked according to the uniformity or coherence of the public and media salience of each risk as set out in Chapter 6, second section.
Extent and distribution of organized groups	Presence of dominant organized groups	Regimes ranked according to the presence of organized groups within each regime as set out in Chapter 7.
	Degree of mobilization of affected stakeholders	Regimes ranked according to the mobilization of organized groups within each regime as set out in Chapter 7.

TABLE 3.1: *Continued*

Regime content		Method
Size	Policy aggression	Regimes ranked according to the degree of risk tolerance implied by standard setting, the extent to which information gathering matched that which would be reasonably required to fully characterize the risk, and the degree of risk toleration found in practice as the outcome of behaviour modification activities. Ranking was based on existing published material, and extensive discussion with regulators and regulatees.
	Overall investment in regulation	Regimes ranked according to the total private and public sector costs for each regime component making use of existing published material, and extensive discussion with regulators and regulatees.
Structure	Proportion of investment in regulation from private or third sector sources	Regimes ranked according to the proportion of non-state costs of the total investment—using the same material as set out in the above row 'overall investment'—for each component of each regime.
	Degree of organizational complexity or fragmentation	Regimes ranked according to the number of departments/organizations involved in each component of each regime combined with the number of associated regimes that had a significant impact on the control of each risk.
Style	Rule orientation	Regimes ranked according to the extent to which each regime component could be characterized as rule driven.
	Zeal of regulators	Regimes ranked according to the extent to which actors in each regime component were zealous in trying to control risk as judged by time and commitment to the task or through the utilization of particular professional/technical skills and knowledges.

TABLE 3.4: *An aggregated comparison of nine United Kingdom and European Union risk regulation regimes on six institutional and instrumental elements across all regulatory control dimensions*

Institutional and instrumental elements	Method for relative rating of regulation regime
Regime context	
Overall risk: pre-regulatory vulnerability	Regimes ranked by combining the ratings in Table 3.1 for the degree of risk—without relevant regime—and the degree of market failure
Overall opinion salience: heat of public concern	Regimes ranked by combining the ratings in Table 3.1 for the media/public salience and the degree of coherence/uniformity of public opinion
Overall interest group pressure: concentrated lobbying pressure	Regimes ranked by combining the ratings in Table 3.1 for the presence of dominant organized groups and the degree of mobilization of affected stakeholders
Regime content	
Size (scale)	Regimes ranked by combining the total ratings for aggression and total investment across control components of each regime as set out in Table 3.1
Structure (complexity)	Regimes ranked by combining the total ratings for the proportion of private investment and organizational complexity and fragmentation across control components of each regime as set out in Table 3.1
Style (intensity or formality)	Regimes ranked by combining the total ratings for the rule orientation and regulatory zeal across control components of each regime as set out in Table 3.1

TABLE 8.1: *Three content elements of nine risk regulation regimes observed against three sets of expectations*

Risk regulation regime	Regulatory control component	Observed	Observed vs market-failure expectation	Observed vs opinion-responsive expectation	Observed vs external interest-driven expectation
Regime	Size	Regimes ranked as summarized in Table 3.4 and discussion in Chapters 5, 6, and 7	Comparison of observed regime content features with expected content features as set out in Chapter 5	Comparison of observed regime content features with expected content features as set out in Chapter 6	Comparison of observed regime content features with expected content features as set out in Chapter 7
	Structure				
	Style				

TABLE 8.2: *Three control components of nine risk regulation regimes observed against three sets of expectations*

Risk regulation regime	Regulatory control component	Observed	Observed vs market-failure expectation	Observed vs opinion-responsive expectation	Observed vs external interest-driven expectation
Regime	Information gathering	Regimes ranked as summarized in Table 3.1 and discussion in Chapters 5, 6, and 7	Comparison of observed control component features with expected control component features as set out in Chapter 5	Comparison of observed control component features with expected control component features as set out in Chapter 6	Comparison of observed control component features with expected control component features as set out in Chapter 7
	Standard setting				
	Behaviour modification				

REFERENCES

Adams, J. (1985). *Risk and Freedom: The Record of Road Safety Regulation*. Cardiff: Transport Publishing Projects.

—— (1995). *Risk*. London: UCL Press.

—— (1999). 'Cars, Cholera and Cows'. *Policy Analysis*, No. 335: 1–49.

AIT/FIA (1998). *The Safety of Visitors to European Camping and Caravan Sites*. Brussels: European Bureau of the Alliance Internationale de Tourisme and Fédération Internationale de l'Automobile.

Anderson, R. (1999). 'A Framework for Strategy', in *Risk and Regulation*, supplement to *LSE Magazine*, December: 11.

Ayres, I. and Braithwaite, J. (1992). *Responsive Regulation: Transcending the Deregulation Debate*. New York: Oxford University Press.

Baker, K. (1993). *The Turbulent Years*. London and Boston: Faber and Faber.

Baldwin, R. (1995). *Rules and Government*. Oxford: Clarendon Press.

—— and Daintith, T. (1992). *Harmonisation and Hazard*. London: Graham and Trotman.

—— and Hawkins, K. (1984). 'Discretionary Justice: Davis Reconsidered'. *Public Law*: 570–99.

——, Scott, C., and Hood, C. (eds) (1998). *A Reader on Regulation*. Oxford: Oxford University Press.

Bardach, E. (1977). *The Implementation Game*. Cambridge, MA: MIT Press.

—— (1999). *Getting Agencies to Work Together*. Washington, DC: Brookings Institution.

Barzelay, M. (2000). *The New Public Management: Improving Research and Policy Dialogue*. Berkeley: University of California Press.

Baumgartner, F. and Jones, B. (1991). 'Agenda Dynamics and Policy Subsystems'. *Journal of Politics* 53(4): 1044–74.

Baxter, D. (1984). 'The Deleterious Effects of Dogs on Human Health: Dog-Associated Injuries'. *Community Medicine*, 6: 29–36.

BBC News Online (1999). 'Road Safety Revealed as "Low Priority"'. 9 December: http://news.bbc.co.uk

Beaumont, P. (1993). *Pesticides, Policies and People*. London: The Pesticides Trust.

Beck, U. (1992). *Risk Society* (trans. M. Ritter). London: Sage.

Beck Jørgensen, T. (1985). 'The Management of Survival and Growth in Public Organizations'. Paper presented at European Consortium for Political Research Joint Sessions, Barcelona.

—— (1987). *Models of Retrenchment Behaviour* (Working Paper No. 24). Brussels: International Institute of Administrative Sciences.

Beer, S. (1966). *Decision and Control*. New York: Wiley.

Bentham, J. (1843). 'On Publicity', in John Bowring (ed.), *Works of Jeremy Bentham*, vi. Edinburgh: W. Tait: 310–17.

—— (1983). *Constitutional Code, Volume 1*. Oxford: Clarendon Press.

Bernstein, M. (1955). *Regulating Business by Independent Commission*. Princeton: Princeton University Press.

Better Regulation Task Force (1998). *Principles of Good Regulation*. London: Better Regulation Task Force.

Black, J. (1997). *Rules and Regulators*. Oxford: Clarendon Press.

Blaxter, M. (1999). 'Risk, Health and Social Research: Lessons from the ESRC Programme on Risk and Human Behaviour'. *Health, Risk and Society*, 1/1: 11–24.

Blythe, A. (1997). *Radon—A Growing Concern*. Brighton: National Society for Clean Air and Environmental Protection (Environmental Protection 1997, 64th NSCA Environmental Protection Conference and Exhibition, 20–3 October, Glasgow.

Brans, M. and Rossbach, S. (1997). 'The Autopoeisis of Administrative Systems: Niklas Luhmann on Public Administration and Public Policy'. *Public Administration*, 75: 417–39.

Breyer, S. (1982). *Regulation and its Reform*. Cambridge, MA, and London: Harvard University Press.

—— (1993). *Breaking the Vicious Cycle*. Cambridge, MA: Harvard University Press.

Brin, D. (1998). *The Transparent Society*. Reading, MA: Addison-Wesley.

Brittan, S. (1964). *The Treasury under the Tories 1951–1964*. Harmondsworth: Penguin.

Bryant, R., Hooper, P., and Mann, C. (1993). *Evaluating Policy Regimes: New Research in Empirical Macroeconomics*. Washington, DC: Brookings Institution.

Burton, T., Chilton, S., Covey, J., Gilbert, H., Jones-Lee, M., Loomes, G., Pidgeon, N., Robinson, A., and Twist, J. (2000). *Valuation of Benefits of Heath and Safety Control: Follow–up Study*. London: Health and Safety Executive.

Calman, K. (1998). Statement No. 179, 12 October: *The BSE Inquiry*, http://www.bse.org.uk/frwit

Carthy, T., Packham, D., Rhodes-Defty, N., Salter, D., and Silcock, D. (1993). Executive Summary, *Risk and Safety on the Roads: Perceptions and Attitudes*. Basingstoke: AA Foundation for Road Safety Research.

Chartered Institute of Housing (1998). *Rehousing Sex Offenders: A Summary of the Legal and Operational Issues*. Coventry: Chartered Institute of Housing.

Cheit, R. (1990). *Setting Safety Standards*. Berkeley: University of California Press.

Clay, E. and Schaffer, B. (1984). *Room for Manoeuvre*. London: Heinemann.

Coase, R (1960). 'The Problem of Social Cost'. *Journal of Law and Economics*, 3: 1–44.

Cohen, B. (1982). 'Failures and Critique of the BEIR-II Lung Cancer Risk Estimates'. *Health Physics*, 42/3: 2670–84.

—— (1985). 'Radon and Lung Cancer in Swedish Miners'. *New England Journal of Medicine*, 313/18: 1158.

Cohen, J. and Cohen, M. (1993). *The Penguin Dictionary of Twentieth-Century Quotations* (revised edn). London: Viking.

Cohen, M., March, J., and Olsen, J. (1972). 'A Garbage Can Model of Organizational Choice'. *Administrative Science Quarterly*, 17/1: 1–23.

Cole, L. (1993). *Element of Risk: The Politics of Radon*. Washington, DC: American Association for the Advancement of Science.

Collingridge, D. and Reeve, C. (1986). *Science Speaks to Power*. London: Francis Pinter.

Commission of the European Communities (1993). *Occupational Exposure Limits: Criteria Document for Benzene* (Report EUR 14491 EN). Brussels: Commission of the European Communities.

—— (2000). 'Amended Proposal for a Directive of the European Parliament and of the Council on Limit Values for Benzene and Carbon Monoxide in Ambient Air'

(Commission Proposal COM (2000). 223 final). Brussels: Commission of the European Communities.

Commission of the European Communities DGXI (1999). *Economic Evaluation of Air Quality Targets for CO and Benzene.* Brussels: Commission of the European Communities, DGXI.

CONCAWE (1996). *Scientific Basis for an Air Quality Standard on Benzene* (Report No. 96/63). Brussels: CONCAWE.

Consumers' Association (1980). *Pesticide Residues and Food.* London: Consumers' Association.

Council of the European Communities (1980). Council Directive 80/778/EEC of 15 July 1980 relating to the quality of water intended for human consumption. *Official Journal of the European Communities,* L 229: 11ff.

—— (1996a). Council Directive 96/62/EC of 27 September 1996 on Ambient Air Quality Assessment and Management, *Official Journal of the European Communities,* L 296: 55–63.

—— (1996b). Council Directive 96/29/Euratom of 13 May 1996 laying down basic safety standards for the protection of the health of workers and the general public against the dangers arising from ionizing radiation. *Official Journal of the European Communities,* No. L 159, 1–114.

Crespi, I. (1989). *Public Opinion, Polls, and Democracy.* Boulder, CO: Westview Press.

Daily Telegraph (1990). 'Car Economy is Vital, Thatcher Tells Greens'. 17 March: 4.

Darby, S., Whitley, E., Silcocks, P., Thakrar, B., Green, M., Lomas, P., Miles, J., Reeves, G., Fearn, T., and Doll, R. (1998). 'Risk of Lung Cancer Associated with Residential Radon Exposure in South-West England: A Case-Control Study'. *British Journal of Cancer,* 78/3: 394–408.

Davis, R. (1992). *Death on the Streets: Cars and the Mythology of Road Safety.* Hawes: Leading Edge Press.

Department of the Environment (1976). *Report of the Working Party on Dogs.* London: HMSO.

—— (1990). *News Release* No. 32/90, January.

Department of the Environment and Welsh Office (1989). *Action on Dogs: The Government's Proposals for Legislation.* London: Department of the Environment.

Derthick, M. and Quirk, P. (1985). *The Politics of Deregulation.* Washington, DC: Brookings Institution.

DETR (Department of the Environment, Transport and the Regions) (1997). *Road Safety Strategy: Current Problems and Future Options.* London: DETR.

—— (1998a). Executive Summary, *The Impact of Large Foodstores on Market Towns and District Centres.* London: DETR.

—— (1998b). *Finance, Management and Policy Review of the Expert Panel on Air Quality Standards: Final Report.* London: DETR.

—— (1998c). *Highways Economics Note No. 1.* London: DETR.

—— (1999). *Road Accidents Great Britain 1998: The Casualty Report.* London: DETR.

—— (2000). *Tomorrow's Roads: Safer for Everyone.* London, DETR.

Department of Transport (1987). *Road Safety: The Next Steps.* London: Department of Transport.

Diver, C. (1983). 'The Optimum Precision of Administrative Rules'. *Yale Law Journal,* 93: 65–109.

DOE/SO (Department of the Environment and Scottish Office) (1997). *The United Kingdom National Air Quality Strategy* (CM3587). London: the Stationery Office Ltd.

Doig, J. and Hargrove, E. (eds) (1987). *Leadership and Innovation: A Biographical Perspective on Entrepreneurs in Government*. Baltimore: Johns Hopkins University Press.

Dorfman, R. (1962). 'Basic Economic and Technologic Concepts: A General Statement', in A. Maass *et al.* (eds), *Design of Water Resource Systems*. Cambridge, MA: Harvard University Press.

Doron, G. (1979). *The Smoking Paradox: Public Regulation in the Cigarette Industry*. Cambridge, MA: Abt Books.

Douglas, M. (1986). *Risk Acceptability According to the Social Sciences*. London: Routledge and Kegan Paul.

—— (1987). *How Institutions Think*. London: Routledge and Kegan Paul.

—— (1990). *Risk and Blame*. London: Routledge.

—— and Wildavsky, A. (1982). *Risk and Culture*. Berkeley: University of California Press.

Dowding, K. (1996). *Power*. Buckingham: Open University Press.

—— (1995). 'Model or Metaphor? A Critical Review of the Policy Network Approach' *Political Studies* 43: 136–58.

Downs, A. (1967). *Inside Bureaucracy*. Boston, MA: Little, Brown and Company.

—— (1972). 'Up and Down with Ecology: The Issue-Attention Cycle'. *Public Interest*, 28/1: 38–50.

Dryzek, J. (1990). *Discursive Democracy: Politics, Policy and Science*. Cambridge: Cambridge University Press.

—— (1996). Review of A. Wildavsky, *But Is It True? A Citizen's Guide to Environmental Health and Safety Issues* (Harvard University Press, 1995). *Journal of Public Policy* 15/2: 299–304.

Dunleavy, P. (1991). *Democracy, Bureaucracy and Public Choice: Economic Explanations in Political Science*. London: Harvester.

Dunsire, A. (1975). *Control in a Bureaucracy* (The Execution Process, 2). Oxford: Martin Robertson.

—— (1990). 'Holistic Governance'. *Public Policy and Administration*, 5/1: 4–19.

DWI (Drinking Water Inspectorate) (2000). *Drinking Water 1999: A Report by the Chief Inspector, Drinking Water Inspectorate*. London: HMSO.

Edelstein, M. and Makofske, W. (1998). *Radon's Deadly Daughters*. Lanham, Maryland: Rowman and Littlefield Publishers, Inc.

Egan, M (1998). 'Regulatory Strategies, Delegation and European Market Integration'. *Journal of European Public Policy*, 5/3: 485–506.

Elkin, S. (1986). 'Regulation and Regime: A Comparative Analysis'. *Journal of Public Policy*, 6/1: 49–72.

EPAQS/DoE (Expert Panel on Air Quality Standards / Department of the Environment) (1994). *Benzene*. London: HMSO.

Esau, A. and Beattie, K. (eds) (1990). *Radon and the Law: Interdisciplinary Perspectives*. Manitoba, Canada: Legal Research Institute, University of Manitoba.

Europe Environment (1999). 'EU/Canada—Canada Challenges France's Asbestos Ban at WTO'. *Europe Environment*, No. 531. Brussels: Europe Information Service.

Evans, A. (1994). Editorial. *Journal of Transport Economics and Policy*, 28/1.

IPCS/WHO (International Programme on Chemical Safety/ World Health Organisation) (1993). *Environmental Health Criteria 150: Benzene*. Geneva: WHO.

Fishkin, J. (1995). *The Voice of the People: Public Opinion and Democracy*. New Haven: Yale University Press.

Foucault, M. (1977). *Discipline and Punish* (trans. A. Sheridan). Harmondsworth: Penguin.

Frewer, L., Howard, C., and Shepherd, R. (1998). 'Understanding Public Attitudes to Technology'. *Journal of Risk Research*, 1/3): 221–35.

Fuller, L. (1964). *The Morality of Law*. New Haven: Yale University Press.

Gallup, G. and Rae, S. (1940). *The Pulse of Democracy*. New York: Simon and Schuster.

Gaskell, G., Bauer, M., Durant, J., and Allum, N. (1999). 'Worlds Apart? The Reception of Genetically Modified Foods In Europe and the U.S.' *Science*, 285/16 July: 384–7.

George, A. (1972). 'The Case for Multiple Advocacy in Making Foreign Policy'. *American Political Science Review*, 66: 751–85.

Gerth, H. and Mills, C. (eds) (1948). *From Max Weber*. London: Routledge.

Gilbert, D. and Macrory, R. (1989). *Pesticide Related Law: A Guide to Pesticide Related Law in the UK with an Historical Account of the Development of Pesticide Safety*. Farnham: British Crop Protection Council.

Gillespie, B. (1979). 'British "Safety Policy" and Pesticides', in R. Johnston and P. Gummett (eds), *Directing Technology: Policies for Promotion and Control*. London: Croom Helm.

Goldstein, J. (1993). *Ideas, Interests and American Trade Policy*. Ithaca, NY: Cornell University Press.

Goodin, R. (ed.) (1996). *The Theory of Institutional Design*. Cambridge: Cambridge University Press.

—— and Klingemann, H. (1996). *A New Handbook of Political Science*. Oxford: Oxford University Press.

Gore, D. (1997). *Radon* (Research Paper 97/37). London: Science and Environment Section, House of Commons Library.

Grabosky, P. (1995). 'Counter-Productive Regulation'. *International Journal of Sociology of Law*, 23: 347–69.

Greenfield, S. and Stricklon, A. (eds) (1986). *Entrepreneurship and Social Change*. Lanham: University Press of America.

Grendstad, G. and Selle, P. (1995). 'Cultural Theory and the New Institutionalism'. *Journal of Theoretical Politics*, 7: 5–27.

Grubin, D (1998). *Sex Offending Against Children: Understanding the Risk* (Police Research Series, Paper 99). London: Home Office Policing and Reducing Crime Unit.

Guardian (1998). 'Voters Beef about New Meat Ban'. 13 January.

—— (1999). 'South-East Asia Faces New Smog Crisis'. 2 July: 1.

—— (2000). 'Tougher Police Line on Speeding'. 25 July: 7.

Gunn, L. (1987). 'Perspectives on Public Management', in J. Kooiman and K. Eliassen (eds), *Managing Public Organizations*. London: Sage.

Haigh, N. (1992). *Manual of Environmental Policy: The EC and Britain*. Harlow: Longman, in association with the Institute for European Environmental Policy.

Hall, C., Scott, C., and Hood , C. (1999). *Telecommunications Regulation: Culture, Chaos and Interdependence Inside the Regulatory Process*. London and New York: Routledge.

Hall, R.H. (1972). *Organizations: Structure and Process*. Englewood Cliffs, NJ: Prentice-Hall.

—— (1999). 7th edition *Organizations: Structure and Process*. Englewood Cliffs, NJ: Prentice-Hall.

Hancher, L., and Moran, M. (1989). *Capitalism, Culture and Regulation*. Oxford: Clarendon Press.

Hansard Society for Parliamentary Government (1993). *The Report of the Hansard Society Commission on the Legislative Process*. London: Hansard Society for Parliamentary Government.

Harrison, K. and Hoberg, G. (1991). 'Setting the Environmental Agenda in Canada and the United States: The Cases of Dioxin and Radon'. *Canadian Journal of Political Science*, 24/1: 3–27.

Hawkins, K. (1984) *Environment and Enforcement*. Oxford: Oxford University Press.

—— and Thomas, J. (eds) (1984). *Enforcing Regulation*. Boston: Kluwer-Nijhoff.

Healey, M. and A. Jones (1989). 'Pesticides in Water Supplies' (memo to Chief Executives of Water Service Companies and Secretaries of Water Companies in England and Wales. Department of the Environment/Welsh Office WP 18/1989). 29 September.

Health and Safety Commission (1995). *Proposed Amendment to the Carcinogens Directive* (Paper HSC/95/171). London: Health and Safety Commission.

Health and Safety Executive (1989). *EH40/1989 Occupational Exposure Limits 1989*. London: Health and Safety Executive.

—— (1991). *EH40/1991 Occupational Exposure Limits 1991*. London: Health and Safety Executive.

—— (1996). *Use of Risk Assessment within Government Departments* (report prepared by the Interdepartmental Liaison Group on Risk Assessment). London: Health and Safety Executive.

—— (1998). *Risk Assessment and Risk Management* (second report prepared by the Interdepartmental Liaison Group on Risk Assessment). London: Health and Safety Executive.

—— (2000). *EH40/2000 Occupational Exposure Limits 2000*. London: Health and Safety Executive.

Health and Safety Executive Advisory Committee on Toxic Substances (1997). *Developing a Consistent and Transparent Approach to Standards for Airborne Contaminants*. London: Health and Safety Executive.

Health Council of the Netherlands: Committee on Risk Measures and Risk Assessment (1996). *Risk is More that Just a Number*. The Hague: Health Council of the Netherlands (publication no. 1996/03E).

Hebenton, B. and Thomas, T. (1996). '"Tracking" Sex Offenders'. *The Howard Journal*, 53/2: 97–112.

—— —— (1997). *Keeping Track? Observations on Sex Offender Registers in the US*. London: Home Office Police Research Group.

Heclo H. (1978). 'Issue Networks and the Executive Establishment' in A. King (ed) *The New American Political System*. Washington, DC: American Enterprise Institute.

Hedges, A. (1993). *Air Quality Information: Report on Consultancy and Research* (report No. JN537). London: DETR.

Heimann, C. (1997). *Acceptable Risks: Politics, Policy, and Risky Technologies*. Ann Arbor: University of Michigan Press.

Hennestad, B. (1990). 'The Symbolic Impact of Double Bind Leadership: Double Bind and the Dynamics of Organizational Culture'. *Journal of Management Studies*, 27/3: 265–80.

Hervey, E. (1977). 'Incidence of Bites Due to Dogs and Other Animals in Leeds'. *British Medical Journal*, 2/6078: 53–4.

Hirschman, A. O. (1982). *Shifting Involvements*. Oxford: Blackwell.

—— (1991). *The Rhetoric of Reaction*. Cambridge: Polity.

HM Factory Inspectorate (1969). *Threshold Limit Values for 1969*. (Technical Data Note 2/69). London: Department of Employment and Productivity.

HM Inspectorate of Probation (1998). *Exercising Constant Vigilance: The Role of the Probation Service in Protecting the Public from Sex Offenders* (Report of a Thematic Inspection). London: Home Office.

HM Treasury (1996). *The Setting of Safety Standards: A Report by an Interdepartmental Group and External Advisers*. London: HM Treasury.

HMIC (Her Majesty's Inspector of Constabulary) (1998). *Road Policing and Traffic*. London: Home Office.

Home Office, Scottish Office, Welsh Office and Department of the Environment (1990). *The Control of Dogs*. London. Home Office.

Hood, C. (1976). *The Limits of Administration*. London: Wiley.

—— (1983). *The Tools of Government*. London: Macmillan.

—— (1986). *Administrative Analysis*. Brighton: Wheatsheaf Books

—— (1994). *Explaining Economic Policy Reversals*. Buckingham: Open University Press.

—— (1996). 'Where Extremes Meet: "SPRAT" versus "SHARK" in Public Risk Management', in C. Hood and D. Jones (eds), *Accident and Design*. London: UCL Press.

—— (2001). 'Transparency', in B. Clarke and J. Foweraker (eds), *Encyclopædia of Democratic Thought*. London: Routledge (forthcoming).

——, Baldwin, R., and Rothstein, H. (2000). 'Assessing the Dangerous Dogs Act: When Does a Regulatory Law Fail?'. *Public Law*: 282–305.

—— and Rothstein, H. (2001). 'Risk Regulation Under Pressure: Problem Solving or Blame-Shifting?', *Administration and Society* 33/1: 21–53.

—— and Schuppert, G.-F. (eds) (1988). *Delivering Public Services in Western Europe*. London: Sage.

——, Rothstein, H and Spackman, M. with Rees, J. and Baldwin, R. (1999*a*). 'Explaining Risk Regulation Regimes: Exploring The "Minimal Feasible Response" Hypothesis'. *Health, Risk and Society*, 1/2: 151–66.

——, Rothstein, H., Baldwin, R., Rees, J., and Spackman, M. (1999*b*). 'Where Risk Society Meets The Regulatory State: Exploring Variations In Risk Regulation Regimes'. *Risk Management: An International Journal*, 1/1: 21–34.

House of Commons Agriculture Committee (1995). *Pesticides Safety Directorate and Veterinary Medicines Directorate*, Vol. II, Appendix 11, HC 391-II. London: HMSO.

House of Commons Environment Committee (1991). *Indoor Pollution (Sixth Report)*, Vols I and II. London: House of Commons.

Huang, D., Tang, D., and Chow, K.W. (1993). 'Public Administration in Hong Kong: Crises and Prospects'. *International Journal of Public Administration*, 16: 1397–430.

Hughes, B., Parker, H., and Gallagher, B. (1996). *Policing Child Sexual Abuse: The View from Police Practitioners*. London: Home Office Policing and Reducing Crime Unit.

Hughes, P. (1998). *Dogs* (Research Paper 98/6). London: Science and Environment Section, House of Commons Library.

Hutter, B. (1997). *Compliance: Regulation and Environment*. Oxford: Clarendon Press.

ICAEW (Institute for Chartered Accountants for England and Wales) (1999). *Internal Control: Guidance for Directors on the Combined Code*. London: ICAEW.

ICRP (International Commission on Radiological Protection) (1977). 'Recommendations of the International Commission on Radiological Protection. ICRP Publication 26'. *Ann. ICRP*, 1/3

—— (1984). 'Principles for Limiting Exposure of the Public to Natural Sources of Radiation. ICRP Publication 39'. *Ann. ICRP*, 14/1: 1–8.

—— (1991). 'Recommendations of the International Commission on Radiological Protection. ICRP Publication 60' *Ann. ICRP*, 21/1-3.

ILGRA (Interdepartmental Liaison Group on Risk Assessment) (1997). 'Draft Report on DoE Methodology for Setting of Safety Standards'. Unpublished: DETR.

Independent (1999). 'Inspectors Sent in as Sellafield Admits to Serious Safety Lapses'. 14 September: 1.

—— (2000). '"Stab Him! Burn Him! Kill Him!" Two Weeks of Mob Hysteria Come to a Vicious Climax'. 5 August: 3.

Independent Expert Group on Mobile Phones (Chairman: Sir William Stewart) (2000). *Mobile Phones and Health*. Didcot: National Radiological Protection Board.

International Research Associates (1991). 'European Attitudes towards Urban Traffic Problems and Public Transport' (Report 60). *Eurobarometer* 35.1. Brussels: INRA.

—— (1998). 'La Securité des Produits Alimentaires' (Report 120). *Eurobarometer* 49. Brussels: INRA.

Institution of Environmental Health Officers (1988). *Radon* (Report of the IEHO Survey on Radon in Homes 1987/8). London: IEHO.

International Federation of Red Cross and Red Crescent Societies (1998). *World Disasters Report*. Geneva: International Federation of Red Cross and Red Crescent Societies.

Ioannou, T. (1992). 'Public Sector Entrepreneurship: Policy and Process Innovators in the UK' (Ph.D. thesis). London: Department of Government, London School of Economics.

IPCS/WHO (International Programme on Chemical Safety/World Health Organization) (1993). *Environmental Health Criteria 150: Benzene*. Geneva: WHO.

Irwin, A., Rothstein, H., Yearley, S., and McCarthy, E. (1997). 'Regulatory Science: Towards a Sociological Framework'. *Futures*, 29/1: 17–31.

Jacobsen, J. (1995). 'Much Ado About Ideas: The Cognitive Factor in Economic Policy'. *World Politics*, 47: 283–310.

Jasanoff, S. (1990). *The Fifth Branch: Science Advisors as Policymakers*. Cambridge, MA: Harvard University Press.

John, P. (1998). *Analysing Public Policy*. London: Pinter.

Joo, J. (1999). 'Dynamics of Social Policy Change: A Korean Case Study from a Comparative Perspective'. *Governance*, 12/1: 57–80.

Kaspersen, R. (1992). 'The Social Amplification of Risk: Progress in Developing an Integrative Framework', in S. Krimsky and D. Golding (eds), *Social Theories of Risk*. Westport, Conn: Praeger.

Kemshall, H. (1998). *Risk in Probation Practice*. Aldershot: Ashgate.

Key, V. (1961). *Public Opinion and American Democracy*. New York: Knopf.

Kingdon, J. (1984). *Agendas, Ideas and Public Policy*. Boston: Little, Brown.

Kitzinger, J. (1999). 'The Ultimate Neighbour from Hell? Stranger-Danger and the Media Framing of Paedophiles', in B. Franklin (ed.), *Misleading Messages: The Media, Misrepresentation and Social Policy*. London: Routledge.

Klaassen, B., Buckley, J., and Esmail, A. (1996). 'Does The Dangerous Dogs Act Protect against Animal Attacks? A Prospective Study Of Mammalian Bites in the Accident and Emergency Department'. *Injury*, 27/2: 89–91.

Krasner, S. (ed.) (1983). *International Regimes*. Ithaca, NY: Cornell University Press.

Landau, M. (1969). 'Redundancy, Rationality and the Problem of Duplication and Overlap'. *Public Administration Review*, 29/4: 346–58.

Landis, J. (1938). *The Administrative Process*. New Haven: Yale University Press.

Lang, T. and Clutterbuck, C. (1991). *P is for Pesticides*. London: Random Century Group.

Laughlin, R. (1991). 'Environmental Disturbances and Organizational Transitions and Transformations: Some Alternative Models'. *Organization Studies*, 12/2: 209–32.

—— and Broadbent, J. (1995). 'The New Public Management Reforms in Schools and GP Practices: Professional Resistance and the Role of Absorption and Absorbing Groups'. Paper presented to the first Asian Pacific Interdisciplinary Perspectives on Accounting Conference, University of New South Wales, Sydney, 2–5 July.

Laver, M. (1983). *Invitation to Politics*. Oxford: Robertson.

Lawrence, P. and Lorsch, J. (1967). *Organization and Environment: Managing Differentiation and Integration*. Boston: Division of Research, Graduate School of Business Administration, Harvard University.

Lawton, R. and Parker, D. (1998). 'Procedures and the Professional: The Case of Medicine'. *Social Science and Medicine*, 49: 353–61.

Leathley, A. (1999). 'Foreign Office and Holiday Firms Disagree over Who is to Blame: Massacre in the Jungle'. *Times*, 3 March: 2.

Lee, T. (1994). *Householders' Response to the Radon Risk*. London: HMSO.

Leiss, W., Massey, C., and Walker L. (1998). 'Communicating the Risks from Radon in Buildings', in P. Gray, R. Stern, and M. Biocca (eds), *Communicating About Risks to Environment and Health in Europe*. Dordrecht, Boston, London: Kluwer.

Letwin, S. (1965). *The Pursuit of Certainty*. Cambridge: Cambridge University Press.

Leung, P.-L. and Harrison, R. M. (1999). 'Roadside and In-Vehicle Concentrations of Monoaromatic Hydrocarbons'. *Atmospheric Environment*, 33: 191–204.

Levy, A. (1986). 'Second-Order Planned Change: Definition and Conceptualisation'. *Organizational Dynamics*, 15/1: 5–23.

Lex Service Plc (1997). *Lex Report on Motoring: Driving for Safety*. London: Lex Service Plc.

Lubin, J. and Boice, J. (1997). 'Lung Cancer Risk from Residential Radon: Meta-Analysis of Eight Epidemiological Studies'. *Journal of the National Cancer Institute*, 89/10: 49–57.

MAAF (Ministry of Agriculture, Fisheries and Food, Pesticides Safety Directorate, Health and Safety Executive) (1999). *Annual Report of the Working Party on Pesticide Residues 1998*. London: Ministry of Agriculture, Fisheries and Food.

Majone, G. (1994). 'The Rise of the Regulatory State in Europe'. *West European Politics*, 17: 77–101.

Malkin, J. and Wildavsky, A. (1991). 'Why the Traditional Distinction between Public and Private Goods should be Abandoned'. *Journal of Theoretical Politics*, 3: 355–78.

Management Advisory Board (Commonwealth of Australia) (1995). *Guidelines for Managing Risk in the Australian Public Service: Exposure Draft* (Joint Publication of the

Management Advisory Board and its Management Improvement Advisory Committee No. 17). Canberra: Australian Government Publishing Service.

March, J. and Olsen, J. (1989). *Rediscovering Institutions*. New York: Free Press.

Marmor, T. and Fellman, P. (1986). 'Policy Entrepreneurship in Government: An American Study'. *Journal of Public Policy*, 6: 225–53.

Marshall, P. (1997). *The Prevalence of Convictions for Sexual Offending*. London: Home Office Research and Statistics Directorate.

Martell E. (1987). 'Critique of Current Lung Dosimetry Models for Radon Progeny Exposure in Radon and its Decay Products: Occurrence, Properties and Health Effects', in P Hopke (ed.), *ACS Symposium Series 331*. Washington: American Chemical Society.

Massuelle, M., Pirard, P., and Hubert, P. (1998). 'Experts and Researchers Faced with Legal Issues in Radon Affairs'. Paper delivered to the Conference of the Society for Risk Analysis Europe, 'Risk Analysis: Opening the Process', Paris, 11–14 October.

May, P. (1991). 'Reconsidering Policy Design: Politics and Publics'. *Journal of Public Policy*, 11/2: 187–206.

McCubbins, M. and Schwarz, T. (1984). 'Congressional Oversight Overlooked: Police Patrols versus Fire Alarms'. *American Journal of Political Science*, 28: 165–79.

Meidinger, E. (1987). 'Regulatory Culture: A Theoretical Outline'. *Law and Policy* 9: 355–86.

Merton, R. (1936). 'The Unintended Effects of Purposive Social Action'. *American Sociological Review* 1: 894–904.

——, Gray, A., Hockey, B., and Slevin, H. (eds) (1952). *Reader in Bureaucracy*. New York: Free Press.

Michael, M. (1991). "Discourses of Danger and Dangerous Discourses: Patrolling the Borders of Science, Nature and Society'. *Discourse and Society*, 2/1: 5–28.

—— (1992). 'Lay Discourses of Science: Science-in-General, Science-in-Particular and Self'. *Science, Technology and Human Values*, 17: 313–33.

Millstone, E. (1986). *Food Additives: Taking the Lid Off What We Really Eat*. Harmondsworth: Penguin.

Mintzberg, H. (1983). *Structure in Fives*. Englewood Cliffs, NJ: Prentice-Hall.

Moran, K (1999). 'Are They Safe—Or Are We Risking Our Lives Every Time We Use Them?'. *Sunday Mirror*, 7 March.

Monroe, A. (1998). 'Public Opinion and Public Policy, 1980–1993'. *Public Opinion Quarterly*, 62: 6–28.

Moore, M. (1995). *Creating Public Value*. Cambridge, MA.: Harvard University Press.

MORI (1998). *Business and the Environment: Attitudes and Behaviour of the General Public. Public Trends: 1989–1998*. London: MORI.

—— (2000). *Naming and Shaming Poll*. London: MORI.

MORI/Better Regulation Task Force (1999). 'Public Attitudes to Risk'. Unpublished survey, February.

MORI/Water UK (1998). *Satisfaction with Water Services*. London: MORI.

Morris, J. (2000). *Rethinking Risk and the Precautionary Principle*. Oxford: Butterworth Heinemann.

Munby, J. and Weetman, D. (1997). 'Benzene and Leukaemia', in R. Bate (ed.), *What Risk? Science, Politics and Public Health*. Oxford: Butterworth Heinemann.

Nelkin, D. (ed.) (1979). *Controversy: Politics of Technical Decisions*. London: Sage.

NERA (National Economic Research Associates) (1998). *Developing a Common UK Approach to Negotiations on Risk Assessment at International Level: Final Report*. London: NERA.

—— (2000). *Safety Regulations and Standards for European Railways*. London: NERA.

Nero, A. (1992). 'A National Strategy for Indoor Radon'. *Issues in Science and Technology*, 9/1: 33–40.

Niskanen, W. (1971). *Bureaucracy and Representative Government*. Chicago: Aldine Atherton.

—— (1973). *Bureaucracy: Servant or Master? Lessons from America*. London: Institute of Economic Affairs.

Noll, R. (1987). 'The Political Foundations of Regulatory Policy', in K. McCubbins and T. Sullivan (eds), *Congress*. Cambridge: Cambridge University Press.

NRPB (National Radiological Protection Board) (1987). *Exposure to Radon Daughters in Dwellings* (ASP 10). London: HMSO.

—— (1990). 'Board Statement on Radon in Homes'. *Documents of the NRPB*, 1/1: 17–32.

—— (1994). *Exposure to Radon in UK Dwellings* (NRPB-R272). London: HMSO.

Observer (1991). 'Harris Poll Reveals 92% Support for Dog Register'. 16 September: 4.

OECD (1986). *Control of Toxic Substances in the Atmosphere—Benzene* (OECD Environment Monographs, No. 5). Paris: OECD.

O'Riordan, M. and Miles, J. (eds) (1992). 'Radon 2000'. *Radiation Protection Dosimetry*, 42/3: 145–262.

Ogilvie-Smith, A., Downey, A., and Ransom, E. (1994). *Traffic Policing: Activity and Organisation* (Police Research Series Paper 12). London: Home Office Police Department.

Ogus, A. (1994). *Regulation: Legal Form and Economic Theory*. Oxford: Clarendon Press.

Olson, M. (1965). The Logic of Collective Action: Public Goods and the Theory of Groups. Cambridge, MA: Harvard University Press.

Ostrom, E. (1965). 'Public Entrepreneurs: A Case Study in Ground Water Basin Management' (Ph.D. thesis). Los Angeles: University of California.

—— (1986). 'A Method of Institutional Analysis', in F-X. Kaufmann, G. Majone, and V. Ostrom (eds), *Guidance, Control and Evaluation in the Public Sector*. Berlin: de Gruyter

Ostrom, V. (1974). *The Intellectual Crisis in American Public Administration* (2nd edn). Tuscaloosa: University of Alabama Press.

Page, E. (1992). Political Authority and Bureaucratic Power (2nd edn). Hemel Hempstead: Harvester Wheatsheaf.

Parliamentary Office of Science and Technology (1993). *Drinking Water Quality*. London: Parliamentary Office of Science and Technology.

Partners in Production Ltd (1999). *Brussels Behind Closed Doors: Something in the Air; The Name of the Game; Jeux Sans Frontières* (TV Documentary Series). London: Partners in Production Ltd.

Peel, M. (1999). 'Redrawing the Curve Reveals New Pattern of Events'. *Financial Times*, 2 September: 10.

Peltzman, S. (1975). 'The Effects of Automobile Safety Regulation'. *Journal of Political Economy*, 83: 677–725.

—— (1976). 'Towards a More General Theory of Regulation'. *Journal of Law and Economics*, 19: 211–40.

Perrow, C. (1984). *Normal Accidents*. New York: Basic Books.

Pesticides Safety Directorate (1999). '1998 Working Party on Pesticide Residues: Pear

Survey' (Pesticides Residues Monitoring Information Sheet, June). York: Pesticides Safety Directorate.

—— (undated). 'Pesticides Residues Surveillance and Brand Naming' (Information Sheet). York: Pesticides Safety Directorate.

Pet Food Manufacturers' Association (1999). *Statistics on UK Pet Population 1965–1998*. London: Pet Food Manufacturers' Association.

Podberscek, A. (1994). 'Dog on a Tightrope: The Position of the Dog in British Society as Influenced by Press Reports on Dog Attacks'. *Anthrozoos*, 7/4: 232–41.

—— and Blackshaw, J. (1993). 'A Survey of Dog Bites in Brisbane, Australia'. *Australian Veterinary Practitioner*, 23/4: 178–83.

Popper, K. (1957). *The Poverty of Historicism*. London: Routledge and Kegan Paul.

Posner, R. (1986). *Economic Analysis of Law*. Boston: Little, Brown and Company.

Powell, W.W. and DiMaggio, P. J. (1991). *The New Institutionalism in Organizational Analysis*. Chicago: University of Chicago Press.

Power, M. (1997). *The Audit Society*. Oxford: Oxford University Press.

—— (1999). 'The New Risk Management' (inaugural lecture of P.D. Leake Professor of Accounting and Director of CARR, December 1999). London: Centre for the Analysis of Risk and Regulation, London School of Economics.

Presidential/Congressional Commission on Risk Assessment and Risk Management (1997). *Framework for Environmental Health Management* and *Risk Assessment and Risk Management in Regulatory Decision-Making*. Washington, DC: Presidential/ Congressional Commission on Risk Assessment and Risk Management.

Pressman, J. and Wildavsky, A. (1973). *Implementation*. Berkeley: University of California Press.

Price, J. L. (1968). *Organizational Effectiveness*. Homewood, Ill.: J. L. Irwin.

Raab, C. (1997). 'Co-Producing Data Protection'. *International Journal of Law, Computers and Technology*, 11/1: 11–24.

Raiffa, H. (1968). *Decision Analysis*. Reading, MA: Addison-Wesley.

Rhodes, R. A. W. (1997). *Understanding Governance: Policy Networks, Governance, Reflexivity and Accountability*. Buckingham: Open University Press.

—— and Marsh, D. (1992) 'New Directions in the Study of Policy Networks'. *European Journal of Political Research*, 21: 181–205.

Robbins, D. and Johnstone, R. (1976). 'The Role of Cognitive and Occupational Differentiation in Scientific Controversies'. *Social Studies of Science*, 6: 349–68.

Roberts, A. (1998). 'Closing the Window: Public Service Restructuring and the Weakening of Freedom of Information Law' (mimeo). Kingston, Canada: Queen's University School of Policy Studies.

Ross, A. (2000). 'Road Safety: A Global View'. *Beyond 2000: A Vision for Road Safety*, conference of the Institute of Road Safety Officers, Durham, 12–15 July.

Rothstein, H. (1994). 'Science in the Policy-Making Process: The Case of the Regulation of Food Contact Plastics in the UK and EC' (D.Phil. thesis). Brighton: Science Policy Research Unit, University of Sussex.

——, Irwin, A., Yearley, S., and McCarthy, E. (1999). 'Regulatory Science, Europeanisation and the Control of Agrochemicals'. *Science, Technology and Human Values*, 27: 241–64.

Rourke, F. (1976). *Bureaucracy, Politics and Public Policy* (2nd edn). Boston: Little, Brown.

Royal Commission on Environmental Pollution (1984). *Tackling Pollution: Experience and Prospects* (Tenth Report). London: HMSO.

—— (1998). *Setting Environmental Standards* (Twenty-first Report, Cm 4053). London: HMSO.

Royal Society (1992). *Risk: Analysis, Perception, Management.* London: Royal Society.

Sagan, S. (1993). *The Limits of Safety: Organizations, Accidents, and Nuclear Weapons.* Princeton, NJ: Princeton University Press.

Salsburg, D. (1983). 'The Lifetime Feeding Study in Mice and Rats: An Examination of its Validity as a Bioassay for Human Carcinogens'. *Fundamental and Applied Toxicology,* 3: 63–7.

Salter, L. (1988). *Mandated Science.* Dordrecht: Kluwer.

Sapolsky, H. (1990). 'The Politics of Risk'. *Daedalus,* 119/4: 83–96.

Schaffer, B. and Lamb, G. (1981). *Can Equity be Organized?* Farnborough: Gower.

Scharpf, F. (1996). 'Negative and Positive Integration in the Political Economy of European Welfare States', in G. Marks *et al.* (eds), *Governance in the European Union.* London: Sage.

Schon, D. (1971). *Beyond the Stable State.* London: Maurice Temple Smith.

Schwarz, M. and Thompson, M. (1990). *Divided We Stand.* Hemel Hempstead: Harvester Wheatsheaf.

Scottish Office (1989). *Action on Dogs.* London: HMSO.

Self, P. (1985). *Political Theories of Modern Government.* London: Macmillan.

Sheail, J. (1991). 'The Regulation of Pesticide Use: An Historical Perspective', in R. Lewis and A. Weale (eds), *Innovation and Environmental Risk.* London: Belhaven.

Sherwell, P. and Nancarrow, J. (1991). 'Dogs that Bite'. *British Medical Journal,* 303: 1512–13.

Showalter, E. (1997). *Hystories: Hysterical Epidemics and Modern Culture.* New York: Columbia University Press; London: Picador.

Shrader-Frechette, K. (1991). *Risk and Rationality.* Berkeley. University of California Press.

Simon, H. (1946). 'The Proverbs of Administration'. *Public Administration Review,* 6: 53–67.

Simpson, H. (1996). *Comparison of Hospital and Police Casualty Data: Implications of the Road Accident Reporting Process For Casualty Target Monitoring.* Crowthorne, Berks.: Transport Research Laboratory.

Slovic, P. Fischoff, B., and Lichtenstein, S. (1980). 'Facts and Fears: Understanding Perceived Risk', in R. Schwing and W. Albers (eds), *Societal Risk Assessment: How Safe is Safe Enough?.* New York and London: Plenum Press.

—— —— —— (1981). 'Perceived Risks, Psychological Factors and Social Implications'. *Proceedings of the Royal Society of London,* A, 376: 17–34.

SCPR (Social and Community Planning Research) (1991). *British Social Attitudes: The 8th Report.* Aldershot: Ashgate.

—— (1998). *British—and European—Social Attitudes: The 15th Report. How Britain Differs.* Aldershot: Ashgate.

Soothill, K, and Walby, S. (1991). *Sex Crime in the News.* London: Routledge.

Sproule-Jones, M. (1982). 'Public Choice Theory and Natural Resources'. *American Political Science Review,* 76: 790–804.

Statutory Instrument No. 1333 (1985). *The Ionising Radiations Regulations 1985.* London: HMSO.

Statutory Instrument No. 1147 (1989). *Water Supply (Water Quality) Regulations 1989*. London: HMSO.

Statutory Instrument No. 3240 (1992). *The Environmental Information Regulations*. London: HMSO.

Statutory Instrument No. 32 (1995). *Pesticides (Maximum Residue Levels in Crops, Food and Feeding Stuffs) (National Limits) Regulations (Northern Ireland)*. London: HMSO.

Statutory Instrument No. 3043 (1997). *Environmental Protection: The Air Quality Regulations*. London: HMSO.

Statutory Instrument No. 3232 (1999). *The Ionising Radiation Regulations 1999*. London: HMSO.

Statutory Instrument No. 3483 (1999). *Pesticides (Maximum Levels in Crops, Food and Feedingstuffs) (England and Wales) Regulations 1999*. London: HMSO

Statutory Instrument No. 22 (2000). *Pesticides (Maximum Levels in Crops, Food and Feedingstuffs) (Scotland) Regulations 2000*. London: HMSO.

Statutory Instrument No. 928 (2000). *The Air Quality (England) Regulations 2000*. London: HMSO.

Statutory Instrument No. 2531 (2000). *Building Regulations 2000*. London: HMSO.

Steinmo, S., Thelen, K., and Longstreth, E. (1992). *Structuring Politics*. Cambridge: Cambridge University Press.

Stigler, G. (1971). 'The Theory of Economic Regulation'. *Bell Journal of Economics and Management Science*, 2/1: 1–21.

Stringer, J. (1967). 'Operational Research for Multi-Organizations'. *Operational Research Quarterly*,18/2: 105–20.

Sun Tzu (1983). *The Art of War* (ed. J. Clavell). New York: Dell Publishing.

Tait, J., Brown, S., and Carr, S. (1991). 'Pesticide Innovation and Public Acceptability: The Role of Regulation', in R. Lewis and A. Weale (eds), *Innovation and Environmental Risk*. London: Belhaven.

Teubner, G. (1987). 'Juridification: Concepts, Aspects, Limits and Solutions', in G. Teubner, *Juridification of Social Spheres*. Berlin: de Gruyter.

Thomas, H. and Banks, J. (1990). 'A Survey of Dog Bites in Thanet'. *Journal Royal Society Health* 5: 173.

Thompson, D. (1961). *On Growth and Form* (abridged edn, ed. J. Bonner). Cambridge: Cambridge University Press.

Thompson, M., Ellis, R., and Wildavsky, A. (1990). *Cultural Theory*. Boulder, CO: Westview.

Today (1991). 'Put Them Down: Thousands Jam *Today* Phone Poll'. 23 May.

Tollison, R. and Wagner, R. (1988). *Smoking and the State: Social Costs, Rent Seeking and Public Policy*. Lexington, MA: Lexington Books.

Toothill, W. and Mackie, A. (1995). *Transport Supplementary Grants for Safety Schemes, Local Authorities' Schemes From 1992/93 Allocations*. Crowthrone, Berks: Transport Research Laboratory.

UK Press Gazette (1991). 'Regional Press Takes Lead in Gathering and Directing "Mad Dog" Public Opinion'. 3 June. London: 16–17.

United Nations Scientific Committee on the Effects of Atomic Radiation (1982). *Ionizing Radiation: Sources and Biological Effects*. New York: United Nations.

van de Wijngaart, G. (1991). *Competing Perspectives on Drug Use: The Dutch Experience*. Amsterdam: Swets and Zeitlinger BV.

Vogel, D. (1986). *National Styles of Regulation: Environmental Policy in Great Britain and The United States*. Ithaca, NY: Cornell University Press.

Ward, N., Buller, H., and Lowe, P. (1995). *Implementing European Environmental Policy at the Local Level: The British Experience with Water Quality Directives*. Newcastle upon Tyne: Centre for Rural Economy, University of Newcastle upon Tyne.

Webster, D. (1998). *Traffic Calming—Public Attitudes Studies: A Literature Review*. Crowthorne, Berks: Transport Research Laboratory.

Weinstein, N., Klotz, M., and Sandman, P. (1989). 'Promoting Remedial Response to the Risk of Radon: Are Information Campaigns Enough?'. *Science, Technology and Human Values*, 14: 360–79.

Weinstein, N. and Sandman, P. (1992). 'Predicting Homeowners' Mitigation Responses to Radon Test Data'. *Journal of Social Issues*, 48/4: 63–83.

Wildavsky, A. (1980). *The Art and Craft of Policy Analysis*. London: Macmillan.

—— (1988). *Searching for Safety*. New Brunswick, NJ: Transaction.

—— (1995). *But Is It True? A Citizen's Guide to Environmental Health and Safety Issues*. Cambridge, MA: Harvard University Press.

Williams, D. (1998). *What Is Safe?: The Risks of Living in a Nuclear Age*. Cambridge: Royal Society of Chemistry Information Services.

Wilson, G. (1990). *Interest Groups*. Oxford: Oxford University Press.

Wilson, J. (1980). *The Politics of Regulation*. New York: Basic Books.

WHO (World Health Organisation) (1990). *Public Health Impact of Pesticides Used in Agriculture*. Geneva: WHO.

Wynne, B. (1982). 'Institutional Mythologies and Dual Societies in the Management of Risk', in H. Kunreuther and E. Ley (eds), *The Risk Analysis Controversy: An Institutional Perspective*. Berlin: Springer-Verlag.

—— (1989). 'Frameworks of Rationality in Risk Management: Towards the Testing of Naïve Sociology', in J. Brown (ed.), *Environmental Threats*. London: Belhaven Press.

INDEX

DATE DUE
